Computer Graphics: Principles and Practice

Computer Graphics: Principles and Practice

Edited by
Ruben Hawkins

Larsen & Keller
www.larsen-keller.com

Computer Graphics: Principles and Practice
Edited by Ruben Hawkins
ISBN: 978-1-63549-074-9 (Hardback)

 Larsen & Keller

Published by Larsen and Keller Education,
5 Penn Plaza,
19th Floor,
New York, NY 10001, USA

Cataloging-in-Publication Data

Computer graphics : principles and practice / edited by Ruben Hawkins.
     p. cm.
Includes bibliographical references and index.
ISBN 978-1-63549-074-9
1. Computer graphics. 2. Computer art. 3. Computer animation.
I. Hawkins, Ruben.
T385 .C66 2017
006.6--dc23

The publisher's policy is to use permanent paper from mills that operate a sustainable forestry policy. Furthermore, the publisher ensures that the text paper and cover boards used have met acceptable environmental accreditation standards.

Printed and bound in the United States of America.

For more information regarding Larsen and Keller Education and its products, please visit the publisher's website www.larsen-keller.com

Table of Contents

Preface

The book aims to shed light on some of the unexplored aspects of computer graphics. It provides thorough insights about the uses and methods relevant in this field of study. Computer graphics is a rapidly growing field of computer science which concerns itself with the creating of pictures and movies using computers. It includes topics like vector graphics, computer vision, 3D graphics, sprite graphics, etc. Such selected concepts redefine the subject that has been presented in this book. This text is a compilation of chapters that discuss the most vital concepts in the field of computer graphics. It unfolds the innovative aspects of this field which will be crucial for the holistic understanding of the subject matter. The text is appropriate for those seeking detailed information in this area.

Given below is the chapter wise description of the book:

Chapter 1- The pictures and moving images created with computers are known as computer graphics. This area is very vast and is recent as well. The chapter on computer graphics offers an insightful focus, keeping in mind the complex subject matter.

Chapter 2- The forms of computer graphics discussed in the following section are 2D computer graphics and 3D computer graphics. 2D is the digital images produced in computers and they are mostly formed by traditional printings and drawings. 3D dimensions are graphics that use three-dimensional representations. The section elucidates the major forms of computer graphics.

Chapter 3- The main components of computer graphics are sprite, vector graphics, 3D modeling, computer vision and user interface design. Vector graphics present images in computers by using polygons. The major components of computer graphics are discussed in the following chapter.

Chapter 4- Processes and techniques are important components of any field of study. Some of the techniques explained in the chapter are volume rendering, motion capture, shader, rasterisation, feathering and visual effects. Volume rendering is a method used to exhibit a 2D projection on a 3D scalar field whereas motion capture is capturing the movement of things or humans. The aspects elucidated in this section are of vital importance, and provide a better understanding of computer graphics.

Chapter 5- Animation is the process of creating an illusion of movement with the help of drawings. Computer animation helps in this process by generating these images. Traditional animation, stop motion, skeletal animation and animation database are some of the aspects of animation that have been elaborately explained in the following section.

Chapter 6- Amira is a software used for 3D and 4D management and visualization. The other software used for computer graphics are Amira, iClone, Indigo Renderer and CityEngine. This chapter helps the reader in understanding the various computer graphics software.

Chapter 7- The applications of computer graphics discussed in the section are special effect, ambient occlusion, web design, texture mapping, molecular graphics, drug design etc. Special effects are the visual tricks used in movies or video games whereas web designing deals with the production of websites. The topics elaborated in the section will help in gaining a better perspective about the applications of computer graphics.

Chapter 8- The history of computer graphics is an important part of the subject of computer graphics. The initial use of this technology was for scientific reasons and research purposes but as this subject grew, the focus shifted to art and media. This chapter helps the readers in understanding the growth and evolution of computer graphics over a period of decades.

At the end, I would like to thank all those who dedicated their time and efforts for the successful completion of this book. I also wish to convey my gratitude towards my friends and family who supported me at every step.

Editor

Understanding Computer Graphics

The pictures and moving images created with computers are known as computer graphics. This area is very vast and is recent as well. The chapter on computer graphics offers an insightful focus, keeping in mind the complex subject matter.

Computer Graphics

Computer graphics are pictures and movies created using computers – usually referring to image data created by a computer specifically with help from specialized graphical hardware and software. It is a vast and recent area in computer science. The phrase was coined by computer graphics researchers Verne Hudson and William Fetter of Boeing in 1960. It is often abbreviated as CG, though sometimes erroneously referred to as CGIcomputer-generated imagery.

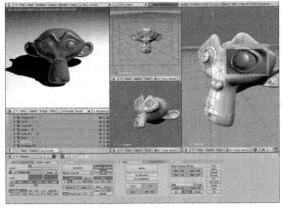

A Blender 2.45 screenshot, displaying the 3D test model Suzanne.

Important topics in computer graphics include user interface design, sprite graphics, vector graphics, 3D modeling, shaders, GPU design, and computer vision, among others. The overall methodology depends heavily on the underlying sciences of geometry, optics, and physics. Computer graphics is responsible for displaying art and image data effectively and meaningfully to the user, and processing image data received from the physical world. The interaction and understanding of computers and interpretation of data has been made easier because of computer graphics. Computer graphic development has had a significant impact on many types of media and has revolutionized animation, movies, advertising, video games, and graphic design generally.

Overview

The term computer graphics has been used a broad sense to describe "almost every-thing on computers that is not text or sound". Typically, the term *computer graphics* refers to several different things:

- the representation and manipulation of image data by a computer

- the various technologies used to create and manipulate images

- the sub-field of computer science which studies methods for digitally synthesiz-ing and manipulating visual content, see study of computer graphics

Computer graphics is widespread today. Computer imagery is found on television, in newspapers, for example in weather reports, or for example in all kinds of medical investigation and surgical procedures. A well-constructed graph can present complex statistics in a form that is easier to understand and interpret. In the media "such graphs are used to illustrate papers, reports, thesis", and other presentation material.

Many powerful tools have been developed to visualize data. Computer generated im-agery can be categorized into several different types: two dimensional (2D), three di-mensional (3D), and animated graphics. As technology has improved, 3D computer graphics have become more common, but 2D computer graphics are still widely used. Computer graphics has emerged as a sub-field of computer science which studies meth-ods for digitally synthesizing and manipulating visual content. Over the past decade, other specialized fields have been developed like information visualization, and scien-tific visualization more concerned with "the visualization of three dimensional phe-nomena (architectural, meteorological, medical, biological, etc.), where the emphasis is on realistic renderings of volumes, surfaces, illumination sources, and so forth, per-haps with a dynamic (time) component".

History

Introduction

The precursor sciences to the development of modern computer graphics were the ad-vances in electrical engineering, electronics, and television that took place during the first half of the twentieth century. Screens could display art since the Lumiere brothers' use of mattes to create special effects for the earliest films dating from 1895, but such displays were limited and not interactive. The first cathode ray tube, the Braun tube, was invented in 1897 - it in turn would permit the oscilloscope and the military control panel - the more direct precursors of the field, as they provided the first two-dimen-sional electronic displays that responded to programmatic or user input. Nevertheless, computer graphics remained relatively unknown as a discipline until the 1950s and the post-World War II period - during which time, the discipline emerged from a combination of both pure university and laboratory academic research into more advanced computers and the United States military's further development of technologies like radar, advanced aviation, and rocketry developed during the war. New kinds of displays were needed to process the wealth of information resulting from such projects, leading to the development of computer graphics as a discipline.

1950s

Early projects like the Whirlwind and SAGE Projects introduced the CRT as a viable display and interaction interface and introduced the light pen as an input device. Douglas T. Ross of the Whirlwind SAGE system performed a personal experiment in 1954 in which a small program he wrote captured the movement of his finger and displayed its vector (his traced name) on a display scope. One of the first interactive video games to feature recognizable, interactive graphics – *Tennis for Two* – was created for an oscilloscope by William Higinbotham to entertain visitors in 1958 at Brookhaven National Laboratory and simulated a tennis match. In 1959, Douglas T. Ross innovated again while working at MIT on transforming mathematic statements into computer generated machine tool vectors, and took the opportunity to create a display scope image of a Disney cartoon character.

SAGE Sector Control Room.

Electronics pioneer Hewlett-Packard went public in 1957 after incorporating the decade prior, and established strong ties with Stanford University through its founders, who were alumni. This began the decades-long transformation of the southern San Francisco Bay Area into the world's leading computer technology hub - now known as Silicon Valley. The field of computer graphics developed with the emergence of computer graphics hardware.

Further advances in computing led to greater advancements in interactive computer graphics. In 1959, the TX-2 computer was developed at MIT's Lincoln Laboratory. The TX-2 integrated a number of new man-machine interfaces. A light pen could be used to draw sketches on the computer using Ivan Sutherland's revolutionary Sketchpad software. Using a light pen, Sketchpad allowed one to draw simple shapes on the computer screen, save them and even recall them later. The light pen itself had a small photoelectric cell in its tip. This cell emitted an electronic pulse whenever it was placed in front of a computer screen and the screen's electron gun fired directly at it. By simply timing the electronic pulse with the current location of the electron gun, it was easy to pinpoint exactly where the pen was on the screen at any given moment. Once that was determined, the computer could then draw a cursor at that location. Sutherland seemed to find the perfect solution for many of the graphics problems he faced. Even today, many standards of computer graphics interfaces got their start with this early Sketchpad program. One example of this is in drawing constraints. If one wants to draw a square for example, they do not have to worry about drawing four lines perfectly to form the edges of the box. One can simply specify that they want to draw a box, and then specify the location and size of the box. The software will then construct a perfect box, with the right dimensions and at the right location. Another example is that Sutherland's software modeled objects - not just a picture of objects. In other words, with a model of a car, one could change the size of the tires without affecting the rest of the car. It could stretch the body of car without deforming the tires.

1960s

The phrase "computer graphics" itself was coined in 1960 by William Fetter, a graphic designer for Boeing. This old quote in many secondary sources comes complete with the following sentence: (*Fetter has said that the terms were actually given to him by Verne Hudson of the Wichita Division of Boeing.*) In 1961 another student at MIT, Steve Russell, created the second video game, *Spacewar*. Written for the DEC PDP-1, Spacewar was an instant success and copies started flowing to other PDP-1 owners and eventually DEC got a copy. The engineers at DEC used it as a diagnostic program on every new PDP-1 before shipping it. The sales force picked up on this quickly enough and when installing new units, would run the "world's first video game" for their new customers. (Higginbotham's *Tennis For Two* had beaten *Spacewar* by almost three years; but it was almost unknown outside of a research or academic setting.)

Spacewar running on the Computer History Museum's PDP-1

E. E. Zajac, a scientist at Bell Telephone Laboratory (BTL), created a film called "Simulation of a two-giro gravity attitude control system" in 1963. In this computer-generated film, Zajac showed how the attitude of a satellite could be altered as it orbits the Earth. He created the animation on an IBM 7090 mainframe computer. Also at BTL, Ken Knowlton, Frank Sinden and Michael Noll started working in the computer graphics field. Sinden created a film called *Force, Mass and Motion* illustrating Newton's laws of motion in operation. Around the same time, other scientists were creating computer graphics to illustrate their research. At Lawrence Radiation Laboratory, Nelson Max created the films *Flow of a Viscous Fluid* and *Propagation of Shock Waves in a Solid Form*. Boeing Aircraft created a film called *Vibration of an Aircraft*.

Also sometime in the early 1960s, automobiles would also provide a boost through the early work of Pierre Bézier at Renault, who used Paul de Casteljau's curves - now called Bézier curves after Bézier's work in the field - to develop 3d modeling techniques for Renault car bodies. These curves would form the foundation for much curve-modeling work in the field, as curves - unlike polygons - are mathematically complex entities to draw and model well.

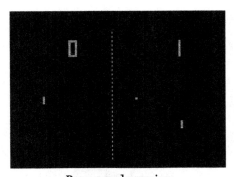

Pong arcade version

It was not long before major corporations started taking an interest in computer graphics. TRW, Lockheed-Georgia, General Electric and Sperry Rand are among the many companies that were getting started in computer graphics by the mid-1960s. IBM was quick to respond to this interest by releasing the IBM 2250 graphics terminal, the first commercially available graphics computer. Ralph Baer, a supervising engineer at Sanders Associates, came up with a home video game in 1966 that was later licensed to Magnavox and called the Odyssey. While very simplistic, and requiring fairly inexpensive electronic parts, it allowed the player to move points of light around on a screen. It was the first consumer computer graphics product. David C. Evans was director of engineering at Bendix Corporation's computer division from 1953 to 1962, after which he worked for the next five years as a visiting professor at Berkeley. There he continued his interest in computers and how they interfaced with people. In 1966, the University of Utah recruited Evans to form a computer science program, and computer graphics quickly became his primary interest. This new department would become the world's primary research center for computer graphics.

Also in 1966, Ivan Sutherland continued to innovate at MIT when he invented the first computer controlled head-mounted display (HMD). Called the Sword of Damocles because of the hardware required for support, it displayed two separate wireframe images, one for each eye. This allowed the viewer to see the computer scene in stereoscopic 3D. After receiving his Ph.D. from MIT, Sutherland became Director of Information Processing at ARPA (Advanced Research Projects Agency), and later became a professor at Harvard. In 1967 Sutherland was recruited by Evans to join the computer science program at the University of Utah. There he perfected his HMD. Twenty years later, NASA would re-discover his techniques in their virtual reality research. At Utah, Sutherland and Evans were highly sought after consultants by large companies but they were frustrated at the lack of graphics hardware available at the time so they started formulating a plan to start their own company. In 1969, the ACM initiated A Special Interest Group on Graphics (SIGGRAPH) which organizes conferences, graphics standards, and publications within the field of computer graphics. In 1973, the first annual SIGGRAPH conference was held, which has become one of the focuses of the organization. SIGGRAPH has grown in size and importance as the field of computer graphics has expanded over time.

1970s

The Utah teapot by Martin Newell and its static renders became emblematic of CGI development during the 1970s.

Many of the most important early breakthroughs in the transformation of graphics from utilitarian to realistic occurred at the University of Utah in the 1970s, which had hired Ivan Sutherland away from MIT. Sutherland's graphics class would contribute a number of significant pioneers to the field, including a student by the name of Edwin Catmull - a later founder of Pixar. Because of David C. Evans' and Sutherland's presence, UU was gaining quite a reputation as the place to be for computer graphics research so Catmull went there to learn 3D animation. Catmull had just come from The Boeing Company and had been working on his degree in physics. Growing up on Disney, Catmull loved animation yet quickly discovered that he did not have the talent for drawing. Now Catmull (along with many others) saw computers as the natural progression of animation and they wanted to be part of the revolution. The first animation that Catmull saw was his own. He created an animation of his hand opening and closing. It became one of his goals to produce a feature-length motion picture using computer graphics. In the same class, Fred Parke created an animation of his wife's face.

As the UU computer graphics laboratory was attracting people from all over, John Warnock was one of those early pioneers; he would later found Adobe Systems and create a revolution in the publishing world with his PostScript page description language, and Adobe would go on later to create the industry standard photo editing software in Adobe Photoshop and the movie industry's special effects standard in Adobe After Effects. Tom Stockham led the image processing group at UU which worked closely with the computer graphics lab. Jim Clark was also there; he would later found Silicon Graphics. The first major advance in 3D computer graphics was created at UU by these early pioneers, the hidden-surface algorithm. In order to draw a representation of a 3D object on the screen, the computer must determine which surfaces are "behind" the object from the viewer's perspective, and thus should be "hidden" when the computer creates (or renders) the image. The 3D Core Graphics System (or Core) was the first graphical standard to be developed. A group of 25 experts of the ACM Special Interest Group SIGGRAPH developed this "conceptual framework". The specifications were published in 1977, and it became a foundation for many future developments in the field.

Also in the 1970s, Henri Gouraud, Jim Blinn and Bui Tuong Phong contributed to the foundations of shading in CGI via the development of the Gouraud shading and Blinn-Phong shading models, allowing graphics to move beyond a "flat" look to a look more accurately portraying depth. Jim Blinn also innovated further in 1978 by introducing bump mapping, a technique for simulating uneven surfaces, and the predecessor to many more advanced kinds of mapping used today.

The modern videogame arcade as is known today was birthed in the 1970s, with the first arcade games using real-time 2D sprite graphics. *Pong* in 1972 was one of the first hit arcade cabinet games. *Speed Race* in 1974 featured sprites moving along a vertically scrolling road. *Gun Fight* in 1975 featured human-looking sprite character graphics, while *Space Invaders* in 1978 featured a large number of sprites on screen; both used an Intel 8080 microprocessor and Fujitsu MB14241 video shifter to accelerate the drawing of sprite graphics.

1980s

The 1980s began to see the modernization and commercialization of computer graphics. As the home computer proliferated, a subject which had previously been an academics-only discipline was adopted by a much larger audience, and the number of computer graphics developers increased significantly.

In the early 1980s, the availability of bit-slice and 16-bit microprocessors started to revolutionise high-resolution computer graphics terminals which now increasingly became intelligent, semi-standalone and standalone workstations. Graphics and application processing were increasingly migrated to the intelligence in the workstation, rather than continuing to rely on central mainframe and mini-computers. Typical of the early move to high resolution computer graphics intelligent workstations for the computer-aided engineering market were the Orca 1000, 2000 and 3000 workstations, developed by Orcatech of Ottawa, a spin-off from Bell-Northern Research, and led by David Pearson, an early workstation pioneer. The Orca 3000 was based on Motorola 68000 and AMD bit-slice processors and had Unix as its operating system. It was targeted squarely at the sophisticated end of the design engineering sector. Artists and graphic designers began to see the personal computer, particularly the Commodore Amiga and Macintosh, as a serious design tool, one that could save time and draw more accurately than other methods. The Macintosh remains a highly popular tool for computer graphics among graphic design studios and businesses. Modern computers, dating from the 1980s, often use graphical user interfaces (GUI) to present data and information with symbols, icons and pictures, rather than text. Graphics are one of the five key elements of multimedia technology.

Dire Straits' 1985 music video for their hit song Money For Nothing - the "I Want My MTV" song – became known as an early example of fully three-dimensional, animated computer-generated imagery.

Japan's Osaka University developed the LINKS-1 Computer Graphics System, a supercomputer that used up to 257 Zilog Z8001 microprocessors, in 1982, for the purpose of rendering realistic 3D computer graphics. According to the Information Processing Society of Japan: "The core of 3D image rendering is calculating the luminance of each pixel making up a rendered surface from the given viewpoint, light source, and object position. The LINKS-1 system was developed to realize an image rendering methodology in which each pixel could be parallel processed independently using ray tracing. By developing a new software methodology specifically for high-speed image rendering, LINKS-1 was able to rapidly render highly realistic images. It was used to create the world's first 3D planetarium-like video of the entire heavens that was made completely with computer graphics. The video was presented at the Fujitsu pavilion at the 1985 International Exposition in Tsukuba." The LINKS-1 was the world's most powerful computer, as of 1984.

The continuing popularity of Star Wars and other science fiction franchises were relevant in cinematic CGI at this time, as Lucasfilm and Industrial Light & Magic became known as the "go-to" house by many other studios for topnotch computer graphics in film. Important advances in chroma keying ("bluescreening", etc.) were made for the later films of the original trilogy. Two other pieces of video would also outlast the era as historically relevant: Dire Straits' iconic, near-fully-CGI video for their song "Money For Nothing" in 1985, which popularized CGI among music fans of that era, and a scene from Young Sherlock Holmes the same year featuring the first fully CGI character in a feature movie (an animated stained-glass knight). In 1988, the first shaders - small programs designed specifically to do shading as a separate algorithm - were developed by Pixar, which had already spun off from Industrial Light & Magic as a separate entity - though the public would not see the results of such technological progress until the next decade. In the late 1980s, SGI computers were used to create some of the first fully computer-generated short films at Pixar, and Silicon Graphics machines were considered a high-water mark for the field during the decade.

The 1980s is also called the golden era of videogames; millions-selling systems from Atari, Nintendo and Sega, among other companies, exposed computer graphics for the first time to a new, young, and impressionable audience - as did MS-DOS-based personal computers, Apple IIs and Macs, and Amigas, which also allowed users to program their own games if skilled enough. Demoscenes and shareware games proliferated; John Carmack, a later 3D innovator, would start out in this period developing sprite-based games. In the arcades, advances were made in commercial, real-time 3D graphics. In 1988, the first dedicated real-time 3D graphics boards were introduced in arcades, with the Namco System 21 and Taito Air System. This innovation would be the precursor of the later home graphics processing unit or GPU, a technology where a separate and very powerful chip is used in parallel processing with a CPU to optimize graphics.

1990s

Quarxs, series poster, Maurice Benayoun, François Schuiten, 1992

The 1990s' overwhelming note was the emergence of 3D modeling on a mass scale, and an impressive rise in the quality of CGI generally. Home computers became able to take on rendering tasks that previously had been limited to workstations costing thousands of dollars; as 3D modelers became available for home systems, the popularity of Silicon Graphics workstations declined and powerful Microsoft Windows and Apple Macintosh machines running Autodesk products like 3D Studio or other home rendering software ascended in importance. By the end of the decade, the GPU would begin its rise to the prominence it still enjoys today.

The field began to see the first rendered graphics that could truly pass as photorealistic to the untrained eye (though they could not yet do so with a trained CGI artist) and 3D graphics became far more popular in gaming, multimedia and animation. At the end of the 1980s and the beginning of the nineties were created, in France, the very first computer graphics TV series: *La Vie des bêtes* by studio Mac Guff Ligne (1988), *Les Fables Géométriques* (1989-1991) by studio Fantôme, and *Quarxs*, the first HDTV computer graphics series by Maurice Benayoun and François Schuiten (studio Z-A production, 1990–1993).

In film, Pixar began its serious commercial rise in this era under Edwin Catmull, with its first major film release, in 1995 - Toy Story - a critical and commercial success of nine-figure magnitude. The studio to invent the programmable shader would go on to have many animated hits, and its work on prerendered video animation is still considered an industry leader and research trailbreaker.

In videogames, in 1992, *Virtua Racing*, running on the Sega Model 1 arcade system board, laid the foundations for fully 3D racing games and popularized real-time 3D polygonal graphics among a wider audience in the video game industry. The Sega Model 2 in 1993 and Sega Model 3 in 1996 subsequently pushed the boundaries of commercial, real-time 3D graphics. Back on the PC, *Wolfenstein 3D*, *Doom* and *Quake*, three of the first massively popular 3D first-person shooter games, were released by id Software to critical and popular acclaim during this decade using a rendering engine innovated primarily by John Carmack. The Sony Playstation and Nintendo 64, among other consoles, sold in the millions and popularized 3D graphics for home gamers. Certain late-90's first-generation 3D titles became seen as influential in popularizing 3D graphics among console users, such as platform games *Super Mario 64* and *The Legend Of Zelda: Ocarina Of Time*, and early 3D fighting games like *Virtua Fighter*, *Battle Arena Toshinden*, and *Tekken*.

Technology and algorithms for rendering continued to improve greatly. In 1996, Krishnamurty and Levoy invented normal mapping - an improvement on Jim Blinn's bump mapping. 1999 saw Nvidia release the seminal GeForce 256, the first home video card billed as a graphics processing unit or GPU, which in its own words contained "integrated transform, lighting, triangle setup/clipping, and rendering engines". By the end of the decade, computers adopted common frameworks for graphics processing such as DirectX and OpenGL. Since then, computer graphics have only become more detailed and realistic, due to more powerful graphics hardware and 3D modeling software. AMD also became a leading developer of graphics boards in this decade, creating a "duopoly" in the field which exists this day.

2000s

CGI became ubiquitous in earnest during this era. Video games and CGI cinema had spread the reach of computer graphics to the mainstream by the late 1990s, and continued to do so at an accelerated pace in the 2000s. CGI was also adopted *en masse* for television advertisements widely in the late 1990s and 2000s, and so became familiar to a massive audience.

Still from Final Fantasy: The Spirits Within, 2001

The continued rise and increasing sophistication of the graphics processing unit was crucial to this decade, and 3D rendering capabilities became a standard feature as 3D-graphics GPUs became considered a necessity for desktop computer makers to offer. The Nvidia GeForce line of graphics cards dominated the market in the early decade with occasional significant competing presence from ATI. As the decade progressed, even low-end machines usually contained a 3D-capable GPU of some kind as Nvidia and AMD both introduced low-priced chipsets and continued to dominate the market. Shaders which had been introduced in the 1980s to perform specialized processing on the GPU would by the end of the decade become supported on most consumer hardware, speeding up graphics considerably and allowing for greatly improved texture and shading in computer graphics via the widespread adoption of normal mapping, bump mapping, and a variety of other techniques allowing the simulation of a great amount of detail.

Computer graphics used in films and video games gradually began to be realistic to the point of entering the uncanny valley. CGI movies proliferated, with traditional animated cartoon films like Ice Age and Madagascar as well as numerous Pixar offerings like Finding Nemo dominating the box office in this field. The *Final Fantasy: The Spirits Within*, released in 2001, was the first fully computer-generated feature film to use photorealistic CGI characters and be fully made with motion capture. The film was not a box-office success, however. Some commentators have suggested this may be partly because the lead CGI characters had facial features which fell into the "uncanny valley". Other animated films like *The Polar Express* drew attention at this time as well. Star Wars also resurfaced with its prequel trilogy and the effects continued to set a bar for CGI in film.

In videogames, the Sony Playstation 2 and 3, the Microsoft Xbox line of consoles, and offerings from Nintendo such as the GameCube maintained a large following, as did the Windows PC. Marquee CGI-heavy titles like the series of Grand Theft Auto, Assassin's Creed, Final Fantasy, Bioshock, Kingdom Hearts, Mirror's Edge and dozens of others continued to approach photorealism, grow the videogame industry and impress, until that industry's revenues became comparable to those of movies. Microsoft made a decision to expose DirectX more easily to the independent developer world with the XNA program, but it was not a success. DirectX itself remained a commercial success, however. OpenGL continued to mature as well, and it and DirectX improved greatly; the second-generation shader languages HLSL and GLSL began to be popular in this decade.

In scientific computing, the GPGPU technique to pass large amounts of data bidirectionally between a GPU and CPU was invented; speeding up analysis on many kinds of bioinformatics and molecular biology experiments. The technique has also been used for Bitcoin mining and has applications in computer vision.

2010s

In the early half of the 2010s, CGI is nearly ubiquitous in video, pre-rendered graphics are nearly scientifically photorealistic, and realtime graphics on a suitably high-end system may simulate photorealism to the untrained eye.

Box art from Titanfall, 2014

Texture mapping has matured into a multistage process with many layers; generally it is not uncommon to implement texture mapping, bump mapping or isosurfaces, normal mapping, lighting maps including specular highlights and reflection techniques, and shadow volumes into one rendering engine using shaders, which are maturing considerably. Shaders are now very nearly a necessity for advanced work in the field, providing considerable complexity in manipulating pixels, vertices, and textures on a per-element basis, and countless possible effects. Their shader languages HLSL and GLSL are active fields of research and development. Physically-based rendering or PBR, which implements even more maps to simulate real optic light flow, is an active research area as well. Experiments into the processing power required to provide graphics in real time at ultra-high-resolution modes like Ultra HD are beginning, though beyond reach of all but the highest-end hardware.

In cinema, most animated movies are CGI now; a great many animated CGI films are made per year, but few, if any, attempt photorealism due to continuing fears of the uncanny valley. Most are 3D cartoons.

In videogames, the Xbox One by Microsoft, Sony Playstation 4, and Nintendo Wii U currently dominate the home space and are all capable of highly advanced 3D graphics; the Windows PC is still one of the most active gaming platforms as well.

Image Types

Two-dimensional

2D computer graphics are the computer-based generation of digital images—mostly from models, such as digital image, and by techniques specific to them.

Raster graphic sprites (left) and masks (right)

2D computer graphics are mainly used in applications that were originally developed upon traditional printing and drawing technologies such as typography. In those applications, the two-dimensional image is not just a representation of a real-world object, but an independent artifact with added semantic value; two-dimensional models are therefore preferred, because they give more direct control of the image than 3D computer graphics, whose approach is more akin to photography than to typography.

Pixel Art

A large form of digital art being pixel art is created through the use of raster graphics software, where images are edited on the pixel level. Graphics in most old (or relatively limited) computer and video games, graphing calculator games, and many mobile phone games are mostly pixel art.

Sprite Graphics

A sprite is a two-dimensional image or animation that is integrated into a larger scene. Initially including just graphical objects handled separately from the memory bitmap of a video display, this now includes various manners of graphical overlays.

Originally, sprites were a method of integrating unrelated bitmaps so that they appeared to be part of the normal bitmap on a screen, such as creating an animated character that can be moved on a screen without altering the data defining the overall screen. Such sprites can be created by either electronic circuitry or software. In circuitry, a hardware sprite is a hardware construct that employs custom DMA channels to integrate visual elements with the main screen in that it super-imposes two discrete video sources. Software can simulate this through specialized rendering methods.

Vector Graphics

Vector graphics formats are complementary to raster graphics. Raster graphics is the representation of images as an array of pixels and is typically used for the representation of photographic images. Vector graphics consists in encoding information about shapes and colors that comprise the image, which can allow for more flexibility in rendering. There are instances when working with vector tools and formats is best practice, and instances when working with raster tools and formats is best practice. There are times when both formats come together. An understanding of the advantages and limitations of each technology and the relationship between them is most likely to result in efficient and effective use of tools.

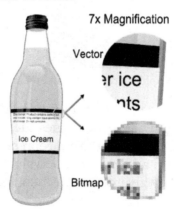

Example showing effect of vector graphics versus raster (bitmap) graphics.

Three-dimensional

3D graphics compared to 2D graphics are graphics that use a three-dimensional representation of geometric data. For the purpose of performance this is stored in the computer. This includes images that may be for later display or for real-time viewing.

Despite these differences, 3D computer graphics rely on similar algorithms as 2D computer graphics do in the frame and raster graphics (like in 2D) in the final rendered display. In computer graphics software, the distinction between 2D and 3D is occasionally blurred; 2D applications may use 3D techniques to achieve effects such as lighting, and primarily 3D may use 2D rendering techniques.

3D computer graphics are the same as 3D models. The model is contained within the graphical data file, apart from the rendering. However, there are differences that include the 3D model is the representation of any 3D object. Until visually displayed a model is not graphic. Due to printing, 3D models are not only confined to virtual space. 3D rendering is how a model can be displayed. Also can be used in non-graphical computer simulations and calculations.

Computer Animation

Computer animation is the art of creating moving images via the use of computers. It is a subfield of computer graphics and animation. Increasingly it is created by means of 3D computer graphics, though 2D computer graphics are still widely used for stylistic, low bandwidth, and faster real-time rendering needs. Sometimes the target of the animation is the computer itself, but sometimes the target is another medium, such as film. It is also referred to as CGI (Computer-generated imagery or computer-generated imaging), especially when used in films.

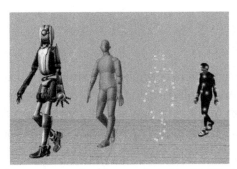

Example of Computer animation produced using Motion capture

Virtual entities may contain and be controlled by assorted attributes, such as transform values (location, orientation, and scale) stored in an object's transformation matrix. Animation is the change of an attribute over time. Multiple methods of achieving animation exist; the rudimentary form is based on the creation and editing of keyframes, each storing a value at a given time, per attribute to be animated. The 2D/3D graphics software will change with each keyframe, creating an editable curve of a value mapped over time, in which results in animation. Other methods of animation include procedural and expression-based techniques: the former consolidates related elements of animated entities into sets of attributes, useful for creating particle effects and crowd simulations; the latter allows an evaluated result returned from a user-defined logical expression, coupled with mathematics, to automate animation in a predictable way (convenient for controlling bone behavior beyond what a hierarchy offers in skeletal system set up).

Fractal landscape, an example of computer-generated imagery.

To create the illusion of movement, an image is displayed on the computer screen then quickly replaced by a new image that is similar to the previous image, but shifted slightly. This technique is identical to the illusion of movement in television and motion pictures.

Concepts and Principles

Images are typically created by devices such as cameras, mirrors, lenses, telescopes, microscopes, etc.

Digital images include both vector images and raster images, but raster images are more commonly used.

Pixel

In digital imaging, a pixel (or picture element) is a single point in a raster image. Pixels are placed on a regular 2-dimensional grid, and are often represented using dots or squares. Each pixel is a sample of an original image, where more samples typically provide a more accurate representation of the original. The intensity of each pixel is variable; in color systems, each pixel has typically three components such as red, green, and blue.

In the enlarged portion of the image individual pixels are rendered as squares and can be easily seen.

Graphics

Graphics are visual presentations on a surface, such as a computer screen. Examples are photographs, drawing, graphics designs, maps, engineering drawings, or other images. Graphics often combine text and illustration. Graphic design may consist of the deliberate selection, creation, or arrangement of typography alone, as in a brochure, flier, poster, web site, or book without any other element. Clarity or effective communication may be the objective, association with other cultural elements may be sought, or merely, the creation of a distinctive style.

Primitives

Primitives are basic units which a graphics system may combine to create more complex images or models. Examples would be sprites and character maps in 2d video games, geometric primitives in CAD, or polygons or triangles in 3d rendering. Primitives may be supported in hardware for efficient rendering, or the building blocks provided by a graphics application

Rendering

Rendering is the generation of a 2D image from a 3D model by means of computer programs. A scene file contains objects in a strictly defined language or data structure; it would contain geometry, viewpoint, texture, lighting, and shading information as a description of the virtual scene. The data contained in the scene file is then passed to a rendering program to be processed and output to a digital image or raster graphics image file. The rendering program is usually built into the computer graphics software, though others are available as plug-ins or entirely separate programs. The term "rendering" may be by analogy with an "artist's rendering" of a scene. Though the technical details of rendering methods vary, the general challenges to overcome in producing a 2D image from a 3D representation stored in a scene file are outlined as the graphics pipeline along a rendering device, such as a GPU. A GPU is a device able to assist the CPU in calculations. If a scene is to look relatively realistic and predictable under virtual lighting, the rendering software should solve the rendering equation. The rendering equation does not account for all lighting phenomena, but is a general lighting model for computer-generated imagery. 'Rendering' is also used to describe the process of calculating effects in a video editing file to produce final video output.

3D projection

> 3D projection is a method of mapping three dimensional points to a two dimensional plane. As most current methods for displaying graphical data are based on planar two dimensional media, the use of this type of projection is widespread, especially in computer graphics, engineering and drafting.

Ray tracing

> Ray tracing is a technique for generating an image by tracing the path of light through pixels in an image plane. The technique is capable of producing a very

high degree of photorealism; usually higher than that of typical scanline rendering methods, but at a greater computational cost.

Shading

Example of shading.

Shading refers to depicting depth in 3D models or illustrations by varying levels of darkness. It is a process used in drawing for depicting levels of darkness on paper by applying media more densely or with a darker shade for darker areas, and less densely or with a lighter shade for lighter areas. There are various techniques of shading including cross hatching where perpendicular lines of varying closeness are drawn in a grid pattern to shade an area. The closer the lines are together, the darker the area appears. Likewise, the farther apart the lines are, the lighter the area appears. The term has been recently generalized to mean that shaders are applied.

Texture mapping

Texture mapping is a method for adding detail, surface texture, or colour to a computer-generated graphic or 3D model. Its application to 3D graphics was pioneered by Dr Edwin Catmull in 1974. A texture map is applied (mapped) to the surface of a shape, or polygon. This process is akin to applying patterned paper to a plain white box. Multitexturing is the use of more than one texture at a time on a polygon. Procedural textures (created from adjusting parameters of an underlying algorithm that produces an output texture), and bitmap textures (created in an image editing application or imported from a digital camera) are, generally speaking, common methods of implementing texture definition on 3D models in computer graphics software, while intended placement of textures onto a model's surface often requires a technique known as UV mapping (arbitrary, manual layout of texture coordinates) for polygon surfaces, while NURBS surfaces have their own intrinsic parameterization used as texture coordinates. Texture mapping as a discipline also encompasses techniques for creating normal maps and bump maps that correspond to a texture to simulate height and specular maps to help simulate shine and light reflections, as well as environment mapping to simulate mirror-like reflectivity, also called gloss.

Anti-aliasing

Rendering resolution-independent entities (such as 3D models) for viewing on a raster (pixel-based) device such as a liquid-crystal display or CRT television inevitably causes aliasing artifacts mostly along geometric edges and the boundaries of texture details; these artifacts are informally called "jaggies". Anti-aliasing methods rectify such problems, resulting in imagery more pleasing to the viewer, but can be somewhat computationally expensive. Various anti-aliasing algorithms (such as supersampling) are able to be employed, then customized for the most efficient rendering performance versus quality of the resultant imagery; a graphics artist should consider this trade-off if anti-aliasing methods are to be used. A pre-anti-aliased bitmap texture being displayed on a screen (or screen location) at a resolution different than the resolution of the texture itself (such as a textured model in the distance from the virtual camera) will exhibit aliasing artifacts, while any procedurally defined texture will always show aliasing artifacts as they are resolution-independent; techniques such as mipmapping and texture filtering help to solve texture-related aliasing problems.

Volume Rendering

Volume rendering is a technique used to display a 2D projection of a 3D discretely sampled data set. A typical 3D data set is a group of 2D slice images acquired by a CT or MRI scanner.

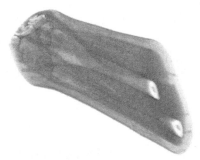

Volume rendered CT scan of a forearm with different colour schemes for muscle, fat, bone, and blood.

Usually these are acquired in a regular pattern (e.g., one slice every millimeter) and usually have a regular number of image pixels in a regular pattern. This is an example of a regular volumetric grid, with each volume element, or voxel represented by a single value that is obtained by sampling the immediate area surrounding the voxel.

3D Modeling

3D modeling is the process of developing a mathematical, wireframe representation of any three-dimensional object, called a "3D model", via specialized software. Models may be created automatically or manually; the manual modeling process of preparing geometric data for 3D computer graphics is similar to plastic arts such as sculpting. 3D models may be created using multiple approaches: use of NURBS curves to generate accurate and smooth surface patches, polygonal mesh modeling (manipulation of faceted geometry), or polygonal mesh subdivision (advanced tessellation of polygons, resulting in smooth surfaces similar to NURBS models). A 3D model can be displayed as a two-dimensional image through a process called *3D rendering*, used in a computer simulation of physical phenomena, or animated directly for other purposes. The model can also be physically created using 3D Printing devices.

Pioneers in Computer Graphics

Charles Csuri

Charles Csuri is a pioneer in computer animation and digital fine art and created the first computer art in 1964. Csuri was recognized by *Smithsonian* as the father of digital art and computer animation, and as a pioneer of computer animation by the Museum of Modern Art (MoMA) and Association for Computing Machinery-SIGGRAPH.

Donald P. Greenberg

Donald P. Greenberg is a leading innovator in computer graphics. Greenberg has authored hundreds of articles and served as a teacher and mentor to many prominent computer graphic artists, animators, and researchers such as Robert L. Cook, Marc Levoy, Brian A. Barsky, and Wayne Lytle. Many of his former students have won Academy Awards for technical achievements and several have won the SIGGRAPH Achievement Award. Greenberg was the founding director of the NSF Center for Computer Graphics and Scientific Visualization.

A. Michael Noll

Noll was one of the first researchers to use a digital computer to create artistic patterns and to formalize the use of random processes in the creation of visual arts. He began creating digital computer art in 1962, making him one of the earliest digital computer artists. In 1965, Noll along with Frieder Nake and Georg Nees were the first to publicly exhibit their computer art. During April 1965, the Howard Wise Gallery exhibited Noll's computer art along with random-dot patterns by Bela Julesz.

Other Pioneers

A modern render of the Utah teapot, an iconic model in 3D computer graphics created by
Martin Newell, 1975

- Pierre Bézier
- Jim Blinn
- Jack Bresenham
- John Carmack
- Paul de Casteljau
- Ed Catmull
- Frank Crow
- James D. Foley
- William Fetter
- Henry Fuchs
- Henri Gouraud
- Nadia Magnenat Thalmann
- Benoît B. Mandelbrot
- Martin Newell
- Fred Parke
- Bui Tuong Phong
- Steve Russell
- Daniel J. Sandin
- Alvy Ray Smith
- Bob Sproull
- Ivan Sutherland
- Daniel Thalmann
- Andries van Dam
- John Warnock
- Lance Williams

Important Organizations

- SIGGRAPH
- SIGGRAPH Asia

- Bell Telephone Laboratories

- United States Armed Forces, particularly the Whirlwind computer and SAGE Project

- Boeing

- IBM

- Renault

- The computer science department of the University of Utah

- Lucasfilm and Industrial Light & Magic

- Autodesk

- Adobe Systems

- Pixar

- Silicon Graphics, Khronos Group & OpenGL

- The DirectX division at Microsoft

- Nvidia and AMD

Study of Computer Graphics

The study of computer graphics is a sub-field of computer science which studies methods for digitally synthesizing and manipulating visual content. Although the term often refers to three-dimensional computer graphics, it also encompasses two-dimensional graphics and image processing.

As an academic discipline, computer graphics studies the manipulation of visual and geometric information using computational techniques. It focuses on the *mathematical* and *computational* foundations of image generation and processing rather than purely aesthetic issues. Computer graphics is often differentiated from the field of visualization, although the two fields have many similarities.

1. *Cinema: A Painstaking Fantasy* Chris Taylor, Time, 31 July 2000 (retrieved 8 August 2012).

2. *Final Fantasy: The Spirits Within* at Box Office Mojo (retrieved 12 August 2012).

3. The uncanny valley is a hypothesis in the field of robotics and 3D computer animation, which holds that when human replicas look and act almost, but not perfectly, like actual human beings, it causes a response of revulsion among human observers. The concept "valley" refers to the dip in a graph of the comfort

level of humans as a function of a robot's human likeness.

4. *Ira Greenberg (2007). Processing: Creative Coding and Computational Art. Apress. ISBN 1-59059-617-X.*

5. *Rudolf F. Graf (1999). Modern Dictionary of Electronics. Oxford: Newnes. p. 569. ISBN 0-7506-4331-5.*

6. Blythe, David. *Advanced Graphics Programming Techniques Using OpenGL.* Siggraph 1999. (see: Multitexture)

Computer Graphics (Computer Science)

Computer graphics is a sub-field of computer science which studies methods for digitally synthesizing and manipulating visual content. Although the term often refers to the study of three-dimensional computer graphics, it also encompasses two-dimensional graphics and image processing.

Overview

Computer graphics studies the manipulation of visual and geometric information using computational techniques. It focuses on the *mathematical* and *computational* foundations of image generation and processing rather than purely aesthetic issues. Computer graphics is often differentiated from the field of visualization, although the two fields have many similarities.

Connected studies include:

*   Applied mathematics

*   Computational geometry

*   Computational topology

*   Computer vision

*   Image processing

*   Information visualization

*   Scientific visualization

Applications of computer graphics include:

*   Digital art

- Special effects

- Video games

- Visual effects

History

One of the first displays of computer animation was *Futureworld* (1976), which included an animation of a human face and hand—produced by Ed Catmull and Fred Parke at the University of Utah. Swedish inventor Håkan Lans applied for the first patent on color graphics in 1979.

There are several international conferences and journals where the most significant results in computer graphics are published. Among them are the SIGGRAPH and Eurographics conferences and the Association for Computing Machinery (ACM) Transactions on Graphics journal. The joint Eurographics and ACM SIGGRAPH symposium series features the major venues for the more specialized sub-fields: Symposium on Geometry Processing, Symposium on Rendering, and Symposium on Computer Animation. As in the rest of computer science, conference publications in computer graphics are generally more significant than journal publications (and subsequently have lower acceptance rates).

Subfields

A broad classification of major subfields in computer graphics might be:

1. Geometry: studies ways to represent and process surfaces

2. Animation: studies with ways to represent and manipulate motion

3. Rendering: studies algorithms to reproduce light transport

4. Imaging: studies image acquisition or image editing

5. Topology:studies the behaviour of spaces and surfaces.

Geometry

Successive approximations of a surface computed using quadric error metrics.

The subfield of geometry studies the representation of three-dimensional objects in a discrete digital setting. Because the appearance of an object depends largely on its exterior, boundary representations are most commonly used. Two dimensional surfaces are a good representation for most objects, though they may be non-manifold. Since surfaces are not finite, discrete digital approximations are used. Polygonal meshes (and to a lesser extent subdivision surfaces) are by far the most common representation, although point-based representations have become more popular recently (see for instance the Symposium on Point-Based Graphics). These representations are *Lagrangian,* meaning the spatial locations of the samples are independent. Recently, *Eulerian* surface descriptions (i.e., where spatial samples are fixed) such as level sets have been developed into a useful representation for deforming surfaces which undergo many topological changes (with fluids being the most notable example).

Geometry Subfields

- Implicit surface modeling – an older subfield which examines the use of algebraic surfaces, constructive solid geometry, etc., for surface representation.

- Digital geometry processing – surface reconstruction, simplification, fairing, mesh repair, parameterization, remeshing, mesh generation, surface compression, and surface editing all fall under this heading.

- Discrete differential geometry – a nascent field which defines geometric quantities for the discrete surfaces used in computer graphics.

- Point-based graphics – a recent field which focuses on points as the fundamental representation of surfaces.

- Subdivision surfaces

- Out-of-core mesh processing – another recent field which focuses on mesh datasets that do not fit in main memory.

Animation

The subfield of animation studies descriptions for surfaces (and other phenomena) that move or deform over time. Historically, most work in this field has focused on parametric and data-driven models, but recently physical simulation has become more popular as computers have become more powerful computationally.

Subfields

- Performance capture

- Character animation

- Physical simulation (e.g. cloth modeling, animation of fluid dynamics, etc.)

Rendering

Rendering generates images from a model. Rendering may simulate light transport to create realistic images or it may create images that have a particular artistic style in non-photorealistic rendering. The two basic operations in realistic rendering are transport (how much light passes from one place to another) and scattering (how surfaces interact with light). See Rendering (computer graphics) for more information.

Indirect diffuse scattering simulated using path tracing and irradiance caching.

Transport

Transport describes how illumination in a scene gets from one place to another. Visibility is a major component of light transport.

Scattering

Models of *scattering* and *shading* are used to describe the appearance of a surface. In graphics these problems are often studied within the context of rendering since they can substantially affect the design of rendering algorithms. Shading can be broken down into two orthogonal issues, which are often studied independently:

1. scattering – how light interacts with the surface *at a given point*

2. shading – how material properties vary across the surface

The former problem refers to scattering, i.e., the relationship between incoming and outgoing illumination at a given point. Descriptions of scattering are usually given in terms of a bidirectional scattering distribution function or BSDF. The latter issue addresses how different types of scattering are distributed across the surface (i.e., which scattering function applies where). Descriptions of this kind are typically expressed with a program called a shader. (Note that there is some confusion since the word "shader" is sometimes used for programs that describe local *geometric* variation.)

Other subfields

*   physically based rendering – concerned with generating images according to the laws of geometric optics

- real time rendering – focuses on rendering for interactive applications, typically using specialized hardware like GPUs

- non-photorealistic rendering

- relighting – recent area concerned with quickly re-rendering scenes

Notable Researchers

- Brian A. Barsky

- Jim Blinn

- Jack E. Bresenham

- Loren Carpenter

- Edwin Catmull

- Robert L. Cook

- Paul Debevec

- Ron Fedkiw

- James D. Foley

- David Forsyth

- Henry Fuchs

- Pat Hanrahan

- Jim Kajiya

- Takeo Kanade

- Kenneth Knowlton

- Marc Levoy

- James O'Brien

- Ken Perlin

- Matt Pharr

- Przemyslaw Prusinkiewicz

- William Reeves

- James Sethian

- Ivan Sutherland

- Greg Turk

- Andries van Dam

- Henrik Wann Jensen

- Lance Williams

References

- Jon Peddie: The History of Visual Magic in Computers: How Beautiful Images are Made in CAD, 3D, VR and AR, Springer, 2013, p. 101, ISBN 978-1447149316

- Information Processing Society of Japan. "LINKS-1 Computer Graphics System-Computer Museum". Retrieved 15 June 2015.

- "Virtua Racing – Arcade (1992)". 15 Most Influential Games of All Time. GameSpot. 14 March 2001. Archived from the original on 2010-04-12. Retrieved 19 January 2014.

Forms of Computer Graphics

The forms of computer graphics discussed in the following section are 2D computer graphics and 3D computer graphics. 2D is the digital images produced in computers and they are mostly formed by traditional printings and drawings. 3D dimensions are graphics that use three-dimensional representations. The section elucidates the major forms of computer graphics.

2D Computer Graphics

2D computer graphics is the computer-based generation of digital images—mostly from two-dimensional models (such as 2D geometric models, text, and digital images) and by techniques specific to them. The word may stand for the branch of computer science that comprises such techniques, or for the models themselves.

2D computer graphics are mainly used in applications that were originally developed upon traditional printing and drawing technologies, such as typography, cartography, technical drawing, advertising, etc. In those applications, the two-dimensional image is not just a representation of a real-world object, but an independent artifact with added semantic value; two-dimensional models are therefore preferred, because they give more direct control of the image than 3D computer graphics (whose approach is more akin to photography than to typography).

In many domains, such as desktop publishing, engineering, and business, a description of a document based on 2D computer graphics techniques can be much smaller than the corresponding digital image—often by a factor of 1/1000 or more. This representation is also more flexible since it can be rendered at different resolutions to suit different output devices. For these reasons, documents and illustrations are often stored or transmitted as 2D graphic files.

2D computer graphics started in the 1950s, based on vector graphics devices. These were largely supplanted by raster-based devices in the following decades. The PostScript language and the X Window System protocol were landmark developments in the field.

2D Graphics Techniques

2D graphics models may combine geometric models (also called vector graphics), digital images (also called raster graphics), text to be typeset (defined by content, font style and size, color, position, and orientation), mathematical functions and equations, and more. These components can be modified and manipulated by two-dimensional geometric transformations such as translation, rotation, scaling. In object-oriented graphics, the image is described indirectly by an object endowed with a self-rendering method—a procedure which assigns colors to the image pixels by an arbitrary algorithm. Complex models can be built by combining simpler objects, in the paradigms of object-oriented programming.

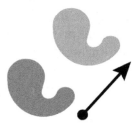

A translation moves every point of a figure or a space by the same amount in a given direction.

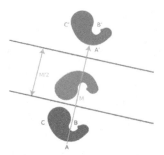

A reflection against an axis followed by a reflection against a second axis parallel to the first one results in a total motion which is a translation.

In Euclidean geometry, a translation moves every point a constant distance in a specified direction. A translation can be described as a rigid motion: other rigid motions include rotations and reflections. A translation can also be interpreted as the addition of a constant vector to every point, or as shifting the origin of the coordinate system. A translation operator is an operator T δ $T_{\mathbf{a}} f(\ddot{\mathbf{u}}) = f(\mathbf{v} +)$.

If v is a fixed vector, then the translation T_v will work as $T_v(\mathrm{p}) = \mathrm{p} + \mathrm{v}$.

If T is a translation, then the image of a subset A under the function T is the translate of A by T. The translate of A by T_v is often written $A + v$.

In a Euclidean space, any translation is an isometry. The set of all translations forms the translation group T, which is isomorphic to the space itself, and a normal subgroup of Euclidean group $E(n)$. The quotient group of $E(n)$ by T is isomorphic to the orthogonal group $O(n)$:

$$E(n) / T \cong O(n).$$

Translation

Since a translation is an affine transformation but not a linear transformation, homogeneous coordinates are normally used to represent the translation operator by a matrix and thus to make it linear. Thus we write the 3-dimensional vector w = (w_x, w_y, w_z) using 4 homogeneous coordinates as w = $(w_x, w_y, w_z, 1)$.

To translate an object by a vector v, each homogeneous vector p (written in homogeneous coordinates) would need to be multiplied by this translation matrix:

$$T_v = \begin{bmatrix} 1 & 0 & 0 & v_x \\ 0 & 1 & 0 & v_y \\ 0 & 0 & 1 & v_z \\ 0 & 0 & 0 & 1 \end{bmatrix}$$

As shown below, the multiplication will give the expected result:

$$T_v p = \begin{bmatrix} 1 & 0 & 0 & v_x \\ 0 & 1 & 0 & v_y \\ 0 & 0 & 1 & v_z \\ 0 & 0 & 0 & 1 \end{bmatrix} \begin{bmatrix} p_x \\ p_y \\ p_z \\ 1 \end{bmatrix} = \begin{bmatrix} p_x + v_x \\ p_y + v_y \\ p_z + v_z \\ 1 \end{bmatrix} = p + v$$

The inverse of a translation matrix can be obtained by reversing the direction of the vector:

$$T_v^{-1} = T_{-v}.$$

Similarly, the product of translation matrices is given by adding the vectors:

$$T_u T_v = T_{u+v}.$$

Because addition of vectors is commutative, multiplication of translation matrices is therefore also commutative (unlike multiplication of arbitrary matrices).

Rotation

In linear algebra, a rotation matrix is a matrix that is used to perform a rotation in Euclidean space.

$$R = \begin{bmatrix} \cos\theta & -\sin\theta \\ \sin\theta & \cos\theta \end{bmatrix}$$

rotates points in the xy-Cartesian plane counterclockwise through an angle θ about the origin of the Cartesian coordinate system. To perform the rotation using a rotation matrix R, the position of each point must be represented by a column vector v, containing the coordinates of the point. A rotated vector is obtained by using the matrix multiplication Rv. Since matrix multiplication has no effect on the zero vector (i.e., on the coordinates of the origin), rotation matrices can only be used to describe rotations about the origin of the coordinate system.

Rotation matrices provide a simple algebraic description of such rotations, and are used extensively for computations in geometry, physics, and computer graphics. In 2-dimensional space, a rotation can be simply described by an angle θ of rotation, but it can be also represented by the 4 entries of a rotation matrix with 2 rows and 2 columns. In 3-dimensional space, every rotation can be interpreted as a rotation by a given angle about a single fixed axis of rotation (see Euler's rotation theorem), and hence it can be simply described by an angle and a vector with 3 entries. However, it can also be represented by the 9 entries of a rotation matrix with 3 rows and 3 columns. The notion of rotation is not commonly used in dimensions higher than 3; there is a notion of a rotational displacement, which can be represented by a matrix, but no associated single axis or angle.

Rotation matrices are square matrices, with real entries. More specifically they can be characterized as orthogonal matrices with determinant 1:

$$R^T = R^{-1}, \det R = 1 .$$

The set of all such matrices of size n forms a group, known as the special orthogonal group SO(n).

In Two Dimensions

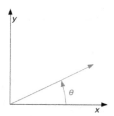

A counterclockwise rotation of a vector through angle θ. The vector is initially aligned with the x-axis.

In two dimensions every rotation matrix has the following form:

$$R(\theta) = \begin{bmatrix} \cos\theta & -\sin\theta \\ \sin\theta & \cos\theta \end{bmatrix} .$$

This rotates column vectors by means of the following matrix multiplication:

$$\begin{bmatrix} x' \\ y' \end{bmatrix} = \begin{bmatrix} \cos\theta & -\sin\theta \\ \sin\theta & \cos\theta \end{bmatrix} \begin{bmatrix} x \\ y \end{bmatrix}.$$

So the coordinates (x',y') of the point (x,y) after rotation are:

$$x' = x\cos\theta - y\sin\theta,$$

$$y' = x\sin\theta + y\cos\theta.$$

The direction of vector rotation is counterclockwise if θ is positive (e.g. 90°), and clockwise if θ is negative (e.g. -90°).

$$R(-\theta) = \begin{bmatrix} \cos\theta & \sin\theta \\ -\sin\theta & \cos\theta \end{bmatrix}.$$

Non-standard Orientation of the Coordinate System

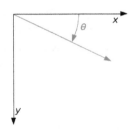

A rotation through angle θ with non-standard axes.

If a standard right-handed Cartesian coordinate system is used, with the x axis to the right and the y axis up, the rotation R(θ) is counterclockwise. If a left-handed Cartesian coordinate system is used, with x directed to the right but y directed down, R(θ) is clockwise. Such non-standard orientations are rarely used in mathematics but are common in 2D computer graphics, which often have the origin in the top left corner and the y-axis down the screen or page.

See below for other alternative conventions which may change the sense of the rotation produced by a rotation matrix.

Common Rotations

Particularly useful are the matrices for 90° and 180° rotations:

$$R(90°) = \begin{bmatrix} 0 & -1 \\ 1 & 0 \end{bmatrix} \text{(90° counterclockwise rotation)}$$

$$R(180°) = \begin{bmatrix} -1 & 0 \\ 0 & -1 \end{bmatrix} (180° \text{ rotation in either direction} - \text{a half-turn})$$

$$R(270°) = \begin{bmatrix} 0 & 1 \\ -1 & 0 \end{bmatrix} (270° \text{ counterclockwise rotation, the same as a 90° clockwise}$$
rotation)

In Euclidean geometry, uniform scaling (isotropic scaling, homogeneous dilation, homothety) is a linear transformation that enlarges (increases) or shrinks (diminishes) objects by a scale factor that is the same in all directions. The result of uniform scaling is similar (in the geometric sense) to the original. A scale factor of 1 is normally allowed, so that congruent shapes are also classed as similar. (Some school text books specifically exclude this possibility, just as some exclude squares from being rectangles or circles from being ellipses.)

More general is scaling with a separate scale factor for each axis direction. Non-uniform scaling (anisotropic scaling, inhomogeneous dilation) is obtained when at least one of the scaling factors is different from the others; a special case is directional scaling or stretching (in one direction). Non-uniform scaling changes the shape of the object; e.g. a square may change into a rectangle, or into a parallelogram if the sides of the square are not parallel to the scaling axes (the angles between lines parallel to the axes are preserved, but not all angles).

Scaling

A scaling can be represented by a scaling matrix. To scale an object by a vector $v = (v_x, v_y, v_z)$, each point $p = (p_x, p_y, p_z)$ would need to be multiplied with this scaling matrix:

$$S_v = \begin{bmatrix} v_x & 0 & 0 \\ 0 & v_y & 0 \\ 0 & 0 & v_z \end{bmatrix}.$$

As shown below, the multiplication will give the expected result:

$$S_v p = \begin{bmatrix} v_x & 0 & 0 \\ 0 & v_y & 0 \\ 0 & 0 & v_z \end{bmatrix} \begin{bmatrix} p_x \\ p_y \\ p_z \end{bmatrix} = \begin{bmatrix} v_x p_x \\ v_y p_y \\ v_z p_z \end{bmatrix}.$$

Such a scaling changes the diameter of an object by a factor between the scale factors, the area by a factor between the smallest and the largest product of two scale factors, and the volume by the product of all three.

The scaling is uniform if and only if the scaling factors are equal ($v_x = v_y = v_z$). If all except one of the scale factors are equal to 1, we have directional scaling.

In the case where $v_x = v_y = v_z = k$, the scaling is also called an enlargement or dilation by a factor k, increasing the area by a factor of k^2 and the volume by a factor of k^3.

A scaling in the most general sense is any affine transformation with a diagonalizable matrix. It includes the case that the three directions of scaling are not perpendicular. It includes also the case that one or more scale factors are equal to zero (projection), and the case of one or more negative scale factors. The latter corresponds to a combination of scaling proper and a kind of reflection: along lines in a particular direction we take the reflection in the point of intersection with a plane that need not be perpendicular; therefore it is more general than ordinary reflection in the plane.

Using Homogeneous Coordinates

In projective geometry, often used in computer graphics, points are represented using homogeneous coordinates. To scale an object by a vector $v = (v_x, v_y, v_z)$, each homogeneous coordinate vector $p = (p_x, p_y, p_z, 1)$ would need to be multiplied with this projective transformation matrix:

$$S_v = \begin{bmatrix} v_x & 0 & 0 & 0 \\ 0 & v_y & 0 & 0 \\ 0 & 0 & v_z & 0 \\ 0 & 0 & 0 & 1 \end{bmatrix}.$$

As shown below, the multiplication will give the expected result:

$$S_v p = \begin{bmatrix} v_x & 0 & 0 & 0 \\ 0 & v_y & 0 & 0 \\ 0 & 0 & v_z & 0 \\ 0 & 0 & 0 & 1 \end{bmatrix} \begin{bmatrix} p_x \\ p_y \\ p_z \\ 1 \end{bmatrix} = \begin{bmatrix} v_x p_x \\ v_y p_y \\ v_z p_z \\ 1 \end{bmatrix}.$$

Since the last component of a homogeneous coordinate can be viewed as the denominator of the other three components, a uniform scaling by a common factor s (uniform scaling) can be accomplished by using this scaling matrix:

$$S_v = \begin{bmatrix} 1 & 0 & 0 & 0 \\ 0 & 1 & 0 & 0 \\ 0 & 0 & 1 & 0 \\ 0 & 0 & 0 & \dfrac{1}{s} \end{bmatrix}.$$

For each vector $p = (p_x, p_y, p_z, 1)$ we would have

$$S_v p = \begin{bmatrix} 1 & 0 & 0 & 0 \\ 0 & 1 & 0 & 0 \\ 0 & 0 & 1 & 0 \\ 0 & 0 & 0 & \dfrac{1}{s} \end{bmatrix} \begin{bmatrix} p_x \\ p_y \\ p_z \\ 1 \end{bmatrix} = \begin{bmatrix} p_x \\ p_y \\ p_z \\ \dfrac{1}{s} \end{bmatrix}$$

which would be homogenized to

$$\begin{bmatrix} Sp_x \\ Sp_y \\ Sp_z \\ 1 \end{bmatrix}$$

Direct Painting

A convenient way to create a complex image is to start with a blank "canvas" raster map (an array of pixels, also known as a bitmap) filled with some uniform background color and then "draw", "paint" or "paste" simple patches of color onto it, in an appropriate order. In particular the canvas may be the frame buffer for a computer display.

Some programs will set the pixel colors directly, but most will rely on some 2D graphics library and/or the machine's graphics card, which usually implement the following operations:

- paste a given image at a specified offset onto the canvas;
- write a string of characters with a specified font, at a given position and angle;
- paint a simple geometric shape, such as a triangle defined by three corners, or a circle with given center and radius;
- draw a line segment, arc, or simple curve with a virtual pen of given width.

Extended Color Models

Text, shapes and lines are rendered with a client-specified color. Many libraries and cards provide color gradients, which are handy for the generation of smoothly-varying backgrounds, shadow effects, etc. (See also Gouraud shading). The pixel colors can also be taken from a texture, e.g. a digital image (thus emulating rub-on screentones and the fabled "checker paint" which used to be available only in cartoons).

Painting a pixel with a given color usually replaces its previous color. However, many systems support painting with transparent and translucent colors, which only modify the previous pixel values. The two colors may also be combined in more complex ways, e.g. by computing their bitwise exclusive or. This technique is known as inverting color or color inversion, and is often used in graphical user interfaces for highlighting, rubber-band drawing, and other volatile painting—since re-painting the same shapes with the same color will restore the original pixel values.

Layers

The models used in 2D computer graphics usually do not provide for three-dimensional shapes, or three-dimensional optical phenomena such as lighting, shadows, reflection, refraction, etc. However, they usually can model multiple *layers* (conceptually of ink, paper, or film; opaque, translucent, or transparent—stacked in a specific order. The ordering is usually defined by a single number (the layer's *depth*, or distance from the viewer).

A 2D animated character composited with 3D backgrounds using layers.

Layered models are sometimes called *2½-D computer graphics*. They make it possible to mimic traditional drafting and printing techniques based on film and paper, such as cutting and pasting; and allow the user to edit any layer without affecting the others. For these reasons, they are used in most graphics editors. Layered models also allow better spatial anti-aliasing of complex drawings and provide a sound model for certain techniques such as mitered joints and the even-odd rule.

Layered models are also used to allow the user to suppress unwanted information when viewing or printing a document, e.g. roads and/or railways from a map, certain process layers from an integrated circuit diagram, or hand annotations from a business letter.

In a layer-based model, the target image is produced by "painting" or "pasting" each layer, in order of decreasing depth, on the virtual canvas. Conceptually, each layer is first rendered on its own, yielding a digital image with the desired resolution which is then painted over the canvas, pixel by pixel. Fully transparent parts of a layer need not be rendered, of course. The rendering and painting may be done in parallel, i.e., each layer pixel may be painted on the canvas as soon as it is produced by the rendering procedure.

Layers that consist of complex geometric objects (such as text or polylines) may be broken down into simpler elements (characters or line segments, respectively), which are then painted as separate layers, in some order. However, this solution may create undesirable aliasing artifacts wherever two elements overlap the same pixel.

2D Graphics Hardware

Modern computer graphics card displays almost overwhelmingly use raster techniques, dividing the screen into a rectangular grid of pixels, due to the relatively low cost of raster-based video hardware as compared with vector graphic hardware. Most graphic hardware has internal support for blitting operations and/or sprite drawing. A co-processor dedicated to blitting is known as a *Blitter chip.*

Classic 2D graphics chips and graphics processing units of the late 1970s to 1980s, used in 8-bit to early 16-bit, arcade games, video game consoles, and home computers, include:

- Atari's TIA, ANTIC, CTIA and GTIA

- Capcom's CPS-A and CPS-B

- Commodore's OCS

- MOS Technology's VIC and VIC-II

- Fujitsu's MB14241

- Hudson Soft's Cynthia and HuC6270

- NEC's µPD7220 and µPD72120

- Ricoh's PPU and S-PPU

- Sega's VDP, Super Scaler, 315-5011/315-5012 and 315-5196/315-5197

- Texas Instruments' TMS9918

- Yamaha's V9938, V9958 and YM7101 VDP

2D Graphics Software

Many graphical user interfaces (GUIs), including Mac OS, Microsoft Windows, or the X Window System, are primarily based on 2D graphical concepts. Such software provides a visual environment for interacting with the computer, and commonly includes some form of window manager to aid the user in conceptually distinguishing between different applications. The user interface within individual software applications is typically 2D in nature as well, due in part to the fact that most common input devices, such as the mouse, are constrained to two dimensions of movement.

2D graphics are very important in the control peripherals such as printers, plotters, sheet cutting machines, etc. They were also used in most early video games; and are still used for card and board games such as solitaire, chess, mahjongg, etc.

2D graphics editors or *drawing programs* are application-level software for the creation of images, diagrams and illustrations by direct manipulation (through the mouse, graphics tablet, or similar device) of 2D computer graphics primitives. These editors generally provide geometric primitives as well as digital images; and some even support procedural models. The illustration is usually represented internally as a layered model, often with a hierarchical structure to make editing more convenient. These editors generally output graphics files where the layers and primitives are separately preserved in their original form. MacDraw, introduced in 1984 with the Macintosh line of computers, was an early example of this class; recent examples are the commercial products Adobe Illustrator and CorelDRAW, and the free editors such as xfig or Inkscape. There are also many 2D graphics editors specialized for certain types of drawings such as electrical, electronic and VLSI diagrams, topographic maps, computer fonts, etc.

Image editors are specialized for the manipulation of digital images, mainly by means of free-hand drawing/painting and signal processing operations. They typically use a direct-painting paradigm, where the user controls virtual pens, brushes, and other free-hand artistic instruments to apply paint to a virtual canvas. Some image editors support a multiple-layer model; however, in order to support signal-processing operations like blurring each layer is normally represented as a digital image. Therefore, any geometric primitives that are provided by the editor are immediately converted to pixels and painted onto the canvas. The name *raster graphics editor* is sometimes used to contrast this approach to that of general editors which also handle *vector graphics*. One of the first popular image editors was Apple's MacPaint, companion to MacDraw. Modern examples are the free GIMP editor, and the commercial products Photoshop and Paint Shop Pro. This class too includes many specialized editors — for medicine, remote sensing, digital photography, etc.

Developmental Animation

With the resurgence of 2D animation, free and proprietary software packages have become widely available for amateurs and professional animators. The principal issue with 2D animation is labor requirements. With software like RETAS and Adobe After Effects, coloring and compositing can be done in less time.

Various approaches have been developed to aid and speed up the process of digital 2D animation. For example, by generating vector artwork in a tool like Adobe Flash an artist may employ software-driven automatic coloring and in-betweening.

3D Computer Graphics

Three-dimensional computer graphics (3D computer graphics, in contrast to 2D computer graphics) are graphics that use a three-dimensional representation of geometric data (often Cartesian) that is stored in the computer for the purposes of performing calculations and rendering 2D images. Such images may be stored for viewing later or displayed in real-time.

3D computer graphics rely on many of the same algorithms as 2D computer vector graphics in the wire-frame model and 2D computer raster graphics in the final rendered display. In computer graphics software, the distinction between 2D and 3D is occasionally blurred; 2D applications may use 3D techniques to achieve effects such as lighting, and 3D may use 2D rendering techniques.

3D computer graphics are often referred to as 3D models. Apart from the rendered graphic, the model is contained within the graphical data file. However, there are differences: a 3D model is the mathematical representation of any three-dimensional object. A model is not technically a graphic until it is displayed. A model can be displayed visually as a two-dimensional image through a process called 3D rendering or used in non-graphical computer simulations and calculations. With 3D printing, 3D models are similarly rendered into a 3D physical representation of the model, with limitations to how accurate the rendering can match the virtual model.

History

William Fetter was credited with coining the term *computer graphics* in 1961 to describe his work at Boeing. One of the first displays of computer animation was *Futureworld* (1976), which included an animation of a human face and a hand that had originally appeared in the 1972 experimental short *A Computer Animated Hand*, created by University of Utah students Edwin Catmull and Fred Parke.

Overview

3D computer graphics creation falls into three basic phases:

- 3D modeling – the process of forming a computer model of an object's shape

- Layout and animation – the motion and placement of objects within a scene

- 3D rendering – the computer calculations that, based on light placement, surface types, and other qualities, generate the image

Modeling

The model describes the process of forming the shape of an object. The two most common sources of 3D models are those that an artist or engineer originates on the computer with some kind of 3D modeling tool, and models scanned into a computer from real-world objects. Models can also be produced procedurally or via physical simulation. Basically, a 3D model is formed from points called vertices (or vertexes) that define the shape and form polygons. A polygon is an area formed from at least three vertexes (a triangle). A polygon of n points is an n-gon. The overall integrity of the model and its suitability to use in animation depend on the structure of the polygons.

Layout and Animation

Before rendering into an image, objects must be laid out (place) in a scene. This defines spatial relationships between objects, including location and size. Animation refers to the temporal description of an object (i.e., how it moves and deforms over time. Popular methods include keyframing, inverse kinematics, and motion capture). These techniques are often used in combination. As with animation, physical simulation also specifies motion.

Rendering

Rendering converts a model into an image either by simulating light transport to get photo-realistic images, or by applying an art style as in non-photorealistic rendering. The two basic operations in realistic rendering are transport (how much light gets from one place to another) and scattering (how surfaces interact with light). This step is usually performed using 3D computer graphics software or a 3D graphics API. Altering the scene into a suitable form for rendering also involves 3D projection, which displays a three-dimensional image in two dimensions.

Examples of 3D Rendering

Left: A 3D rendering with ray tracing and ambient occlusion using Blender and YafaRay.
Center: A 3d model of a *Dunkerque*-class battleship rendered with flat shading.
2-nd Center: During the 3D rendering step, the number of reflections "light rays" can take, as well as various other attributes, can be tailored to achieve a desired visual effect. Rendered with Cobalt.
Right: Experience Curiosity, a real-time web application which leverages 3D rendering capabilities of browsers (WebGL).

Communities

There are a multitude of websites designed to help, educate and support 3D graphic artists. Some are managed by software developers and content providers, but there are standalone sites as well. These communities allow for members to seek advice, post tutorials, provide product reviews or post examples of their own work.

Differences with Other Types of Computer Graphics

Distinction from Photorealistic 2D Graphics

Not all computer graphics that appear 3D are based on a wireframe model. 2D computer graphics with 3D photorealistic effects are often achieved without wireframe modeling and are sometimes indistinguishable in the final form. Some graphic art software includes filters that can be applied to 2D vector graphics or 2D raster graphics on transparent layers. Visual artists may also copy or visualize 3D effects and manually render photorealistic effects without the use of filters.

Pseudo-3D and *True 3D*

Some video games use restricted projections of three-dimensional environments, such as isometric graphics or virtual cameras with fixed angles, either as a way to improve performance of the game engine, or for stylistic and gameplay concerns. Such games are said to use pseudo-3D graphics. By contrast, games using 3D computer graphics without such restrictions are said to use true 3D.

References

- Pile Jr, John (May 2013). 2D Graphics Programming for Games. New York, NY: CRC Press. ISBN 1466501898.

- "Pixar founder's Utah-made Hand added to National Film Registry". The Salt Lake Tribune. December 28, 2011. Retrieved January 8, 2012.

Components of Computer Graphics

The main components of computer graphics are sprite, vector graphics, 3D modeling, computer vision and user interface design. Vector graphics present images in computers by using polygons. The major components of computer graphics are discussed in the following chapter.

Sprite (Computer Graphics)

In computer graphics, a sprite is a two-dimensional bitmap that is integrated into a larger scene.

Originally sprites referred to independent objects that are composited together, by hardware, with other elements such as a background. This occurs as each scan line is prepared for the video output device, such as a CRT, without involvement of the main CPU and without the need for a full-screen frame buffer. Sprites can be positioned or altered by setting attributes used during the hardware composition process. Examples of systems with hardware sprites include the Atari 8-bit family, Commodore 64, Nintendo Entertainment System, Sega Genesis, and many coin-operated arcade machines of the 1980s.

Use of the term "sprite" has expanded to refer to any two-dimensional bitmap used as part of a graphics display, even if drawn into a frame buffer (by either software or a GPU) instead of being composited on-the-fly at display time.

History

In the mid-1970s, Signetics devised the first video/graphics processors capable of generating sprite graphics. The Signetics 2636 video processors were first used in the 1976 Radofin 1292 Advanced Programmable Video System.

The Atari VCS, released in 1977, features a hardware sprite implementation where five graphical objects can be moved independently of the game playfield. The term *sprite* was not in use at the time. The VCS's sprites are called *movable objects* in the programming manual, further identified as two *players*, two *missiles*, and one *ball*. These each consist of a single row of pixels that are displayed on a scan line. To produce a two-dimensional shape, the sprite's single-row bitmap is altered by software from one scanline to the next.

The Atari 400 and 800 home computers of 1979 feature similar, but more elaborate, circuitry capable of moving eight single-color objects per scan line: four 8-bit wide *players* and four 2-bit wide *missiles*. Each is the full height of the display—a long, thin strip. DMA from a table in memory automatically sets the graphics pattern registers for each scan line. Hardware registers control the horizontal position of each player and missile. Vertical motion is achieved by moving the bitmap data within a player or missile's strip. The feature was called "player/missile graphics" by Atari.

The Elektor TV Games Computer was an early microcomputer capable of generating sprite graphics, which Signetics referred to as "objects".

The term *sprite* was first used in the graphic sense by one of the definers of the Texas Instruments 9918(A) video display processor (VDP). The term was derived from the fact that sprites, rather than being part of the bitmap data in the framebuffer, instead "floated" around on top without affecting the data in the framebuffer below, much like a ghost or "sprite". By this time, sprites had advanced to the point where complete two-dimensional shapes could be moved around the screen horizontally and vertically with minimal software overhead.

The CPU would instruct the external chips to fetch source images and integrate them into the main screen using direct memory access channels. Calling up external hardware, instead of using the processor alone, greatly improved graphics performance. Because the processor was not occupied by the simple task of transferring data from one place to another, software could run faster; and because the hardware provided certain innate abilities, programs were also smaller.

Hardware Sprites

Many early graphics chips had true spriting use capabilities in which the sprite images were integrated into the screen, often with priority control with respect to the background graphics, at the time the video signal was being generated by the graphics chip.

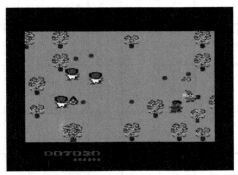

A simple C64 game with few sprites (hardware sprites)

These contrasted with software and blitter methods of 2D animation which modify a framebuffer held in RAM, which required more memory cycles to load and store the pixels, sometimes with an additional mask, and refresh backgrounds behind moving objects. These methods frequently required double buffering to avoid flickering and tearing, but placed fewer restrictions on the size and number of moving objects.

The sprite engine is a hardware implementation of scanline rendering. For each scanline the appropriate scanlines of the sprites are first copied (the number of pixels is limited by the memory bandwidth and the length of the horizontal retrace) into very fast, small, multiple (limiting the number of sprites on a line), and costly caches (the size of which limit the horizontal width) and as the pixels are sent to the screen, these caches are combined with each other and the background. It may be larger than the screen and is usually tiled, where the tile map is cached, but the tile set is not. For every pixel, every sprite unit signals its presence onto its line on a bus, so every other unit can notice a collision with it. Some sprite engines can automatically reload their "sprite units" from a display list. The sprite engine has synergy with the palette. To save registers, the height of the sprite, the location of the texture, and the zoom factors are often limited. On systems where the word size is the same as the texel there is no penalty for doing unaligned reads needed for rotation. This leads to the limitations of the known implementations:

Sprite hardware features													
Computer, chip	Year	Sprites on screen	Sprites on line	Max. texels on line	Texture width	Texture height	Colors	Hardware zoom	Rotation	Background	Collision detection	Transparency	Source
Amiga, Denise	1985	Display list	8	?	16	Arbitrary	3, 15	Vertical by display list	No	2 bitmap layers	Yes	Color key	
Amiga (AGA), Lisa	1992	Display list	8	?	16, 32, 64	Arbitrary	3, 15	Vertical by display list	No	2 bitmap layers	Yes	Color key	
Amstrad Plus, Asic	1990	Display list run by CPU	16 min.	?	16	16	15	1, 2, 4× vertical, 1, 2, 4× horizontal	No	Bitmap layer	No	Color key	
Atari 2600, TIA	1977	Multiplied by CPU	9 (with triplication)	51 (with triplication)	1, 8	262	1	1, 2, 4, 8× horizontal	Horizontal mirroring	1 bitmap layer	Yes	Color key	
Atari 8-bit, GTIA/AN-TIC	1979	Display list	8	40	2, 8	128, 256	1,3	1, 2× vertical, 1, 2, 4× horizontal	No	1 tile or bitmap layer	Yes	Color key	
C64, VIC-II	1982	Display list run by CPU	8	96, 192	12, 24	21	1, 3	1, 2× integer	No	1 tile or bitmap layer	Yes	Color key	
Game Boy	1989	40	10	80	8	8, 16	3	No	Horizontal and vertical mirroring	1 tile layer	No	Color key	

Sprite hardware features													
Computer, chip	Year	Sprites on screen	Sprites on line	Max. texels on line	Texture width	Texture height	Colors	Hardware zoom	Rota-tion	Back-ground	Collision detec-tion	Trans-parency	Source
Game Boy Advance	2001	128	128	1210	8, 16, 32, 64	8, 16, 32, 64	15, 255	Yes, affine	Yes, affine	4 layers, 2 layers, and 1 affine layer, 2 affine layers	No	Color key, blending	
Gameduino	2011	256	96	1,536	16	16	255	No	Yes	1 tile layer	Yes	Color key	
NES, RP2C0x	1983	64	8	64	8	8, 16	3	No	Horizon-tal and vertical mirroring	1 tile layer	Partial	Color key	
Neo Geo	1990	384	96	1536	16	16 to 512	15	Sprite shrinking	Horizon-tal and vertical mirroring	1 tile layer	Partial	Color key	
PC Engine, HuC6270A	1987	64	16	256	16, 32	16, 32, 64	15	No	No	1 tile layer	Yes	Color key	
Master System, Game Gear	1985	64	8	128	8, 16	8, 16	15	1, 2× inte-ger, 1, 2× vertical	Back-ground tile mir-roring	1 tile layer	Yes	Color key	
Genesis	1988	80	20	320	8, 16, 24, 32	8, 16, 24, 32	15	Integer, up to full screen	Horizon-tal and vertical mirroring	2 tile layers	Yes	Color key	
OutRun, dedicated hardware	1986	128	128	1600	8 to 512	8 to 256	15	Yes, anisotro-pic	Horizon-tal and vertical mirroring	2 tile layers and 1 bitmap layer	Yes	Alpha	
Sega Saturn, Sega ST-V	1994	16,384	555	4443	8 to 504	1 to 255	15 to 32,768	Yes	Yes, rotation and dis-tortion	3-6 tile layers and 1-4 bitmap layers	Yes	Alpha	
X68000	1987	128 (512 with raster interrupt)	32	512	16	16	15	1, 2× integer	Horizon-tal and vertical mirroring	1-2 tile layers and 1-4 bitmap layers	Partial	Color key	
PlaySta-tion, Namco System 11	1994	4000	128	1024	8, 16, 256	8, 16, 256	15, 255	Yes	Yes	1 bitmap layer	Partial	Alpha	
SNES	1990	128	34	272	8, 16, 32, 64	8, 16, 32, 64	15	Back-ground only	Back-ground only	3 tile layers or 1 affine mapped tile layer	Yes	Color key, averaging	
Texas Instruments TMS9918	1979	32	4	64	8, 16	8, 16	1	1, 2× integer	No	1 tile layer	Partial	Color key	

Sprite hardware features													
Computer, chip	Year	Sprites on screen	Sprites on line	Max. texels on line	Texture width	Texture height	Colors	Hardware zoom	Rota-tion	Back-ground	Collision detec-tion	Trans-parency	Source
Yamaha V9938	1986	32	8	128	8, 16	8,16	1, 3, 7, 15 per line	1, 2× integer	No	1 tile or bitmap layer	Partial	Color key	
Yamaha V9958	1988	32	8	128	8,16	8,16	1, 3, 7, 15 per line	1, 2× integer	No	1 tile or bitmap layer	Partial	Color key	
Computer, chip	Year	Sprites on screen	Sprites on line	Max. texels on line	Texture width	Texture height	Colors	Hardware zoom	Rota-tion	Back-ground	Collision detec-tion	Trans-parency	Source

Many third party graphics cards offered sprite capabilities. Sprite engines often scale badly, starting to flicker as the number of sprites increases above the number of sprite units, or uses more and more silicon as the designer of the chip implements more units and bigger caches.

Use in 3D Rendering

2D images with alpha channels constrained to face the camera may be used in 3D graphics. They are common for rendering vegetation, to approximate distant objects, or for particle effects. These are sometimes called billboards or Z-sprites. The technique was most heavily used in sega 3d game machines in the late 1990s, prior to the era of polygon rendering. If rendered on the fly to cache an approximate view of an underlying 3D model, such sprites are called impostors. Modern hardware may have a specific mode for rendering such point sprites without needing each corner to be defined, or these may be generated by vertex shaders.

Synonyms

Some hardware makers used terms other than *sprite*, and other terms exist to describe various forms of software-rendering of sprites:

- Player-Missile Graphics was a term used by Atari, Inc. for hardware-generated sprites in the company's early coin-op games, the Atari 2600 and 5200 consoles and the Atari 8-bit computers. The term reflected the usage for both characters ("players") and other objects ("missiles"). They had restricted horizontal size (8 or 2 pixels, albeit with scalability) and vertical size equal to height of the entire screen.

- Movable Object Block, or MOB, was used in MOS Technology's graphics chip literature (data sheets, etc.) However, Commodore, the main user of MOS chips and the owner of MOS for most of the chip maker's lifetime, applied the common term "sprite", except for Amiga line of home computers, where MOB was the preferred term.

- The developer manuals for the Nintendo Entertainment System, Super NES, and Game Boy referred to sprites as OBJs (short for "objects"), and the region of RAM used to store sprite attributes and coordinates was known as OAM (Object Attribute Memory). This still applies today on the Game Boy Advance and Nintendo DS handheld systems. However, *Nintendo Power* referred to them as sprites in articles about the NES architecture in the magazine's third year.

- Software sprites were used to refer to subroutines that used bit blitting to accomplish the same goal on systems such as the Atari ST and the Apple II whose graphics hardware had no sprite capability.

Vector Graphics

Vector graphics is the use of polygons to represent images in computer graphics. Vector graphics are based on vectors, which lead through locations called control points or nodes. Each of these points has a definite position on the x and y axes of the work plane and determines the direction of the path; further, each path may be assigned various attributes, including such values as stroke color, shape, curve, thickness, and fill.

Overview

One of the first uses of vector graphic displays was the US SAGE air defense system. Vector graphics systems were only retired from U.S. en route air traffic control in 1999, and are likely still in use in military and specialised systems. Vector graphics were also used on the TX-2 at the MIT Lincoln Laboratory by computer graphics pioneer Ivan Sutherland to run his program Sketchpad in 1963.

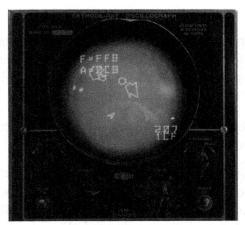

A free software Asteroids-like video game played on a vector monitor.

Subsequent vector graphics systems, most of which iterated through dynamically modifiable stored lists of drawing instructions, include the IBM 2250, Imlac PDS-1, and

DEC GT40. There was a home gaming system that used vector graphics called Vectrex as well as various arcade games like *Asteroids*, *Space Wars* and many cinematronics titles such as *Rip-Off*, and *Tail Gunner* using vector monitors. Storage scope displays, such as the Tektronix 4014, could display vector images but not modify them without first erasing the display.

In computer typography, modern outline fonts describe printable characters (glyphs) by cubic or quadratic mathematical curves with control points. Nevertheless, bitmap fonts are still in use. Converting outlines requires filling them in; converting to bitmaps is not trivial, because bitmaps often don't have sufficient resolution to avoid "stairstepping" ("aliasing"), especially with smaller visible character sizes. Processing outline character data in sophisticated fashion to create satisfactory bitmaps for rendering is called "hinting". Although the term implies suggestion, the process is deterministic, and done by executable code, essentially a special-purpose computer language. While automatic hinting is possible, results can be inferior to that done by experts.

Modern vector graphics displays can sometimes be found at laser light shows, where two fast-moving X-Y mirrors position the beam to rapidly draw shapes and text as straight and curved strokes on a screen.

Vector graphics can be created in form using a pen plotter, a special type of printer that uses a series of ballpoint and felt-tip pens on a servo-driven mount that moves horizontally across the paper, with the plotter moving the paper back and forth through its paper path for vertical movement. Although a typical plot might easily require a few thousand paper motions, back and forth, the paper doesn't slip. In a tiny roll-fed plotter made by Alps in Japan, teeth on thin sprockets indented the paper near its edges on the first pass, and maintained registration on subsequent passes.

Some Hewlett-Packard pen plotters had two-axis pen carriers and stationery paper (plot size was limited). However, the moving-paper H-P plotters had grit wheels (akin to machine-shop grinding wheels) which, on the first pass, indented the paper surface, and collectively maintained registration.

Present-day vector graphic files such as engineering drawings are typically printed as bitmaps, after vector-to-raster conversion.

The term "vector graphics" is mainly used today in the context of two-dimensional computer graphics. It is one of several modes an artist can use to create an image on a raster display. Other modes include text, multimedia, and 3D rendering. Virtually all modern 3D rendering is done using extensions of 2D vector graphics techniques. Plotters used in technical drawing still draw vectors directly to paper.

A vector-based image of a round four-color swirl.

Standards

The World Wide Web Consortium (W3C) standard for vector graphics is Scalable Vector Graphics (SVG). The standard is complex and has been relatively slow to be established at least in part owing to commercial interests. Many web browsers now have some support for rendering SVG data, but full implementations of the standard are still comparatively rare.

In recent years, SVG has become a significant format that is completely independent of the resolution of the rendering device, typically a printer or display monitor. SVG files are essentially printable text that describes both straight and curved paths, as well as other attributes. Wikipedia prefers SVG for images such as simple maps, line illustrations, coats of arms, and flags, which generally are not like photographs or other continuous-tone images. Rendering SVG requires conversion to raster format at a resolution appropriate for the current task. SVG is also a format for animated graphics.

There is also a version of SVG for mobile phones. In particular, the specific format for mobile phones is called SVGT (SVG Tiny version). These images can count links and also exploit anti-aliasing. They can also be displayed as wallpaper.

Conversion

Detail can be added to or removed from vector art.

Original reference photo before vectorization

To raster

From raster

Modern displays and printers are raster devices; vector formats have to be converted to raster format (bitmaps – pixel arrays) before they can be rendered (displayed or printed). The size of the bitmap/raster-format file generated by the conversion will depend on the resolution required, but the size of the vector file generating the bitmap/raster file will always remain the same. Thus, it is easy to convert from a vector file to a range of bitmap/raster file formats but it is much more difficult to go in the opposite direction, especially if subsequent editing of the vector picture is required. It might be an advantage to save an image created from a vector source file as a bitmap/raster format, because different systems have different (and incompatible) vector formats, and some might not support vector graphics at all. However, once a file is converted from the vector format, it is likely to be bigger, and it loses the advantage of scalability without loss of resolution. It will also no longer be possible to edit individual parts of the image as discrete objects. The file size of a vector graphic image depends on the number of graphic elements it contains; it is a list of descriptions.

Printing

Vector art is ideal for printing since the art is made from a series of mathematical curves, it will print very crisply even when resized. For instance, one can print a vector logo on a small sheet of copy paper, and then enlarge the same vector logo to billboard size and keep the same crisp quality. A low-resolution raster graphic would blur or pixelate excessively if it were enlarged from business card size to billboard size. (The precise resolution of a raster graphic necessary for high-quality results depends on the viewing distance; e.g., a billboard may still appear to be of high quality even at low resolution if the viewing distance is great enough.)

If we regard typographic characters as images, then the same considerations that we have made for graphics apply even to composition of written text for printing (typesetting). Older character sets were stored as bitmaps. Therefore, to achieve maximum print quality they had to be used at a given resolution only; these font formats are said to be non-scalable. High quality typography is nowadays based on character drawings (fonts) which are typically stored as vector graphics, and as such are scalable to any size. Examples of these vector formats for characters are Postscript fonts and TrueType fonts.

Operation

Advantages to this style of drawing over raster graphics:

- This minimal amount of information translates to a much smaller file size compared to large raster images (the size of representation does not depend on the dimensions of the object), though a vector graphic with a small file size is often said to lack detail compared with a real world photo.

- Correspondingly, one can infinitely zoom in on e.g., a circle arc, and it remains smooth. On the other hand, a polygon representing a curve will reveal being not really curved.

- On zooming in, lines and curves need not get wider proportionally. Often the width is either not increased or less than proportional. On the other hand, irregular curves represented by simple geometric shapes may be made proportionally wider when zooming in, to keep them looking smooth and not like these geometric shapes.

- The parameters of objects are stored and can be later modified. This means that moving, scaling, rotating, filling etc. doesn't degrade the quality of a drawing. Moreover, it is usual to specify the dimensions in device-independent units, which results in the best possible rasterization on raster devices.

- From a 3-D perspective, rendering shadows is also much more realistic with vector graphics, as shadows can be abstracted into the rays of light from which they are formed. This allows for photo realistic images and renderings.

For example, consider a circle of radius r. The main pieces of information a program needs in order to draw this circle are

1. an indication that what is to be drawn is a circle

2. the radius r

3. the location of the center point of the circle

4. stroke line style and color (possibly transparent)

5. fill style and color (possibly transparent)

Vector formats are not always appropriate in graphics work and also have numerous disadvantages. For example, devices such as cameras and scanners produce essentially continuous-tone raster graphics that are impractical to convert into vectors, and so for this type of work, an image editor will operate on the pixels rather than on drawing objects defined by mathematical expressions. Comprehensive graphics tools will combine images from vector and raster sources, and may provide editing tools for both, since some parts of an image could come from a camera source, and others could have been drawn using vector tools.

Some authors have criticized the term *vector graphics* as being confusing. In particular, *vector graphics* does not simply refer to graphics described by Euclidean vectors. Some authors have proposed to use *object-oriented graphics* instead. However this term can also be confusing as it can be read as any kind of graphics implemented using object-oriented programming.

Typical Primitive Objects

Any particular vector file format supports only some kinds of primitive objects. Nearly all vector file formats support simple and fast-rendering primitive objects:

- Lines, polylines and polygons

- Bézier curves and bezigons

- Circles and ellipses

Most vector file formats support

- Text (in computer font formats such as TrueType where each letter is created from Bézier curves) or quadratics.

- Color gradients

- Often, a bitmap image is considered as a primitive object. From the conceptual view, it behaves as a rectangle.

A few vector file formats support more complex objects as primitives:

- Many computer-aided design applications support splines and other curves, such as:

    o Catmull–Rom splines

    o NURBS

- iterated function systems

- superellipses and superellipsoids

- metaballs

- etc.

If an image stored in one vector file format is converted to another file format that supports all the primitive objects used in that particular image, then the conversion can be lossless.

Vector Operations

Vector graphics editors typically allow rotation, movement (without rotation), mirroring, stretching, skewing, affine transformations, changing of z-order (loosely, what's in front of what) and combination of primitives into more complex objects.

More sophisticated transformations include set operations on closed shapes (union, difference, intersection, etc.).

Vector graphics are ideal for simple or composite drawings that need to be device-independent, or do not need to achieve photo-realism. For example, the PostScript and PDF page description languages use a vector graphics model.

3D Modeling

In 3D computer graphics, 3D modeling (or three-dimensional modelling) is the process of developing a mathematical representation of any three-dimensional *surface* of an object (either inanimate or living) via specialized software. The product is called a 3D model. It can be displayed as a two-dimensional image through a process called *3D rendering* or used in a computer simulation of physical phenomena. The model can also be physically created using 3D printing devices.

Models may be created automatically or manually. The manual modeling process of preparing geometric data for 3D computer graphics is similar to plastic arts such as sculpting.

3D modeling software is a class of 3D computer graphics software used to produce 3D models. Individual programs of this class are called modeling applications or modelers.

Models

3D models represent a physical body using a collection of points in 3D space, connected by various geometric entities such as triangles, lines, curved surfaces, etc. Being a collection of data (points and other information), 3D models can be created by hand, algorithmically (procedural modeling), or scanned. Their surfaces may be further defined with texture mapping.

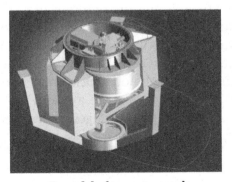

3D model of a spectrograph

3D models are widely used anywhere in 3D graphics and CAD. Actually, their use predates the widespread use of 3D graphics on personal computers. Many computer games used pre-rendered images of 3D models as sprites before computers could render them in real-time.

Today, 3D models are used in a wide variety of fields. The medical industry uses detailed models of organs; these may be created with multiple 2-D image slices from an MRI or CT scan. The movie industry uses them as characters and objects for animated and real-life motion pictures. The video game industry uses them as assets for computer and video games. The science sector uses them as highly detailed models of chemical compounds. The architecture industry uses them to demonstrate proposed buildings and landscapes in lieu of traditional, physical architectural models. The engineering community uses them as designs of new devices, vehicles and structures as well as a host of other uses. In recent decades the earth science community has started to construct 3D geological models as a standard practice. 3D models can also be the basis for physical devices that are built with 3D printers or CNC machines.

Representation

Almost all 3D models can be divided into two categories.

- Solid - These models define the volume of the object they represent (like a rock). These are more realistic, but more difficult to build. Solid models are mostly used for nonvisual simulations such as medical and engineering simulations, for CAD and specialized visual applications such as ray tracing and constructive solid geometry

- Shell/boundary - these models represent the surface, e.g. the boundary of the object, not its volume (like an infinitesimally thin eggshell). These are easier to work with than solid models. Almost all visual models used in games and film are shell models.

Because the appearance of an object depends largely on the exterior of the object, boundary representations are common in computer graphics. Two dimensional surfaces are a good analogy for the objects used in graphics, though quite often these objects are non-manifold. Since surfaces are not finite, a discrete digital approximation is required: polygonal meshes (and to a lesser extent subdivision surfaces) are by far the most common representation, although point-based representations have been gaining some popularity in recent years. Level sets are a useful representation for deforming surfaces which undergo many topological changes such as fluids.

The process of transforming representations of objects, such as the middle point coordinate of a sphere and a point on its circumference into a polygon representation of a sphere, is called tessellation. This step is used in polygon-based rendering, where objects are broken down from abstract representations ("primitives") such as spheres, cones etc., to so-called *meshes*, which are nets of interconnected triangles. Meshes of triangles (instead of e.g. squares) are popular as they have proven to be easy to rasterise (the surface described by each triangle is planar, so the projection is always convex); . Polygon representations are not used in all rendering techniques, and in these cases the tessellation step is not included in the transition from abstract representation to rendered scene.

Modeling Process

There are three popular ways to represent a model:

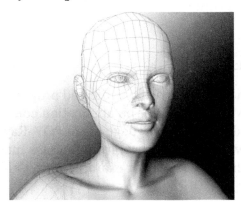

3D polygonal modelling of a human face.

1. Polygonal modeling - Points in 3D space, called vertices, are connected by line segments to form a polygon mesh. The vast majority of 3D models today are built as textured polygonal models, because they are flexible and because computers can render them so quickly. However, polygons are planar and can only approximate curved surfaces using many polygons.

2. Curve modeling - Surfaces are defined by curves, which are influenced by weighted control points. The curve follows (but does not necessarily interpolate) the points. Increasing the weight for a point will pull the curve closer to that point. Curve types include nonuniform rational B-spline (NURBS), splines, patches, and geometric primitives

3. Digital sculpting - Still a fairly new method of modeling, 3D sculpting has become very popular in the few years it has been around. There are currently three types of digital sculpting: Displacement, which is the most widely used among applications at this moment, uses a dense model (often generated by subdivision surfaces of a polygon control mesh) and stores new locations for the vertex positions through use of a 32bit image map that stores the adjusted locations. Volumetric, loosely based on voxels, has similar capabilities as displacement but does not suffer from polygon stretching when there are not enough polygons in a region to achieve a deformation. Dynamic tessellation is similar to voxel but divides the surface using triangulation to maintain a smooth surface and allow finer details. These methods allow for very artistic exploration as the model will have a new topology created over it once the models form and possibly details have been sculpted. The new mesh will usually have the original high

resolution mesh information transferred into displacement data or normal map data if for a game engine.

The modeling stage consists of shaping individual objects that are later used in the scene. There are a number of modeling techniques, including:

- Constructive solid geometry

- Implicit surfaces

- Subdivision surfaces

Modeling can be performed by means of a dedicated program (e.g., Cinema 4D, Maya, 3ds Max, Blender, LightWave, Modo) or an application component (Shaper, Lofter in 3ds Max) or some scene description language (as in POV-Ray). In some cases, there is no strict distinction between these phases; in such cases modeling is just part of the scene creation process (this is the case, for example, with Caligari trueSpace and Real-soft 3D).

Complex materials such as blowing sand, clouds, and liquid sprays are modeled with particle systems, and are a mass of 3D coordinates which have either points, polygons, texture splats, or sprites assigned to them.

Compared to 2D Methods

3D photorealistic effects are often achieved without wireframe modeling and are some-times indistinguishable in the final form. Some graphic art software includes filters that can be applied to 2D vector graphics or 2D raster graphics on transparent layers.

A fully textured and lit rendering of a 3D model.

Advantages of wireframe 3D modeling over exclusively 2D methods include:

- *Flexibility,* ability to change angles or animate images with quicker rendering of the changes;

- *Ease of rendering,* automatic calculation and rendering photorealistic effects rather than mentally visualizing or estimating;

- *Accurate photorealism,* less chance of human error in misplacing, overdoing, or forgetting to include a visual effect.

Disadvantages compare to 2D photorealistic rendering may include a software learning curve and difficulty achieving certain photorealistic effects. Some photorealistic effects may be achieved with special rendering filters included in the 3D modeling software. For the best of both worlds, some artists use a combination of 3D modeling followed by editing the 2D computer-rendered images from the 3D model.

3D Model Market

A large market for 3D models (as well as 3D-related content, such as textures, scripts, etc.) still exists - either for individual models or large collections. Online marketplaces for 3D content, such as TurboSquid, The3DStudio, 3DExport, CreativeCrash, CGTrader, FlatPyramid, NoneCG, CGPeopleNetwork, Design Connected and DAZ 3D, allow individual artists to sell content that they have created. Often, the artists' goal is to get additional value out of assets they have previously created for projects. By doing so, artists can earn more money out of their old content, and companies can save money by buying pre-made models instead of paying an employee to create one from scratch. These marketplaces typically split the sale between themselves and the artist that created the asset, artists get 40% to 95% of the sales according to the marketplace. In most cases, the artist retains ownership of the 3d model; the customer only buys the right to use and present the model. Some artists sell their products directly in its own stores offering their products at a lower price by not using intermediaries.

Over the last several years numerous marketplaces specialized in 3D printing models have emerged. Some of the 3D printing marketplaces are combination of models sharing sites, with or without a built in e-com capability. Some of those platforms also offer 3D printing services on demand, software for model rendering and dynamic viewing of items, etc. Among the most popular 3D printing file sharing platforms are Shapeways, Pinshape, Thingiverse, 3DExport, CGTrader, Treatstock, Threeding, MyMiniFactory and GrabCAD.

3D Printing

3D printing is a form of additive manufacturing technology where a three dimensional object is created by laying down or build from successive layers of material.

In recent years, there has been an upsurge in the number of companies offering personalized 3D printed models of objects that have been scanned, designed in CAD software, and then printed to the customer's requirements. As previously mentioned, 3D models can be purchased from online marketplaces and printed by individuals or companies using commercially available 3D printers, enabling the home-production of objects such as spare parts, mathematical models, and even medical equipment.

Human Models

The first widely available commercial application of human virtual models appeared in 1998 on the Lands' End web site. The human virtual models were created by the company My Virtual Mode Inc. and enabled users to create a model of themselves and try on 3D clothing. There are several modern programs that allow for the creation of virtual human models (Poser being one example).

3D Clothing

The development of cloth simulation software such as Marvelous Designer, CLO3D and Optitex, has enabled artists and fashion designers to model dynamic 3D clothing on the computer. Dynamic 3D clothing is used for virtual fashion catalogs, as well as for dressing 3D characters for video games, 3D animation movies, for digital doubles in movies as well as for making clothes for avatars in virtual worlds such as SecondLife.

Dynamic 3D Clothing Model made in Marvelous Designer

Uses

Steps of forensic facial reconstruction of a mummy made in Blender by the Brazilian 3D designer Cícero Moraes.

3D modelling is also used in the field of Industrial Design, wherein products are 3D modeled before representing them to the clients. In Media and Event industries, 3D modelling is used in Stage/Set Design.

Graphics Processing Unit

A graphics processing unit (GPU), also occasionally called visual processing unit (VPU), is a specialized electronic circuit designed to rapidly manipulate and alter memory to accelerate the creation of images in a frame buffer intended for output to a display. GPUs are used in embedded systems, mobile phones, personal computers, workstations, and game consoles. Modern GPUs are very efficient at manipulating computer graphics and image processing, and their highly parallel structure makes them more efficient than general-purpose CPUs for algorithms where the processing of large blocks of data is done in parallel. In a personal computer, a GPU can be present on a video card, or it can be embedded on the motherboard or—in certain CPUs—on the CPU die.

GeForce 6600GT (NV43) GPU

The term GPU was popularized by Nvidia in 1999, who marketed the GeForce 256 as "the world's first GPU", or Graphics Processing Unit. It was presented as a "single-chip processor with integrated transform, lighting, triangle setup/clipping, and rendering engines that are capable of processing a minimum of 10 million polygons per second". Rival ATI Technologies coined the term "visual processing unit" or VPU with the release of the Radeon 9700 in 2002.

History

1970s

Arcade system boards have been using specialized graphics chips since the 1970s. The key to understanding early video games hardware is that the RAM for frame buffers was too expensive, so video chips composited data together as the display was being scanned out on the monitor.

Fujitsu's MB14241 video shifter was used to accelerate the drawing of sprite graphics for various 1970s arcade games from Taito and Midway, such as *Gun Fight* (1975), *Sea Wolf* (1976) and *Space Invaders* (1978). The Namco Galaxian arcade system in 1979 used specialized graphics hardware supporting RGB color, multi-colored sprites and tilemap backgrounds. The Galaxian hardware was widely used during the golden age of arcade video games, by game companies such as Namco, Centuri, Gremlin, Irem, Konami, Midway, Nichibutsu, Sega and Taito.

In the home market, the Atari 2600 in 1977 used a video shifter called the Television Interface Adaptor. The Atari 8-bit computers (1979) had ANTIC, a video processor which interpreted instructions describing a "display list"—the way the scan lines map to specific bitmapped or character modes and where the memory is stored (so there did not need to be a contiguous frame buffer). 6502 machine code subroutines could be triggered on scan lines by setting a bit on a display list instruction. ANTIC also supported smooth vertical and horizontal scrolling independent of the CPU.

1980s

The Williams Electronics arcade games *Robotron: 2084* , *Joust*, *Sinistar*, and *Bubbles*, all released in 1982, contain custom blitter chips for operating on 16-color bitmaps.

In 1985, the Commodore Amiga featured a custom graphics chip, with a blitter unit accelerating bitmap manipulation, line draw, and area fill functions. Also included is a coprocessor with its own primitive instruction set, capable of manipulating graphics hardware registers in sync with the video beam (e.g. for per-scanline palette switches, sprite multiplexing, and hardware windowing), or driving the blitter.

In 1986, Texas Instruments released the TMS34010, the first microprocessor with on-chip graphics capabilities. It could run general-purpose code, but it had a very graphics-oriented instruction set. In 1990-1992, this chip would become the basis of the Texas Instruments Graphics Architecture ("TIGA") Windows accelerator cards.

In 1987, the IBM 8514 graphics system was released as one of the first video cards for IBM PC compatibles to implement fixed-function 2D primitives in electronic hardware. The same year, Sharp released the X68000, which used a custom graphics chipset that was powerful for a home computer at the time, with a 65,536 color palette and hardware support for sprites, scrolling and multiple playfields, eventually serving as a development machine for Capcom's CP System arcade board. Fujitsu later competed with the FM Towns computer, released in 1989 with support for a full 16,777,216 color palette.

In 1988, the first dedicated polygonal 3D graphics boards were introduced in arcades with the Namco System 21 and Taito Air System.

1990s

In 1991, S3 Graphics introduced the *S3 86C911*, which its designers named after the Porsche 911 as an implication of the performance increase it promised. The 86C911 spawned a host of imitators: by 1995, all major PC graphics chip makers had added 2D acceleration support to their chips. By this time, fixed-function *Windows accelerators* had surpassed expensive general-purpose graphics coprocessors in Windows performance, and these coprocessors faded away from the PC market.

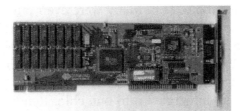

Tseng Labs ET4000/W32p

Voodoo3 2000 AGP card

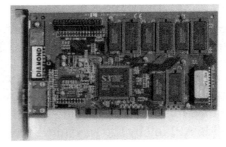

S3 Graphics ViRGE

Throughout the 1990s, 2D GUI acceleration continued to evolve. As manufacturing capabilities improved, so did the level of integration of graphics chips. Additional application programming interfaces (APIs) arrived for a variety of tasks, such as Microsoft's WinG graphics library for Windows 3.x, and their later DirectDraw interface for hardware acceleration of 2D games within Windows 95 and later.

In the early- and mid-1990s, CPU-assisted real-time 3D graphics were becoming increasingly common in arcade, computer and console games, which led to an increasing public demand for hardware-accelerated 3D graphics. Early examples of mass-market 3D graphics hardware can be found in arcade system boards such as the Sega Model 1, Namco System 22, and Sega Model 2, and the fifth-generation video game consoles such as the Saturn, PlayStation and Nintendo 64. Arcade systems such as the Sega Model 2 and Namco Magic Edge Hornet Simulator in 1993 were capable of hardware T&L (transform, clipping, and lighting) years before appearing in consumer graphics cards. Other systems used DSPs to accelerate transformations.Fujitsu, which worked on the Sega Model 2 arcade system, began working on integrating T&L into a single LSI solution for use in home computers in 1995; the Fujitsu Pinolite, the first 3D geometry processor for personal computers, released in 1997. The first hardware T&L GPU on home video game consoles was the Nintendo 64's Reality Coprocessor, released in 1996. In 1997, Mitsubishi released the 3Dpro/2MP, a fully featured GPU capable of transformation and lighting, for workstations and Windows NT desktops; AMD utilized it for their FireGL 4000 graphics card, released in 1997.

In the PC world, notable failed first tries for low-cost 3D graphics chips were the S3 *ViRGE*, ATI *Rage*, and Matrox *Mystique*. These chips were essentially previous-generation 2D accelerators with 3D features bolted on. Many were even pin-compatible with the earlier-generation chips for ease of implementation and minimal cost. Initially, performance 3D graphics were possible only with discrete boards dedicated to accelerating 3D functions (and lacking 2D GUI acceleration entirely) such as the PowerVR and the 3dfx *Voodoo*. However, as manufacturing technology continued to progress, video, 2D GUI acceleration and 3D functionality were all integrated into one chip. Rendition's *Verite* chipsets were among the first to do this well enough to be worthy of note. In 1997, Rendition went a step further by collaborating with Hercules and Fujitsu on a "Thriller Conspiracy" project which combined a Fujitsu FXG-1 Pinolite geometry processor with a Vérité V2200 core to create a graphics card with a full T&L engine years before Nvidia's GeForce 256. This card, designed to reduce the load placed upon the system's CPU, never made it to market.

OpenGL appeared in the early '90s as a professional graphics API, but originally suffered from performance issues which allowed the Glide API to step in and become a dominant force on the PC in the late '90s. However, these issues were quickly overcome and the Glide API fell by the wayside. Software implementations of OpenGL were common during this time, although the influence of OpenGL eventually led to widespread hardware support. Over time, a parity emerged between features offered in hardware and those offered in OpenGL. DirectX became popular among Windows game developers during the late 90s. Unlike OpenGL, Microsoft insisted on providing strict one-to-one support of hardware. The approach made DirectX less popular as a standalone graphics API initially, since many GPUs provided their own specific features, which existing OpenGL applications were already able to benefit from, leaving DirectX often one generation behind.

Over time, Microsoft began to work more closely with hardware developers, and started to target the releases of DirectX to coincide with those of the supporting graphics hardware. Direct3D 5.0 was the first version of the burgeoning API to gain widespread adoption in the gaming market, and it competed directly with many more-hardware-specific, often proprietary graphics libraries, while OpenGL maintained a strong following. Direct3D 7.0 introduced support for hardware-accelerated transform and lighting (T&L) for Direct3D, while OpenGL had this capability already exposed from its inception. 3D accelerator cards moved beyond being just simple rasterizers to add another significant hardware stage to the 3D rendering pipeline. The Nvidia *GeForce 256* (also known as NV10) was the first consumer-level card released on the market with hardware-accelerated T&L, while professional 3D cards already had this capability. Hardware transform and lighting, both already existing features of OpenGL, came to consumer-level hardware in the '90s and set the precedent for later pixel shader and vertex shader units which were far more flexible and programmable.

2000 to 2010

Nvidia was first to produce a chip capable of programmable shading, the *GeForce 3* (code named NV20). Each pixel could now be processed by a short program that could include additional image textures as inputs, and each geometric vertex could likewise be processed by a short program before it was projected onto the screen. Used in the Xbox console, it competed with the PlayStation 2, which used a custom vector DSP for hardware accelerated vertex processing.

By October 2002, with the introduction of the ATI *Radeon 9700* (also known as R300), the world's first Direct3D 9.0 accelerator, pixel and vertex shaders could implement looping and lengthy floating point math, and were quickly becoming as flexible as CPUs, yet orders of magnitude faster for image-array operations. Pixel shading is often used for bump mapping, which adds texture, to make an object look shiny, dull, rough, or even round or extruded.

With the introduction of the GeForce 8 series, which was produced by Nvidia, and then new generic stream processing unit GPUs became a more generalized computing device. Today, parallel GPUs have begun making computational inroads against the CPU, and a subfield of research, dubbed GPU Computing or GPGPU for *General Purpose Computing on GPU*, has found its way into fields as diverse as machine learning, oil exploration, scientific image processing, linear algebra, statistics, 3D reconstruction and even stock options pricing determination. Over the years, the energy consumption of GPUs has increased and to manage it, several techniques have been proposed.

Nvidia's CUDA platform, first introduced in 2007, was the earliest widely adopted programming model for GPU computing. More recently OpenCL has become broadly supported. OpenCL is an open standard defined by the Khronos Group which allows for the development of code for both GPUs and CPUs with an emphasis on portability. OpenCL solutions are supported by Intel, AMD, Nvidia, and ARM, and according to a recent report by Evan's Data, OpenCL is the GPGPU development platform most widely used by developers in both the US and Asia Pacific.

2010 to Present

In 2010, Nvidia began a partnership with Audi to power their cars' dashboards. These Tegra GPUs were powering the cars' dashboard, offering increased functionality to cars' navigation and entertainment systems. Advancements in GPU technology in cars has helped push self-driving technology. AMD's Radeon HD 6000 Series cards were released in 2010 and in 2011, AMD released their 6000M Series dicreate GPUs to be used in mobile devices. The Kepler line of graphics cards by Nvidia came out in 2012 and were used in the 600 series, 700 series, and 800 series of graphics cards by Nvidia. A new feature in this new GPU microarchitecture included gpu boost, a technology adjusts the clock-speed of a video card to increase or decrease it according to its power draw. The Kepler microarchitecture was manufactured on the 28 nm process.

The PS4 and Xbox One were released in 2013, they both use GPUs based on AMD's Radeon HD 7850 and 7790. Nvidia's Kepler line of GPUs was followed by the Maxwell line, manufactured on the same process. 28 nm chips by Nvidia were manufactured by TSMC, a Taiwanese Semiconductor Manufacturing Company, that was manufacturing using the 28 nm process at the time. Compared to the 40 nm technology from the past, this new manufacturing process allowed a 20 percent boost in performance while drawing less power. Virtual reality headsets like the Oculus Rift and the HTC Vive have very high system requirements. Headset manufactures have recommended GPUs for good virtual reality experiences. At their release, they had the GTX 970 from Nvidia and the R9 290 from AMD as the recommended GPUs. Pascal is the newest generation of graphics cards by Nvidia released in 2016. The GeForce 10 series of cards are under this generation of graphics cards. They are made using the 16 nm manufacturing process which improves upon previous microarchitectures. The Polaris 11 and Polaris 10 GPUs from AMD are made with a 14 nm process. Their release results in a big increase in the performance per watt of AMD video cards.

GPU Companies

Many companies have produced GPUs under a number of brand names. In 2009, Intel, Nvidia and AMD/ATI were the market share leaders, with 49.4%, 27.8% and 20.6% market share respectively. However, those numbers include Intel's integrated graphics solutions as GPUs. Not counting those numbers, Nvidia and ATI control nearly 100% of the market as of 2008. In addition, S3 Graphics (owned by VIA Technologies) and Matrox produce GPUs.

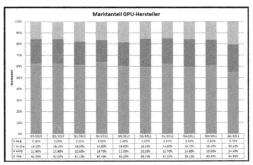

GPU manufacturers market share

Computational Functions

Modern GPUs use most of their transistors to do calculations related to 3D computer graphics. They were initially used to accelerate the memory-intensive work of texture mapping and rendering polygons, later adding units to accelerate geometric calculations such as the rotation and translation of vertices into different coordinate systems. Recent developments in GPUs include support for programmable shaders which can manipulate vertices and textures with many of the same operations supported by CPUs, oversampling and interpolation techniques to reduce aliasing, and very high-precision color spaces. Because most of these computations involve matrix and vector operations, engineers and scientists have increasingly studied the use of GPUs for non-graphical calculations; they are especially suited to other embarrassingly parallel problems.

In addition to the 3D hardware, today's GPUs include basic 2D acceleration and framebuffer capabilities (usually with a VGA compatibility mode). Newer cards like AMD/ATI HD5000-HD7000 even lack 2D acceleration; it has to be emulated by 3D hardware.

GPU Accelerated Video Decoding

The ATI HD5470 GPU (above) features UVD 2.1 which enables it to decode AVC and VC-1 video formats

Most GPUs made since 1995 support the YUV color space and hardware overlays, important for digital video playback, and many GPUs made since 2000 also support

MPEG primitives such as motion compensation and iDCT. This process of hardware accelerated video decoding, where portions of the video decoding process and video post-processing are offloaded to the GPU hardware, is commonly referred to as "GPU accelerated video decoding", "GPU assisted video decoding", "GPU hardware accelerated video decoding" or "GPU hardware assisted video decoding".

More recent graphics cards even decode high-definition video on the card, offloading the central processing unit. The most common APIs for GPU accelerated video decoding are DxVA for Microsoft Windows operating system and VDPAU, VAAPI, XvMC, and XvBA for Linux-based and UNIX-like operating systems. All except XvMC are capable of decoding videos encoded with MPEG-1, MPEG-2, MPEG-4 ASP (MPEG-4 Part 2), MPEG-4 AVC (H.264 / DivX 6), VC-1, WMV3/WMV9, Xvid / OpenDivX (DivX 4), and DivX 5 codecs, while XvMC is only capable of decoding MPEG-1 and MPEG-2.

Video Decoding Processes that Can be Accelerated

The video decoding processes that can be accelerated by today's modern GPU hardware are:

- Motion compensation (mocomp)

- Inverse discrete cosine transform (iDCT)

    o   Inverse telecine 3:2 and 2:2 pull-down correction

- Inverse modified discrete cosine transform (iMDCT)

- In-loop deblocking filter

- Intra-frame prediction

- Inverse quantization (IQ)

- Variable-length decoding (VLD), more commonly known as slice-level acceleration

- Spatial-temporal deinterlacing and automatic interlace/progressive source detection

- Bitstream processing (Context-adaptive variable-length coding/Context-adaptive binary arithmetic coding) and perfect pixel positioning.

GPU Forms

Dedicated Graphics Cards

The GPUs of the most powerful class typically interface with the motherboard by means of an expansion slot such as PCI Express (PCIe) or Accelerated Graphics Port (AGP) and can usually be replaced or upgraded with relative ease, assuming the motherboard is capable of supporting the upgrade. A few graphics cards still use Peripheral Component Interconnect (PCI) slots, but their bandwidth is so limited that they are generally used only when a PCIe or AGP slot is not available.

A dedicated GPU is not necessarily removable, nor does it necessarily interface with the motherboard in a standard fashion. The term "dedicated" refers to the fact that dedicated graphics cards have RAM that is dedicated to the card's use, not to the fact that *most* dedicated GPUs are removable. Dedicated GPUs for portable computers are most commonly interfaced through a non-standard and often proprietary slot due to size and weight constraints. Such ports may still be considered PCIe or AGP in terms of their logical host interface, even if they are not physically interchangeable with their counterparts.

Technologies such as SLI by Nvidia and CrossFire by AMD allow multiple GPUs to draw images simultaneously for a single screen, increasing the processing power available for graphics.

Integrated Graphics Solutions

Integrated graphics solutions, shared graphics solutions, or *integrated graphics processors* (IGP) utilize a portion of a computer's system RAM rather than dedicated graphics memory. IGPs can be integrated onto the motherboard as part of the chipset, or within the same die as CPU (like AMD APU or Intel HD Graphics). On certain motherboards AMD's IGPs can use dedicated sideport memory. This is a separate fixed block of high performance memory that is dedicated for use by the GPU. In early 2007, computers with integrated graphics account for about 90% of all PC shipments.These solutions are less costly to implement than dedicated graphics solutions, but tend to be less capable. Historically, integrated solutions were often considered unfit to play 3D games or run graphically intensive programs but could run less intensive programs such as Adobe Flash. Examples of such IGPs would be offerings from SiS and VIA circa 2004. However, modern integrated graphics processors such as AMD Accelerated Processing Unit and Intel HD Graphics are more than capable of handling 2D graphics or low stress 3D graphics.

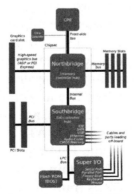

The position of an integrated GPU in a northbridge/southbridge system layout

As a GPU is extremely memory intensive, an integrated solution may find itself competing for the already relatively slow system RAM with the CPU, as it has minimal or no dedicated video memory. IGPs can have up to 29.856 GB/s of memory bandwidth from system RAM, however graphics cards can enjoy up to 264 GB/s of bandwidth between its RAM and GPU core. This bandwidth is what is referred to as the memory bus and can be performance limiting. Older integrated graphics chipsets lacked hardware transform and lighting, but newer ones include it.

An ASRock motherboard with integrated graphics, which has HDMI, VGA and DVI outs.

Hybrid Solutions

This newer class of GPUs competes with integrated graphics in the low-end desktop and notebook markets. The most common implementations of this are ATI's Hyper-Memory and Nvidia's TurboCache.

Hybrid graphics cards are somewhat more expensive than integrated graphics, but much less expensive than dedicated graphics cards. These share memory with the system and have a small dedicated memory cache, to make up for the high latency of the system RAM. Technologies within PCI Express can make this possible. While these solutions are sometimes advertised as having as much as 768MB of RAM, this refers to how much can be shared with the system memory.

Stream Processing and General Purpose GPUs (GPGPU)

It is becoming increasingly common to use a general purpose graphics processing unit (GPGPU) as a modified form of stream processor (or a vector processor), running compute kernels. This concept turns the massive computational power of a modern graphics accelerator's shader pipeline into general-purpose computing power, as opposed to being hard wired solely to do graphical operations. In certain applications requiring massive vector operations, this can yield several orders of magnitude higher performance than a conventional CPU. The two largest discrete (see "Dedicated graphics cards" above) GPU designers, ATI and Nvidia, are beginning to pursue this approach with an array of applications. Both Nvidia and ATI have teamed with Stanford University to create a GPU-based client for the Folding@home distributed computing project, for protein folding calculations. In certain circumstances the GPU calculates forty times faster than the conventional CPUs traditionally used by such applications.

GPGPU can be used for many types of embarrassingly parallel tasks including ray tracing. They are generally suited to high-throughput type computations that exhibit data-parallelism to exploit the wide vector width SIMD architecture of the GPU.

Furthermore, GPU-based high performance computers are starting to play a significant role in large-scale modelling. Three of the 10 most powerful supercomputers in the world take advantage of GPU acceleration.

NVIDIA cards support API extensions to the C programming language such as CUDA and OpenCL. CUDA is specifically for NVIDIA GPUs whilst OpenCL is designed to work across a multitude of architectures including GPU, CPU and DSP (using vendor specific SDKs). These technologies allow specified functions called compute kernels from a normal C program to run on the GPU's stream processors. This makes C programs capable of taking advantage of a GPU's ability to operate on large buffers in parallel, while still making use of the CPU when appropriate. CUDA is also the first API to allow CPU-based applications to directly access the resources of a GPU for more general purpose computing without the limitations of using a graphics API.

Since 2005 there has been interest in using the performance offered by GPUs for evolutionary computation in general, and for accelerating the fitness evaluation in genetic programming in particular. Most approaches compile linear or tree programs on the host PC and transfer the executable to the GPU to be run. Typically the performance advantage is only obtained by running the single active program simultaneously on many example problems in parallel, using the GPU's SIMD architecture. However, substantial acceleration can also be obtained by not compiling the programs, and instead transferring them to the GPU, to be interpreted there. Acceleration can then be obtained by either interpreting multiple programs simultaneously, simultaneously running multiple example problems, or combinations of both. A modern GPU (*e.g.* 8800 GTX or later) can readily simultaneously interpret hundreds of thousands of very small programs.

External GPU (eGPU)

An external GPU is a graphics processor located outside of the housing of the computer. External graphics processors are sometimes used with laptop computers. Laptops might have a substantial amount of RAM and a sufficiently powerful central processing unit (CPU), but often lack a powerful graphics processor (and instead have a less powerful but more energy-efficient on-board graphics chip). On-board graphics chips are often not powerful enough for playing the latest games, or for other tasks (video editing, ...).

Therefore, it is desirable to be able to attach a GPU to some external bus of a notebook. PCI Express is the only bus commonly used for this purpose. The port may be, for example, an ExpressCard or mPCIe port (PCIe ×1, up to 5 or 2.5 Gbit/s respectively) or a Thunderbolt 1, 2, or 3 port (PCIe ×4, up to 10, 20, or 40 Gbit/s respectively). Those ports are only available on certain notebook systems.

External GPUs have had little official vendor support. This has not stopped enthusiasts from creating their own DIY eGPU solutions.

Sales

In 2013, 438.3 million GPUs were shipped globally and the forecast for 2014 was 414.2 million.

Computer Vision

Computer vision is an interdisciplinary field that deals with how computers can be made to gain high-level understanding from digital images or videos. From the perspective of engineering, it seeks to automate tasks that the human visual system can do.

Computer vision tasks include methods for acquiring, processing, analyzing and understanding digital images, and in general, deal with the extraction of high-dimensional data from the real world in order to produce numerical or symbolic information, *e.g.*, in the forms of decisions. Understanding in this context means the transformation of visual images (the input of the retina) into descriptions of the world that can interface with other thought processes and elicit appropriate action. This image understanding can be seen as the disentangling of symbolic information from image data using models constructed with the aid of geometry, physics, statistics, and learning theory.

As a scientific discipline, computer vision is concerned with the theory behind artificial systems that extract information from images. The image data can take many forms, such as video sequences, views from multiple cameras, or multi-dimensional data from a medical scanner. As a technological discipline, computer vision seeks to apply its theories and models for the construction of computer vision systems.

Sub-domains of computer vision include scene reconstruction, event detection, video tracking, object recognition, object pose estimation, learning, indexing, motion estimation, and image restoration.

History

In the late 1960s, computer vision began at universities that were pioneering artificial intelligence. It was meant to mimic the human visual system, as a stepping stone to endowing robots with intelligent behavior. In 1966, it was believed that this could be achieved through a summer project, by attaching a camera to a computer and having it "describe what it saw".

What distinguished computer vision from the prevalent field of digital image processing at that time was a desire to extract three-dimensional structure from images with the goal of achieving full scene understanding. Studies in the 1970s formed the early foundations for many of the computer vision algorithms that exist today, including extraction of edges from images, labeling of lines, non-polyhedral and polyhedral modeling, representation of objects as interconnections of smaller structures, optical flow, and motion estimation.

The next decade saw studies based on more rigorous mathematical analysis and quantitative aspects of computer vision. These include the concept of scale-space, the inference of shape from various cues such as shading, texture and focus, and contour models known as snakes. Researchers also realized that many of these mathematical concepts could be treated within the same optimization framework as regularization and Markov random fields.

By the 1990s, some of the previous research topics became more active than the others. Research in projective 3-D reconstructions led to better understanding of camera calibration. With the advent of optimization methods for camera calibration, it was realized that a lot of the ideas were already explored in bundle adjustment theory from the field of photogrammetry. This led to methods for sparse 3-D reconstructions of scenes from multiple images. Progress was made on the dense stereo correspondence problem and further multi-view stereo techniques. At the same time, variations of graph cut were used to solve image segmentation. This decade also marked the first time statistical learning techniques were used in practice to recognize faces in images (see Eigenface). Toward the end of the 1990s, a significant change came about with the increased interaction between the fields of computer graphics and computer vision. This included image-based rendering, image morphing, view interpolation, panoramic image stitching and early light-field rendering.

Recent work has seen the resurgence of feature-based methods, used in conjunction with machine learning techniques and complex optimization frameworks.

Related Fields

Areas of artificial intelligence deal with autonomous planning or deliberation for robotical systems to navigate through an environment. A detailed understanding of these environments is required to navigate through them. Information about the environment could be provided by a computer vision system, acting as a vision sensor and providing high-level information about the environment and the robot.

Artificial intelligence and computer vision share other topics such as pattern recognition and learning techniques. Consequently, computer vision is sometimes seen as a part of the artificial intelligence field or the computer science field in general.

Solid-state physics is another field that is closely related to computer vision. Most computer vision systems rely on image sensors, which detect electromagnetic radiation, which is typically in the form of either visible or infra-red light. The sensors are designed using quantum physics. The process by which light interacts with surfaces is explained using physics. Physics explains the behavior of optics which are a core part of most imaging systems. Sophisticated image sensors even require quantum mechanics to provide a complete understanding of the image formation process. Also, various measurement problems in physics can be addressed using computer vision, for example motion in fluids.

A third field which plays an important role is neurobiology, specifically the study of the biological vision system. Over the last century, there has been an extensive study of eyes, neurons, and the brain structures devoted to processing of visual stimuli in both humans and various animals. This has led to a coarse, yet complicated, description of how "real" vision systems operate in order to solve certain vision related tasks. These results have led to a subfield within computer vision where artificial systems are designed to mimic the processing and behavior of biological systems, at different levels of complexity. Also, some of the learning-based methods developed within computer vision (*e.g.* neural net and deep learning based image and feature analysis and classification) have their background in biology.

Some strands of computer vision research are closely related to the study of biological vision – indeed, just as many strands of AI research are closely tied with research into human consciousness, and the use of stored knowledge to interpret, integrate and utilize visual information. The field of biological vision studies and models the physiological processes behind visual perception in humans and other animals. Computer vision, on the other hand, studies and describes the processes implemented in software and hardware behind artificial vision systems. Interdisciplinary exchange between biological and computer vision has proven fruitful for both fields.

Yet another field related to computer vision is signal processing. Many methods for processing of one-variable signals, typically temporal signals, can be extended in a natural way to processing of two-variable signals or multi-variable signals in computer vision. However, because of the specific nature of images there are many methods developed within computer vision which have no counterpart in processing of one-variable signals. Together with the multi-dimensionality of the signal, this defines a subfield in signal processing as a part of computer vision.

Beside the above-mentioned views on computer vision, many of the related research topics can also be studied from a purely mathematical point of view. For example, many methods in computer vision are based on statistics, optimization or geometry. Finally, a significant part of the field is devoted to the implementation aspect of computer vision; how existing methods can be realized in various combinations of software and hardware, or how these methods can be modified in order to gain processing speed without losing too much performance.

The fields most closely related to computer vision are image processing, image analysis and machine vision. There is a significant overlap in the range of techniques and applications that these covers. This implies that the basic techniques that are used and developed in these fields are more or less identical, something which can be interpreted as there is only one field with different names. On the other hand, it appears to be necessary for research groups, scientific journals, conferences and companies to present or market themselves as belonging specifically to one of these fields and, hence, various characterizations which distinguish each of the fields from the others have been presented.

Computer vision is, in some ways, the inverse of computer graphics. While computer graphics produces image data from 3D models, computer vision often produces 3D models from image data. There is also a trend towards a combination of the two disciplines, *e.g.*, as explored in augmented reality.

The following characterizations appear relevant but should not be taken as universally accepted:

- Image processing and image analysis tend to focus on 2D images, how to transform one image to another, *e.g.*, by pixel-wise operations such as contrast enhancement, local operations such as edge extraction or noise removal, or geometrical transformations such as rotating the image. This characterization implies that image processing/analysis neither require assumptions nor produce interpretations about the image content.

- Computer vision includes 3D analysis from 2D images. This analyzes the 3D scene projected onto one or several images, *e.g.*, how to reconstruct structure or other information about the 3D scene from one or several images. Computer vision often relies on more or less complex assumptions about the scene depicted in an image.

- Machine vision is the process of applying a range of technologies & methods to provide imaging-based automatic inspection, process control and robot guidance in industrial applications. Machine vision tends to focus on applications, mainly in manufacturing, *e.g.*, vision based autonomous robots and systems for vision-based inspection or measurement. This implies that image sensor technologies and control theory often are integrated with the processing of image data to control a robot and that real-time processing is emphasised by means of efficient implementations in hardware and software. It also implies that the external conditions such as lighting can be and are often more controlled in machine vision than they are in general computer vision, which can enable the use of different algorithms.

- There is also a field called imaging which primarily focus on the process of producing images, but sometimes also deals with processing and analysis of images. For example, medical imaging includes substantial work on the analysis of image data in medical applications.

- Finally, pattern recognition is a field which uses various methods to extract information from signals in general, mainly based on statistical approaches and artificial neural networks. A significant part of this field is devoted to applying these methods to image data.

Photogrammetry also overlaps with computer vision, e.g., stereophotogrammetry vs. stereo computer vision.

Applications

Applications range from tasks such as industrial machine vision systems which, say, inspect bottles speeding by on a production line, to research into artificial intelligence and computers or robots that can comprehend the world around them. The computer vision and machine vision fields have significant overlap. Computer vision covers the core technology of automated image analysis which is used in many fields. Machine vision usually refers to a process of combining automated image analysis with other methods and technologies to provide automated inspection and robot guidance in industrial applications. In many computer vision applications, the computers are pre-programmed to solve a particular task, but methods based on learning are now becoming increasingly common. Examples of applications of computer vision include systems for:

- Controlling processes, *e.g.*, an industrial robot;
- Navigation, *e.g.*, by an autonomous vehicle or mobile robot;
- Detecting events, *e.g.*, for visual surveillance or people counting;
- Organizing information, *e.g.*, for indexing databases of images and image sequences;
- Modeling objects or environments, *e.g.*, medical image analysis or topographical modeling;
- Interaction, *e.g.*, as the input to a device for computer-human interaction, and
- Automatic inspection, *e.g.*, in manufacturing applications.

One of the most prominent application fields is medical computer vision or medical image processing. This area is characterized by the extraction of information from image data for the purpose of making a medical diagnosis of a patient. Generally, image data is in the form of microscopy images, X-ray images, angiography images, ultrasonic images, and tomography images. An example of information which can be extracted from such image data is detection of tumours, arteriosclerosis or other malign changes. It can also be measurements of organ dimensions, blood flow, etc. This application area also supports medical research by providing new information, *e.g.*, about the structure of the brain, or about the quality of medical treatments. Applications of computer vision in the medical area also includes enhancement of images that are interpreted by humans, for example ultrasonic images or X-ray images, to reduce the influence of noise.

A second application area in computer vision is in industry, sometimes called machine vision, where information is extracted for the purpose of supporting a manufacturing process. One example is quality control where details or final products are being automatically inspected in order to find defects. Another example is the measurement of position and orientation of details to be picked up by a robot arm. Machine vision is also heavily used in agricultural process to remove undesirable food stuff from bulk material, a process called optical sorting.

Military applications are probably one of the largest areas for computer vision. The obvious example is the detection of enemy soldiers or vehicles and missile guidance. More advanced systems for missile guidance send the missile to an area rather than a specific target, and target selection is made when the missile reaches the area based on locally acquired image data. Modern military concepts, such as "battlefield awareness", imply that various sensors, including image sensors, provide a rich set of information about a combat scene which can be used to support strategic decisions. In this case, automatic processing of the data is used to reduce complexity and to fuse information from multiple sensors to increase reliability.

Artist's Concept of Rover on Mars, an example of an unmanned land-based vehicle. Notice the stereo cameras mounted on top of the Rover.

One of the newer application areas is autonomous vehicles, which include submersibles, land-based vehicles (small robots with wheels, cars or trucks), aerial vehicles, and unmanned aerial vehicles (UAV). The level of autonomy ranges from fully autonomous (unmanned) vehicles to vehicles where computer vision based systems support a driver or a pilot in various situations. Fully autonomous vehicles typically use computer vision for navigation, i.e. for knowing where it is, or for producing a map of its environment

(SLAM) and for detecting obstacles. It can also be used for detecting certain task specific events, *e.g.*, a UAV looking for forest fires. Examples of supporting systems are obstacle warning systems in cars, and systems for autonomous landing of aircraft. Several car manufacturers have demonstrated systems for autonomous driving of cars, but this technology has still not reached a level where it can be put on the market. There are ample examples of military autonomous vehicles ranging from advanced missiles, to UAVs for recon missions or missile guidance. Space exploration is already being made with autonomous vehicles using computer vision, *e.g.*, NASA's Mars Exploration Rover and ESA's ExoMars Rover.

Other application areas include:

- Support of visual effects creation for cinema and broadcast, *e.g.*, camera tracking (matchmoving).

- Surveillance.

Representational and Control Requirements

Image-understanding systems (IUS) include three levels of abstraction as follows: Low level includes image primitives such as edges, texture elements, or regions; intermediate level includes boundaries, surfaces and volumes; and high level includes objects, scenes, or events. Many of these requirements are really topics for further research.

The representational requirements in the designing of IUS for these levels are: representation of prototypical concepts, concept organization, spatial knowledge, temporal knowledge, scaling, and description by comparison and differentiation.

While inference refers to the process of deriving new, not explicitly represented facts from currently known facts, control refers to the process that selects which of the many inference, search, and matching techniques should be applied at a particular stage of processing. Inference and control requirements for IUS are: search and hypothesis activation, matching and hypothesis testing, generation and use of expectations, change and focus of attention, certainty and strength of belief, inference and goal satisfaction.

Typical Tasks

Each of the application areas described above employ a range of computer vision tasks; more or less well-defined measurement problems or processing problems, which can be solved using a variety of methods. Some examples of typical computer vision tasks are presented below.

Recognition

The classical problem in computer vision, image processing, and machine vision is that of determining whether or not the image data contains some specific object, feature, or activity. Different varieties of the recognition problem are described in the literature:

- Object recognition (also called object classification) – one or several pre-specified or learned objects or object classes can be recognized, usually together with their 2D positions in the image or 3D poses in the scene. Blippar, Google Goggles and LikeThat provide stand-alone programs that illustrate this functionality.

- Identification – an individual instance of an object is recognized. Examples include identification of a specific person›s face or fingerprint, identification of handwritten digits, or identification of a specific vehicle.

- Detection – the image data are scanned for a specific condition. Examples include detection of possible abnormal cells or tissues in medical images or detection of a vehicle in an automatic road toll system. Detection based on relatively simple and fast computations is sometimes used for finding smaller regions of interesting image data which can be further analyzed by more computationally demanding techniques to produce a correct interpretation.

Currently, the best algorithms for such tasks are based on convolutional neural networks. An illustration of their capabilities is given by the ImageNet Large Scale Visual Recognition Challenge; this is a benchmark in object classification and detection, with millions of images and hundreds of object classes. Performance of convolutional neural networks, on the ImageNet tests, is now close to that of humans. The best algorithms still struggle with objects that are small or thin, such as a small ant on a stem of a flower or a person holding a quill in their hand. They also have trouble with images that have been distorted with filters (an increasingly common phenomenon with modern digital cameras). By contrast, those kinds of images rarely trouble humans. Humans, however, tend to have trouble with other issues. For example, they are not good at classifying objects into fine-grained classes, such as the particular breed of dog or species of bird, whereas convolutional neural networks handle this with ease.

Several specialized tasks based on recognition exist, such as:

- Content-based image retrieval – finding all images in a larger set of images which have a specific content. The content can be specified in different ways, for example in terms of similarity relative a target image (give me all images similar to image X), or in terms of high-level search criteria given as text input (give me all images which contains many houses, are taken during winter, and have no cars in them).

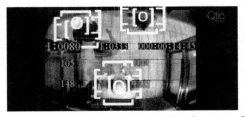

Computer vision for people counter purposes in public places, malls, shopping centres

- Pose estimation – estimating the position or orientation of a specific object relative to the camera. An example application for this technique would be assisting a robot arm in retrieving objects from a conveyor belt in an assembly line situation or picking parts from a bin.

- Optical character recognition (OCR) – identifying characters in images of printed or handwritten text, usually with a view to encoding the text in a format more amenable to editing or indexing (*e.g.* ASCII).

- 2D Code reading Reading of 2D codes such as data matrix and QR codes.

- Facial recognition

- Shape Recognition Technology (SRT) in people counter systems differentiating human beings (head and shoulder patterns) from objects

Motion Analysis

Several tasks relate to motion estimation where an image sequence is processed to produce an estimate of the velocity either at each points in the image or in the 3D scene, or even of the camera that produces the images . Examples of such tasks are:

- Egomotion – determining the 3D rigid motion (rotation and translation) of the camera from an image sequence produced by the camera.

- Tracking – following the movements of a (usually) smaller set of interest points or objects (*e.g.*, vehicles or humans) in the image sequence.

- Optical flow – to determine, for each point in the image, how that point is moving relative to the image plane, i.e., its apparent motion. This motion is a result both of how the corresponding 3D point is moving in the scene and how the camera is moving relative to the scene.

Scene Reconstruction

Given one or (typically) more images of a scene, or a video, scene reconstruction aims at computing a 3D model of the scene. In the simplest case the model can be a set of 3D points. More sophisticated methods produce a complete 3D surface model. The advent of 3D imaging not requiring motion or scanning, and related processing algorithms is enabling rapid advances in this field. Grid-based 3D sensing can be used to acquire 3D images from multiple angles. Algorithms are now available to stitch multiple 3D images together into point clouds and 3D models.

Image Restoration

The aim of image restoration is the removal of noise (sensor noise, motion blur, etc.) from images. The simplest possible approach for noise removal is various types of filters such as low-pass filters or median filters. More sophisticated methods assume a model of how the local image structures look like, a model which distinguishes them from the noise. By first analysing the image data in terms of the local image structures, such as lines or edges, and then controlling the filtering based on local information from the analysis step, a better level of noise removal is usually obtained compared to the simpler approaches.

An example in this field is inpainting.

System Methods

The organization of a computer vision system is highly application dependent. Some systems are stand-alone applications which solve a specific measurement or detection problem, while others constitute a sub-system of a larger design which, for example, also contains sub-systems for control of mechanical actuators, planning, information databases, man-machine interfaces, etc. The specific implementation of a computer vision system also depends on if its functionality is pre-specified or if some part of it can be learned or modified during operation. Many functions are unique to the application. There are, however, typical functions which are found in many computer vision systems.

- Image acquisition – A digital image is produced by one or several image sensors, which, besides various types of light-sensitive cameras, include range sensors, tomography devices, radar, ultra-sonic cameras, etc. Depending on the type of sensor, the resulting image data is an ordinary 2D image, a 3D volume, or an image sequence. The pixel values typically correspond to light intensity in one or several spectral bands (gray images or colour images), but can also be related to various physical measures, such as depth, absorption or reflectance of sonic or electromagnetic waves, or nuclear magnetic resonance.

- Pre-processing – Before a computer vision method can be applied to image data in order to extract some specific piece of information, it is usually necessary to process the data in order to assure that it satisfies certain assumptions implied by the method. Examples are

    o Re-sampling in order to assure that the image coordinate system is correct.

    o Noise reduction in order to assure that sensor noise does not introduce false information.

    o Contrast enhancement to assure that relevant information can be detected.

    o Scale space representation to enhance image structures at locally appropriate scales.

- Feature extraction – Image features at various levels of complexity are extracted from the image data. Typical examples of such features are

- o   Lines, edges and ridges.

- o   Localized interest points such as corners, blobs or points.

More complex features may be related to texture, shape or motion.

- Detection/segmentation – At some point in the processing a decision is made about which image points or regions of the image are relevant for further processing. Examples are

  - o   Selection of a specific set of interest points

  - o   Segmentation of one or multiple image regions which contain a specific object of interest.

  - o   Segmentation of image into nested scene architecture comprised foreground, object groups, single objects or salient object parts (also referred to as spatial-taxon scene hierarchy)

- High-level processing – At this step the input is typically a small set of data, for example a set of points or an image region which is assumed to contain a specific object. The remaining processing deals with, for example:

  - o   Verification that the data satisfy model-based and application specific assumptions.

  - o   Estimation of application specific parameters, such as object pose or object size.

  - o   Image recognition – classifying a detected object into different categories.

  - o   Image registration – comparing and combining two different views of the same object.

- Decision making Making the final decision required for the application, for example:

  - o   Pass/fail on automatic inspection applications

  - o   Match / no-match in recognition applications

  - o   Flag for further human review in medical, military, security and recognition applications

Hardware

There are many kinds of computer vision systems, nevertheless all of them contain these basic elements: a power source, at least one image acquisition device (i.e. camera, ccd, etc.), a processor as well as control and communication cables or some kind of wireless interconnection mechanism. In addition, a practical vision system contains software, as well as a display in order to monitor the system. Vision systems for inner spaces, as most industrial ones, contain an illumination system and may be placed in a controlled environment. Furthermore, a completed system includes many accessories like camera supports, cables and connectors.

While traditional broadcast and consumer video systems operate at a rate of 30 frames per second, advances in digital signal processing and consumer graphics hardware has made high-speed image acquisition, processing, and display possible for real-time systems on the order of hundreds to thousands of frames per second. For applications in robotics, fast, real-time video systems are critically important and often can simplify the processing needed for certain algorithms. When combined with a high-speed projector, fast image acquisition allows 3D measurement and feature tracking to be realised.

As of 2016, vision processing units are emerging as a new class of processor, to complement CPUs and GPUs in this role.

User Interface Design

User interface design (UI) or user interface engineering is the design of user interfaces for machines and software, such as computers, home appliances, mobile devices, and other electronic devices, with the focus on maximizing usability and the user experience. The goal of user interface design is to make the user's interaction as simple and efficient as possible, in terms of accomplishing user goals (user-centered design).

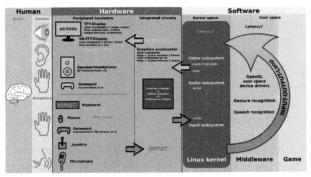

The graphical user interface is presented (displayed) on the computer screen. It is the result of processed user input and usually the primary interface for human-machine interaction. The touch user interfaces popular on small mobile devices are an overlay of the visual output to the visual input.

Good user interface design facilitates finishing the task at hand without drawing unnecessary attention to itself. Graphic design and typography are utilized to support its usability, influencing how the user performs certain interactions and improving the aesthetic appeal of the design; design aesthetics may enhance or detract from the abili-

ty of users to use the functions of the interface. The design process must balance technical functionality and visual elements (e.g., mental model) to create a system that is not
only operational but also usable and adaptable to changing user needs.

Interface design is involved in a wide range of projects from computer systems, to cars,
to commercial planes; all of these projects involve much of the same basic human interactions yet also require some unique skills and knowledge. As a result, designers
tend to specialize in certain types of projects and have skills centered on their expertise,
whether that be software design, user research, web design, or industrial design.

Processes

User interface design requires a good understanding of user needs. There are several
phases and processes in the user interface design, some of which are more demanded
upon than others, depending on the project. (Note: for the remainder of this section,
the word *system* is used to denote any project whether it is a website, application, or
device.)

- Functionality requirements gathering – assembling a list of the functionality
  required by the system to accomplish the goals of the project and the potential
  needs of the users.

- User and task analysis – a form of field research, it's the analysis of the potential
  users of the system by studying how they perform the tasks that the design must
  support, and conducting interviews to elucidate their goals. Typical questions
  involve:

  o   What would the user want the system to do?

  o   How would the system fit in with the user's normal workflow or daily
      activities?

  o   How technically savvy is the user and what similar systems does the user
      already use?

  o   What interface look & feel styles appeal to the user?

- Information architecture – development of the process and/or information flow
  of the system (i.e. for phone tree systems, this would be an option tree flowchart
  and for web sites this would be a site flow that shows the hierarchy of the pages).

- Prototyping – development of wire-frames, either in the form of paper prototypes or simple interactive screens. These prototypes are stripped of all look &
  feel elements and most content in order to concentrate on the interface.

- Usability inspection – letting an evaluator inspect a user interface. This is generally considered to be cheaper to implement than usability testing (see step below), and can be used early on in the development process since it can be used to evaluate prototypes or specifications for the system, which usually can't be tested on users. Some common usability inspection methods include cognitive walkthrough, which focuses the simplicity to accomplish tasks with the system for new users, heuristic evaluation, in which a set of heuristics are used to identify usability problems in the UI design, and pluralistic walkthrough, in which a selected group of people step through a task scenario and discuss usability issues.

- Usability testing – testing of the prototypes on an actual user—often using a technique called think aloud protocol where you ask the user to talk about their thoughts during the experience. User interface design testing allows the designer to understand the reception of the design from the viewer's standpoint, and thus facilitates creating successful applications.

- Graphical user interface design – actual look and feel design of the final graphical user interface (GUI). It may be based on the findings developed during the user research, and refined to fix any usability problems found through the results of testing.

Requirements

The dynamic characteristics of a system are described in terms of the dialogue requirements contained in seven principles of part 10 of the ergonomics standard, the ISO 9241. This standard establishes a framework of ergonomic "principles" for the dialogue techniques with high-level definitions and illustrative applications and examples of the principles. The principles of the dialogue represent the dynamic aspects of the interface and can be mostly regarded as the "feel" of the interface. The seven dialogue principles are:

- Suitability for the task: the dialogue is suitable for a task when it supports the user in the effective and efficient completion of the task.

- Self-descriptiveness: the dialogue is self-descriptive when each dialogue step is immediately comprehensible through feedback from the system or is explained to the user on request.

- Controllability: the dialogue is controllable when the user is able to initiate and control the direction and pace of the interaction until the point at which the goal has been met.

- Conformity with user expectations: the dialogue conforms with user expectations when it is consistent and corresponds to the user characteristics, such as task knowledge, education, experience, and to commonly accepted conventions.

- Error tolerance: the dialogue is error tolerant if despite evident errors in input, the intended result may be achieved with either no or minimal action by the user.

- Suitability for individualization: the dialogue is capable of individualization when the interface software can be modified to suit the task needs, individual preferences, and skills of the user.

- Suitability for learning: the dialogue is suitable for learning when it supports and guides the user in learning to use the system.

The concept of usability is defined of the ISO 9241 standard by effectiveness, efficiency, and satisfaction of the user. Part 11 gives the following definition of usability:

- Usability is measured by the extent to which the intended goals of use of the overall system are achieved (effectiveness).

- The resources that have to be expended to achieve the intended goals (efficiency).

- The extent to which the user finds the overall system acceptable (satisfaction).

Effectiveness, efficiency, and satisfaction can be seen as quality factors of usability. To evaluate these factors, they need to be decomposed into sub-factors, and finally, into usability measures.

The information presentation is described in Part 12 of the ISO 9241 standard for the organization of information (arrangement, alignment, grouping, labels, location), for the display of graphical objects, and for the coding of information (abbreviation, color, size, shape, visual cues) by seven attributes. The "attributes of presented information" represent the static aspects of the interface and can be generally regarded as the "look" of the interface. The attributes are detailed in the recommendations given in the standard. Each of the recommendations supports one or more of the seven attributes. The seven presentation attributes are:

- Clarity: the information content is conveyed quickly and accurately.

- Discriminability: the displayed information can be distinguished accurately.

- Conciseness: users are not overloaded with extraneous information.

- Consistency: a unique design, conformity with user's expectation.

- Detectability: the user's attention is directed towards information required.

- Legibility: information is easy to read.

- Comprehensibility: the meaning is clearly understandable, unambiguous, interpretable, and recognizable.

The user guidance in Part 13 of the ISO 9241 standard describes that the user guidance information should be readily distinguishable from other displayed information and should be specific for the current context of use. User guidance can be given by the following five means:

- Prompts indicating explicitly (specific prompts) or implicitly (generic prompts) that the system is available for input.

- Feedback informing about the user's input timely, perceptible, and non-intrusive.

- Status information indicating the continuing state of the application, the system's hardware and software components, and the user's activities.

- Error management including error prevention, error correction, user support for error management, and error messages.

- On-line help for system-initiated and user initiated requests with specific information for the current context of use.

Research

User interface design has been a topic of considerable research, including on its aesthetics. Standards have been developed as far back as the 1980s for defining the usability of software products. One of the structural bases has become the IFIP user interface reference model. The model proposes four dimensions to structure the user interface:

- The input/output dimension (the look)

- The dialogue dimension (the feel)

- The technical or functional dimension (the access to tools and services)

- The organizational dimension (the communication and co-operation support)

This model has greatly influenced the development of the international standard ISO 9241 describing the interface design requirements for usability. The desire to understand application-specific UI issues early in software development, even as an application was being developed, led to research on GUI rapid prototyping tools that might offer convincing simulations of how an actual application might behave in production use. Some of this research has shown that a wide variety of programming tasks for GUI-based software can, in fact, be specified through means other than writing program code.

Research in recent years is strongly motivated by the increasing variety of devices that can, by virtue of Moore's law, host very complex interfaces.

Research has also been conducted on generating user interfaces automatically, to match a user's level of ability for different levels of interaction.

At the moment, in addition to traditional prototypes the literature proposes new solutions, such as an experimental mixed prototype based on a configurable physical prototype that allow to achieve a complete sense of touch, thanks to the physical mock-up, and a realistic visual experience, thanks to the superimposition of the virtual interface on the physical prototype with Augmented Reality techniques.

References

- Arie Kaufman (1993). Rendering, Visualization and Rasterization Hardware. Springer Science & Business Media. pp. 86–87. ISBN 978-3-540-56787-5.

- Ted Landau (2000). Sad Macs, Bombs and Other Disasters (4th ed.). Peachpit Press. p. 409. ISBN 978-0-201-69963-0.

- Sanders, Jason; Kandrot, Edward (2010-07-19). CUDA by Example: An Introduction to General-Purpose GPU Programming, Portable Documents. Addison-Wesley Professional. ISBN 9780132180139.

- Huang, T. (1996-11-19). Vandoni, Carlo, E, ed. Computer Vision : Evolution And Promise (PDF). 19th CERN School of Computing. Geneva: CERN. pp. 21–25. doi:10.5170/CERN-1996-008.21. ISBN 978-9290830955.

- Milan Sonka; Vaclav Hlavac; Roger Boyle (2008). Image Processing, Analysis, and Machine Vision. Thomson. ISBN 0-495-08252-X.

- Bernd Jähne; Horst Haußecker (2000). Computer Vision and Applications, A Guide for Students and Practitioners. Academic Press. ISBN 0-13-085198-1.

- Richard Szeliski (30 September 2010). Computer Vision: Algorithms and Applications. Springer Science & Business Media. pp. 10–16. ISBN 978-1-84882-935-0.

- Margaret Ann Boden (2006). Mind as Machine: A History of Cognitive Science. Clarendon Press. p. 781. ISBN 978-0-19-954316-8.

- Takeo Kanade (6 December 2012). Three-Dimensional Machine Vision. Springer Science & Business Media. ISBN 978-1-4613-1981-8.

- Nicu Sebe; Ira Cohen; Ashutosh Garg; Thomas S. Huang (3 June 2005). Machine Learning in Computer Vision. Springer Science & Business Media. ISBN 978-1-4020-3274-5.

- Steger, Carsten; Markus Ulrich & Christian Wiedemann (2008). Machine Vision Algorithms and Applications. Weinheim: Wiley-VCH. p. 1. ISBN 978-3-527-40734-7. Retrieved 2010-11-05.

- Shapiro, Stuart C. (1992). Encyclopedia of Artificial Intelligence, Volume 1. New York: John WIley & Sons, Inc. pp. 643–646. ISBN 0-471-50306-1.

- "NVIDIA Launches the World's First Graphics Processing Unit: GeForce 256". Nvidia. 31 August 1999. Retrieved 28 March 2016.

- Pabst, Thomas (18 July 2002). "ATi Takes Over 3D Technology Leadership With Radeon 9700". Tom's Hardware. Retrieved 29 March 2016.

- "AMD RX 480, 470 & 460 Polaris GPUs To Deliver The "Most Revolutionary Jump In Performance" Yet". 2016-01-16. Retrieved 2016-08-03.

Processes and Techniques of Computer Graphics

Processes and techniques are important components of any field of study. Some of the techniques explained in the chapter are volume rendering, motion capture, shader, rasterisation, feathering and visual effects. Volume rendering is a method used to exhibit a 2D projection on a 3D scalar field whereas motion capture is capturing the movement of things or humans. The aspects elucidated in this section are of vital importance, and provide a better understanding of computer graphics.

Volume Rendering

In scientific visualization and computer graphics, volume rendering is a set of techniques used to display a 2D projection of a 3D discretely sampled data set, typically a 3D scalar field.

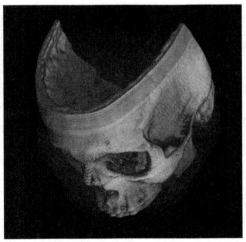

A volume rendered cadaver head using view-aligned texture mapping and diffuse reflection

A typical 3D data set is a group of 2D slice images acquired by a CT, MRI, or MicroCT scanner. Usually these are acquired in a regular pattern (e.g., one slice every millimeter) and usually have a regular number of image pixels in a regular pattern. This is an example of a regular volumetric grid, with each volume element, or voxel represented by a single value that is obtained by sampling the immediate area surrounding the voxel.

To render a 2D projection of the 3D data set, one first needs to define a camera in space relative to the volume. Also, one needs to define the opacity and color of every voxel. This is usually defined using an RGBA (for red, green, blue, alpha) transfer function that defines the RGBA value for every possible voxel value.

For example, a volume may be viewed by extracting isosurfaces (surfaces of equal values) from the volume and rendering them as polygonal meshes or by rendering the volume directly as a block of data. The marching cubes algorithm is a common technique for extracting an isosurface from volume data. Direct volume rendering is a computationally intensive task that may be performed in several ways.

Direct Volume Rendering

A direct volume renderer requires every sample value to be mapped to opacity and a color. This is done with a "transfer function" which can be a simple ramp, a piecewise linear function or an arbitrary table. Once converted to an RGBA (for red, green, blue, alpha) value, the composed RGBA result is projected on corresponding pixel of the frame buffer. The way this is done depends on the rendering technique.

A combination of these techniques is possible. For instance, a shear warp implementation could use texturing hardware to draw the aligned slices in the off-screen buffer.

Volume Ray Casting

Volume Ray Casting. Crocodile mummy provided by the Phoebe A. Hearst Museum of Anthropology, UC Berkeley. CT data was acquired by Dr. Rebecca Fahrig, Department of Radiology, StanfordUniversity, using a Siemens SOMATOM Definition, Siemens Healthcare. The image was rendered by Fovia's High Definition Volume Rendering® engine

The technique of volume ray casting can be derived directly from the rendering equation. It provides results of very high quality, usually considered to provide the best image quality. Volume ray casting is classified as image based volume rendering technique, as the computation emanates from the output image, not the input volume data as is the case with object based techniques. In this technique, a ray is generated for each desired image pixel. Using a simple camera model, the ray starts at the center of projection of the camera (usually the eye point) and passes through the image pixel on the imaginary image plane floating in between the camera and the volume to be rendered. The ray is clipped by the boundaries of the volume in order to save time. Then the ray is sampled at regular or adaptive intervals throughout the volume. The data is interpolated at each sample point, the transfer function applied to form an RGBA sample, the sample is composited onto the accumulated RGBA of the ray, and the process repeated until the ray exits the volume. The RGBA color is converted to an RGB color and deposited in the corresponding image pixel. The process is repeated for every pixel on the screen to form the completed image.

Splatting

This is a technique which trades quality for speed. Here, every volume element is splatted, as Lee Westover said, like a snow ball, on to the viewing surface in back to front order. These splats are rendered as disks whose properties (color and transparency) vary diametrically in normal (Gaussian) manner. Flat disks and those with other kinds of property distribution are also used depending on the application.

Shear Warp

The shear warp approach to volume rendering was developed by Cameron and Undrill, popularized by Philippe Lacroute and Marc Levoy. In this technique, the viewing transformation is transformed such that the nearest face of the volume becomes axis aligned with an off-screen image buffer with a fixed scale of voxels to pixels. The volume is then rendered into this buffer using the far more favorable memory alignment and fixed scaling and blending factors. Once all slices of the volume have been rendered, the buffer is then warped into the desired orientation and scaled in the displayed image.

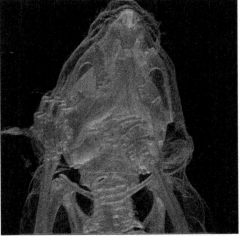

Example of a mouse skull (CT) rendering using the shear warp algorithm

This technique is relatively fast in software at the cost of less accurate sampling and potentially worse image quality compared to ray casting. There is memory overhead for storing multiple copies of the volume, for the ability to have near axis aligned volumes. This overhead can be mitigated using run length encoding.

Texture-based Volume Rendering

Many 3D graphics systems use texture mapping to apply images, or textures, to geometric objects. Commodity PC graphics cards are fast at texturing and can efficiently render slices of a 3D volume, with real time interaction capabilities. Workstation GPUs are even faster, and are the basis for much of the production volume visualization used in medical imaging, oil and gas, and other markets (2007). In earlier years, dedicated 3D texture mapping systems were used on graphics systems such as Silicon Graphics InfiniteReality, HP Visualize FX graphics accelerator, and others. This technique was first described by Bill Hibbard and Dave Santek.

These slices can either be aligned with the volume and rendered at an angle to the viewer, or aligned with the viewing plane and sampled from unaligned slices through the volume. Graphics hardware support for 3D textures is needed for the second technique.

Volume aligned texturing produces images of reasonable quality, though there is often a noticeable transition when the volume is rotated.

Maximum Intensity Projection

As opposed to direct volume rendering, which requires every sample value to be mapped to opacity and a color, *maximum intensity projection* picks out and projects only the voxels with maximum intensity that fall in the way of parallel rays traced from the viewpoint to the plane of projection.

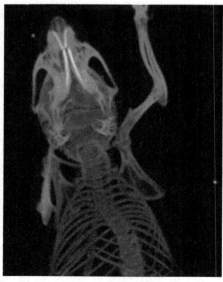

CT visualized by a maximum intensity projection of a mouse

This technique is computationally fast, but the 2D results do not provide a good sense of depth of the original data. To improve the sense of 3D, animations are usually rendered of several MIP frames in which the viewpoint is slightly changed from one to the other, thus creating the illusion of rotation. This helps the viewer's perception to find the relative 3D positions of the object components. This implies that two MIP renderings from opposite viewpoints are symmetrical images, which makes it impossible for the viewer to distinguish between left or right, front or back and even if the object is rotating clockwise or counterclockwise even though it makes a significant difference for the volume being rendered.

MIP imaging was invented for use in nuclear medicine by Jerold Wallis, MD, in 1988, and subsequently published in IEEE Transactions in Medical Imaging.

Surprisingly, an easy improvement to MIP is Local maximum intensity projection. In this technique we don't take the global maximum value, but the first maximum value that is above a certain threshold. Because - in general - we can terminate the ray earlier this technique is faster and also gives somehow better results as it approximates occlusion.

Hardware-accelerated Volume Rendering

Due to the extremely parallel nature of direct volume rendering, special purpose volume rendering hardware was a rich research topic before GPU volume rendering became fast enough. The most widely cited technology was VolumePro, which used high memory bandwidth and brute force to render using the ray casting algorithm.

A recently exploited technique to accelerate traditional volume rendering algorithms such as ray-casting is the use of modern graphics cards. Starting with the programmable pixel shaders, people recognized the power of parallel operations on multiple pixels and began to perform *general-purpose computing on (the) graphics processing units* (GPGPU). The pixel shaders are able to read and write randomly from video memory and perform some basic mathematical and logical calculations. These SIMD processors were used to perform general calculations such as rendering polygons and signal processing. In recent GPU generations, the pixel shaders now are able to function as MIMD processors (now able to independently branch) utilizing up to 1 GB of texture memory with floating point formats. With such power, virtually any algorithm with steps that can be performed in parallel, such as volume ray casting or tomographic reconstruction, can be performed with tremendous acceleration. The programmable pixel shaders can be used to simulate variations in the characteristics of lighting, shadow, reflection, emissive color and so forth. Such simulations can be written using high level shading languages.

Optimization Techniques

The primary goal of optimization is to skip as much of the volume as possible. A typical medical data set can be 1 GB in size. To render that at 30 frame/s requires an extremely fast memory bus. Skipping voxels means that less information needs to be processed.

Empty Space Skipping

Often, a volume rendering system will have a system for identifying regions of the volume containing no visible material. This information can be used to avoid rendering these transparent regions.

Early Ray Termination

This is a technique used when the volume is rendered in front to back order. For a ray through a pixel, once sufficient dense material has been encountered, further samples will make no significant contribution to the pixel and so may be neglected.

Octree and BSP Space Subdivision

The use of hierarchical structures such as octree and BSP-tree could be very helpful for both compression of volume data and speed optimization of volumetric ray casting process.

Volume Segmentation

By sectioning out large portions of the volume that one considers uninteresting before rendering, the amount of calculations that have to be made by ray casting or texture blending can be significantly reduced. This reduction can be as much as from $O(n)$ to $O(\log n)$ for n sequentially indexed voxels. Volume segmentation also has significant performance benefits for other ray tracing algorithms.

Multiple and Adaptive Resolution Representation

By representing less interesting regions of the volume in a coarser resolution, the data input overhead can be reduced. On closer observation, the data in these regions can be populated either by reading from memory or disk, or by interpolation. The coarser resolution volume is resampled to a smaller size in the same way as a 2D mipmap image is created from the original. These smaller volume are also used by themselves while rotating the volume to a new orientation.

Pre-integrated Volume Rendering

Pre-integrated volume rendering is a method that can reduce sampling artifacts by pre-computing much of the required data. It is especially useful in hardware-accelerated applications because it improves quality without a large performance impact. Unlike most other optimizations, this does not skip voxels. Rather it reduces the number of samples needed to accurately display a region of voxels. The idea is to render the intervals between the samples instead of the samples themselves. This technique captures rapidly changing material, for example the transition from muscle to bone with much less computation.

Image-based Meshing

Image-based meshing is the automated process of creating computer models from 3D image data (such as MRI, CT, Industrial CT or microtomography) for computational analysis and design, e.g. CAD, CFD, and FEA.

Temporal Reuse of Voxels

For a complete display view, only one voxel per pixel (the front one) is required to be shown (although more can be used for smoothing the image), if animation is needed, the front voxels to be shown can be cached and their location relative to the camera can be recalculated as it moves. Where display voxels become too far apart to cover all the pixels, new front voxels can be found by ray casting or similar, and where two voxels are in one pixel, the front one can be kept.

Motion Capture

Motion capture (Mo-cap for short) is the process of recording the movement of objects or people. It is used in military, entertainment, sports, medical applications, and for validation of computer vision and robotics. In filmmaking and video game development, it refers to recording actions of human actors, and using that information to animate digital character models in 2D or 3D computer animation. When it includes face and fingers or captures subtle expressions, it is often referred to as performance capture. In many fields, motion capture is sometimes called motion tracking, but in filmmaking and games, motion tracking usually refers more to match moving.

In motion capture sessions, movements of one or more actors are sampled many times per second. Whereas early techniques used images from multiple cameras to calculate 3D positions, often the purpose of motion capture is to record only the movements of the actor, not his or her visual appearance. This *animation data* is mapped to a 3D model so that the model performs the same actions as the actor. This process may be contrasted with the older technique of rotoscoping, as seen in Ralph Bakshi's *The Lord of the Rings* (1978) and *American Pop* (1981). The animated character movements were achieved in these films by tracing over a live-action actor, capturing the actor's motions and movements. To explain, an actor is filmed performing an action, and then the recorded film is projected onto an animation table frame-by-frame. Animators trace the live-action footage onto animation cels, capturing the actor's outline and motions frame-by-frame, and then they fill in the traced outlines with the animated character. The completed animation cels are then photographed frame-by-frame, exactly matching the movements and actions of the live-action footage. The end result of which is that the animated character replicates exactly the live-action movements of the actor. However, this process takes a considerable amount of time and effort.

Camera movements can also be motion captured so that a virtual camera in the scene will pan, tilt, or dolly around the stage driven by a camera operator while the actor is performing, and the motion capture system can capture the camera and props as well as the actor's performance. This allows the computer-generated characters, images and sets to have the same perspective as the video images from the camera. A computer processes the data and displays the movements of the actor, providing the desired camera positions in terms of objects in the set. Retroactively obtaining camera movement data from the captured footage is known as *match moving* or *camera tracking*.

Advantages

Motion capture offers several advantages over traditional computer animation of a 3D model:

- Low latency, close to real time, results can be obtained. In entertainment applications this can reduce the costs of keyframe-based animation. The Hand Over technique is an example of this.

- The amount of work does not vary with the complexity or length of the performance to the same degree as when using traditional techniques. This allows many tests to be done with different styles or deliveries, giving a different personality only limited by the talent of the actor.

- Complex movement and realistic physical interactions such as secondary motions, weight and exchange of forces can be easily recreated in a physically accurate manner.

- The amount of animation data that can be produced within a given time is extremely large when compared to traditional animation techniques. This contributes to both cost effectiveness and meeting production deadlines.

- Potential for free software and third party solutions reducing its costs.

Disadvantages

- Specific hardware and special software programs are required to obtain and process the data.

- The cost of the software, equipment and personnel required can be prohibitive for small productions.

- The capture system may have specific requirements for the space it is operated in, depending on camera field of view or magnetic distortion.

- When problems occur, it is easier to reshoot the scene rather than trying to manipulate the data. Only a few systems allow real time viewing of the data to decide if the take needs to be redone.

- The initial results are limited to what can be performed within the capture volume without extra editing of the data.

- Movement that does not follow the laws of physics cannot be captured.

- Traditional animation techniques, such as added emphasis on anticipation and follow through, secondary motion or manipulating the shape of the character, as with squash and stretch animation techniques, must be added later.

- If the computer model has different proportions from the capture subject, artifacts may occur. For example, if a cartoon character has large, oversized hands, these may intersect the character's body if the human performer is not careful with their physical motion.

History

An introduction to the history of motion capture technology starting at Aristotle (384-322 B.C.).

Applications

Video games often use motion capture to animate athletes, martial artists, and other in-game characters. This has been done since the Sega Model 2 arcade game *Virtua Fighter 2* in 1994. By mid-1995 the use of motion capture in video game development had become commonplace, and developer/publisher Acclaim Entertainment had gone so far as to have its own in-house motion capture studio built into its headquarters. Namco's 1995 arcade game *Soul Edge* used passive optical system markers for motion capture.

Motion Capture Performers from Buckinghamshire New University

Movies use motion capture for CG effects, in some cases replacing traditional cel animation, and for completely computer-generated creatures, such as Gollum, The Mummy, King Kong, Davy Jones from *Pirates of the Caribbean*, the Na'vi from the film *Avatar*, and Clu from *Tron: Legacy*. The Great Goblin, the three Stone-trolls, many of the orcs and goblins in the 2012 film The Hobbit: An Unexpected Journey, and Smaug were created using motion capture.

Sinbad: Beyond the Veil of Mists was the first movie made primarily with motion capture, although many character animators also worked on the film, which had a very limited release. 2001's *Final Fantasy: The Spirits Within* was the first widely released movie to be made primarily with motion capture technology. Despite its poor box-office intake, supporters of motion capture technology took notice.

The Lord of the Rings: The Two Towers was the first feature film to utilize a real-time motion capture system. This method streamed the actions of actor Andy Serkis into the computer generated skin of Gollum / Smeagol as it was being performed.

Out of the three nominees for the 2006 Academy Award for Best Animated Feature, two of the nominees (*Monster House* and the winner *Happy Feet*) used motion capture, and only Disney·Pixar's *Cars* was animated without motion capture. In the ending credits of Pixar's film *Ratatouille*, a stamp appears labelling the film as "100% Pure Animation – No Motion Capture!"

Since 2001, motion capture is being used extensively to produce films which attempt to simulate or approximate the look of live-action cinema, with nearly photorealistic digital character models. *The Polar Express* used motion capture to allow Tom Hanks to perform as several distinct digital characters (in which he also provided the voices). The 2007 adaptation of the saga *Beowulf* animated digital characters whose appearances were based in part on the actors who provided their motions and voices. James Cameron's highly popular *Avatar* used this technique to create the Na'vi that inhabit Pandora. The Walt Disney Company has produced Robert Zemeckis's *A Christmas Carol* using this technique. In 2007, Disney acquired Zemeckis' ImageMovers Digital (that produces motion capture films), but then closed it in 2011, after a string of failures.

Television series produced entirely with motion capture animation include *Laflaque* in Canada, *Sprookjesboom* and *Cafe de Wereld* in The Netherlands, and *Headcases* in the UK.

Virtual Reality and Augmented Reality allow users to interact with digital content in real-time. This can be useful for training simulations, visual perception tests, or performing a virtual walk-throughs in a 3D environment. Motion capture technology is frequently used in digital puppetry systems to drive computer generated characters in real-time.

Gait analysis is the major application of motion capture in clinical medicine. Techniques allow clinicians to evaluate human motion across several biometric factors, often while streaming this information live into analytical software.

During the filming of James Cameron's *Avatar* all of the scenes involving this process were directed in realtime using Autodesk Motion Builder software to render a screen image which allowed the director and the actor to see what they would look like in the movie, making it easier to direct the movie as it would be seen by the viewer. This method allowed views and angles not possible from a pre-rendered animation. Cameron was so proud of his results that he even invited Steven Spielberg and George Lucas on set to view the system in action.

In Marvel's critically acclaimed *The Avengers*, Mark Ruffalo used motion capture so he could play his character the Hulk, rather than have him be only CGI like previous films, making Ruffalo the first actor to play both the human and the Hulk versions of Bruce Banner.

FaceRig software uses facial recognition technology from ULSee.Inc to map a player's facial expressions to a 3D or 2D character's motion onscreen.

During *Game Developers Conference* 2016 in San Francisco *Epic Games* demonstrated full-body motion capture live in Unreal Engine. The whole scene from the upcoming game *Hellblade* was rendered in real-time and centers around a woman warrior, Senua, who is battling madness. The keynote was a collaboration between *Unreal Engine, Ninja Theory, 3Lateral, Cubic Motion, IKinema* and *Xsens*.

Methods and Systems

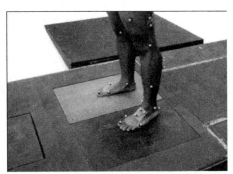

Reflective markers attached to skin to identify bony landmarks and the 3D motion of body segments

Silhouette Tracking

Motion tracking or motion capture started as a photogrammetric analysis tool in biome-chanics research in the 1970s and 1980s, and expanded into education, training, sports and recently computer animation for television, cinema, and video games as the technol-ogy matured. Since the 20th century the performer has to wear markers near each joint to identify the motion by the positions or angles between the markers. Acoustic, inertial, LED, magnetic or reflective markers, or combinations of any of these, are tracked, opti-mally at least two times the frequency rate of the desired motion. The resolution of the system is important in both the spatial resolution and temporal resolution as motion blur causes almost the same problems as low resolution. Since the beginning of the 21st century and because of the rapidly growth of technology new methods were developed. Most modern systems can extract the silhouette of the performer from the background. Afterwards all joint angles are calculated by fitting in a mathematic model into the silhou-ette. For movements you can't see a change of the silhouette, there are hybrid Systems available who can do both (marker and silhouette), but with less marker.

Optical Systems

Optical systems utilize data captured from image sensors to triangulate the 3D position of a subject between two or more cameras calibrated to provide overlapping projec-tions. Data acquisition is traditionally implemented using special markers attached to an actor; however, more recent systems are able to generate accurate data by track-ing surface features identified dynamically for each particular subject. Tracking a large number of performers or expanding the capture area is accomplished by the addition of more cameras. These systems produce data with 3 degrees of freedom for each marker, and rotational information must be inferred from the relative orientation of three or more markers; for instance shoulder, elbow and wrist markers providing the angle of the elbow. Newer hybrid systems are combining inertial sensors with optical sensors to reduce occlusion, increase the number of users and improve the ability to track without having to manually clean up data.

Passive Markers

Passive optical system use markers coated with a retroreflective material to reflect light that is generated near the cameras lens. The camera's threshold can be adjusted so only the bright reflective markers will be sampled, ignoring skin and fabric.

The centroid of the marker is estimated as a position within the two-dimensional im-age that is captured. The grayscale value of each pixel can be used to provide sub-pixel accuracy by finding the centroid of the Gaussian.

An object with markers attached at known positions is used to calibrate the cameras and obtain their positions and the lens distortion of each camera is measured. If two calibrated cameras see a marker, a three-dimensional fix can be obtained. Typically a system will consist of around 2 to 48 cameras. Systems of over three hundred cameras exist to try to reduce marker swap. Extra cameras are required for full coverage around the capture subject and multiple subjects.

A dancer wearing a suit used in an optical motion capture system

Vendors have constraint software to reduce the problem of marker swapping since all passive markers appear identical. Unlike active marker systems and magnetic systems, passive systems do not require the user to wear wires or electronic equipment. Instead, hundreds of rubber balls are attached with reflective tape, which needs to be replaced periodically. The markers are usually attached directly to the skin (as in biomechanics), or they are velcroed to a performer wearing a full body spandex/lycra suit designed specifically for motion capture. This type of system can capture large numbers of markers at frame rates usually around 120 to 160 fps although by lowering the resolution and tracking a smaller region of interest they can track as high as 10000 fps.

Several markers are placed at specific points on an actor's face during facial optical motion capture

Active Marker

Active optical systems triangulate positions by illuminating one LED at a time very quickly or multiple LEDs with software to identify them by their relative positions, somewhat akin to celestial navigation. Rather than reflecting light back that is generated externally, the markers themselves are powered to emit their own light. Since Inverse Square law provides 1/4 the power at 2 times the distance, this can increase the distances and volume for capture. This also enables high signal-to-noise ratio, resulting in very low marker jitter and a resulting high measurement resolution (often down to 0.1 mm within the calibrated volume).

The TV series ("Stargate SG1") produced episodes using an active optical system for the VFX allowing the actor to walk around props that would make motion capture difficult for other non-active optical systems.

ILM used active Markers in Van Helsing to allow capture of Dracula's flying brides on very large sets similar to Weta's use of active markers in "Rise of the Planet of the Apes". The power to each marker can be provided sequentially in phase with the capture system providing a unique identification of each marker for a given capture frame at a cost to the resultant frame rate. The ability to identify each marker in this manner is useful in realtime applications. The alternative method of identifying markers is to do it algorithmically requiring extra processing of the data.

There are also possibilities to find the position by using coloured LED-Markers. In these Systems, each colour is assigned to a specific point of the body.

One of the earliest active marker systems in the 1980s was a hybrid passive-active mocap system with rotating mirrors and colored glass reflective markers and which used masked linear array detectors.

Time Modulated Active Marker

A high-resolution uniquely identified active marker system with 3,600 × 3,600 resolution at 960 hertz providing real time submillimeter positions.

Active marker systems can further be refined by strobing one marker on at a time, or tracking multiple markers over time and modulating the amplitude or pulse width to provide marker ID. 12 megapixel spatial resolution modulated systems show more subtle movements than 4 megapixel optical systems by having both higher spatial and temporal resolution. Directors can see the actors performance in real time, and watch the results on the motion capture driven CG character. The unique marker IDs reduce the turnaround, by eliminating marker swapping and providing much cleaner data than other technologies. LEDs with onboard processing and a radio synchronization allow motion capture outdoors in direct sunlight, while capturing at 120 to 960 frames per second due to a high speed electronic shutter. Computer processing of modulated IDs allows less hand cleanup or filtered results for lower operational costs. This higher accuracy and resolution requires more processing than passive technologies, but the additional processing is done at the camera to improve resolution via a subpixel or centroid processing, providing both high resolution and high speed. These motion capture systems are typically $20,000 for an eight camera, 12 megapixel spatial resolution 120 hertz system with one actor.

IR sensors can compute their location when lit by mobile multi-LED emitters, e.g. in a moving car. With Id per marker, these sensor tags can be worn under clothing and tracked at 500 Hz in broad daylight.

Semi-passive Imperceptible Marker

One can reverse the traditional approach based on high speed cameras. Systems such as Prakash use inexpensive multi-LED high speed projectors. The specially built multi-LED IR projectors optically encode the space. Instead of retro-reflective or active light emitting diode (LED) markers, the system uses photosensitive marker tags to decode the optical signals. By attaching tags with photo sensors to scene points, the tags can compute not only their own locations of each point, but also their own orientation, incident illumination, and reflectance.

These tracking tags work in natural lighting conditions and can be imperceptibly embedded in attire or other objects. The system supports an unlimited number of tags in a scene, with each tag uniquely identified to eliminate marker reacquisition issues. Since the system eliminates a high speed camera and the corresponding high-speed image stream, it requires significantly lower data bandwidth. The tags also provide incident illumination data which can be used to match scene lighting when inserting synthetic elements. The technique appears ideal for on-set motion capture or real-time broadcasting of virtual sets but has yet to be proven.

Underwater Motion Capture System

Motion capture technology has been available for researchers and scientists for a few decades, which has given new insight into many fields.

Underwater Cameras

The vital part of the system, the Underwater camera, has a waterproof housing. The housing has a finish that withstands corrosion and chlorine which makes it perfect for use in basins and swimming pools. There are two types of cameras. Industrial high-speed-cameras can also be used as infrared cameras. The infrared underwater cameras comes with a cyan light strobe instead of the typical IR light—for minimum falloff under water and the high-speed-cameras cone with an LED-light or with the option of using image processing.

Underwater, motion capture camera.

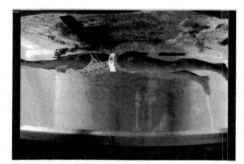

Motion tracking in swimming by using image processing

Measurement Volume

A Underwater camera is typically able to measure 15–20 meters depending on the water quality, the camera and the type of marker used. Unsurprisingly, the best range is achieved when the water is clear, and like always, the measurement volume is also dependent on the number of cameras. A range of underwater markers are available for different circumstances.

Tailored

Different pools require different mountings and fixtures. Therefore, all underwater motion capture systems are uniquely tailored to suit each specific pool installment. For cameras placed in the center of the pool, specially designed tripods, using suction cups, are provided.

Markerless

Emerging techniques and research in computer vision are leading to the rapid development of the markerless approach to motion capture. Markerless systems such as those developed at Stanford University, the University of Maryland, MIT, and the Max Planck Institute, do not require subjects to wear special equipment for tracking. Special computer algorithms are designed to allow the system to analyze multiple streams of optical input and identify human forms, breaking them down into constituent parts for tracking. ESC entertainment, a subsidiary of Warner Brothers Pictures created specially to enable virtual cinematography, including photorealistic digital look-alikes for filming the Matrix Reloaded and Matrix Revolutions movies, used a technique called Universal Capture that utilized 7 camera setup and the tracking the optical flow of all pixels over all the 2-D planes of the cameras for motion, gesture and facial expression capture leading to photorealistic results.

Traditional Systems

Traditionally markerless optical motion tracking is used to keep track on various objects, including airplanes, launch vehicles, missiles and satellites. Many of such optical motion tracking applications occur outdoors, requiring differing lens and camera configurations. High resolution images of the target being tracked can thereby provide more information than just motion data. The image obtained from NASA's long-range tracking system on space shuttle Challenger's fatal launch provided crucial evidence about the cause of the accident. Optical tracking systems are also used to identify known spacecraft and space debris despite the fact that it has a disadvantage over radar in that the objects must be reflecting or emitting sufficient light.

An optical tracking system typically consists of 3 subsystems: the optical imaging system, the mechanical tracking platform and the tracking computer.

The optical imaging system is responsible for converting the light from the target area into digital image that the tracking computer can process. Depending on the design of the optical tracking system, the optical imaging system can vary from as simple as a standard digital camera to as specialized as an astronomical telescope on the top of a mountain. The specification of the optical imaging system determines the upper-limit of the effective range of the tracking system.

The mechanical tracking platform holds the optical imaging system and is responsible for manipulating the optical imaging system in such a way that it always points to the target being tracked. The dynamics of the mechanical tracking platform combined with the optical imaging system determines the tracking system's ability to keep the lock on a target that changes speed rapidly.

The tracking computer is responsible for capturing the images from the optical imaging system, analyzing the image to extract target position and controlling the mechanical tracking platform to follow the target. There are several challenges. First the tracking computer has to be able to capture the image at a relatively high frame rate. This posts a requirement on the bandwidth of the image capturing hardware. The second challenge is that the image processing software has to be able to extract the target image from its background and calculate its position. Several textbook image processing algorithms are designed for this task. This problem can be simplified if the tracking system can expect certain characteristics that is common in all the targets it will track. The next problem down the line is to control the tracking platform to follow the target. This is a typical control system design problem rather than a challenge, which involves modeling the system dynamics and designing controllers to control it. This will however become a challenge if the tracking platform the system has to work with is not designed for real-time.

The software that runs such systems are also customized for the corresponding hardware components. One example of such software is OpticTracker, which controls computerized telescopes to track moving objects at great distances, such as planes and satellites. An other option is the software SimiShape, which can also be used hybrid in combination with markers.

Non-optical Systems

Inertial Systems

Inertial Motion Capture technology is based on miniature inertial sensors, biomechanical models and sensor fusion algorithms. The motion data of the inertial sensors (inertial guidance system) is often transmitted wirelessly to a computer, where the motion is recorded or viewed. Most inertial systems use inertial measurement units (IMUs) containing a combination of gyroscope, magnetometer, and accelerometer, to measure rotational rates. These rotations are translated to a skeleton in the software. Much like optical markers, the more IMU sensors the more natural the data. No external cameras, emitters or markers are needed for relative motions, although they are required to give the absolute position of the user if desired. Inertial motion capture systems capture the full six degrees of freedom body motion of a human in real-time and can give limited direction information if they include a magnetic bearing sensor, although these are much lower resolution and susceptible to electromagnetic noise. Benefits of using Inertial systems include: capturing in a variety of environments including tight spaces, no solving, portability, and large capture areas. Disadvantages include lower positional accuracy and positional drift which can compound over time. These systems are similar to the Wii controllers but are more sensitive and have greater resolution and update rates. They can accurately measure the direction to the ground to within a degree. The popularity of inertial systems is rising amongst independent game developers, mainly because of the quick and easy set up resulting in a fast pipeline. A range of suits are now available from various manufacturers and base prices range from $5,000 to $80,000 USD.

Mechanical Motion

Mechanical motion capture systems directly track body joint angles and are often referred to as exoskeleton motion capture systems, due to the way the sensors are attached to the body. A performer attaches the skeletal-like structure to their body and as they move so do the articulated mechanical parts, measuring the performer's relative motion. Mechanical motion capture systems are real-time, relatively low-cost, free-of-occlusion, and wireless (untethered) systems that have unlimited capture volume. Typically, they are rigid structures of jointed, straight metal or plastic rods linked together with potentiometers that articulate at the joints of the body. These suits tend to be in the $25,000 to $75,000 range plus an external absolute positioning system. Some suits provide limited force feedback or haptic input.

Magnetic Systems

Magnetic systems calculate position and orientation by the relative magnetic flux of three orthogonal coils on both the transmitter and each receiver. The relative intensity of the voltage or current of the three coils allows these systems to calculate both range and orientation by meticulously mapping the tracking volume. The sensor output is 6DOF, which provides useful results obtained with two-thirds the number of markers required in optical systems; one on upper arm and one on lower arm for elbow position and angle. The markers are not occluded by nonmetallic objects but are susceptible to magnetic and electrical interference from metal objects in the environment, like re-bar (steel reinforcing bars in concrete) or wiring, which affect the magnetic field, and electrical sources such as monitors, lights, cables and computers. The sensor response is nonlinear, especially toward edges of the capture area. The wiring from the sensors tends to preclude extreme performance movements. The capture volumes for magnetic systems are dramatically smaller than they are for optical systems. With the magnetic systems, there is a distinction between "AC" and "DC" systems: one uses square pulses, the other uses sine wave pulse.

Related Techniques

Facial Motion Capture

Most traditional motion capture hardware vendors provide for some type of low resolution facial capture utilizing anywhere from 32 to 300 markers with either an active or passive marker system. All of these solutions are limited by the time it takes to apply the markers, calibrate the positions and process the data. Ultimately the technology also limits their resolution and raw output quality levels.

High fidelity facial motion capture, also known as performance capture, is the next generation of fidelity and is utilized to record the more complex movements in a human face in order to capture higher degrees of emotion. Facial capture is currently arranging itself in several distinct camps, including traditional motion capture data, blend shaped based solutions, capturing the actual topology of an actor's face, and proprietary systems.

The two main techniques are stationary systems with an array of cameras capturing the facial expressions from multiple angles and using software such as the stereo mesh solver from OpenCV to create a 3D surface mesh, or to use light arrays as well to calculate the surface normals from the variance in brightness as the light source, camera position or both are changed. These techniques tend to be only limited in feature resolution by the camera resolution, apparent object size and number of cameras. If the users face is 50 percent of the working area of the camera and a camera has megapixel resolution, then sub millimeter facial motions can be detected by comparing frames. Recent work is focusing on increasing the frame rates and doing optical flow to allow the motions to be retargeted to other computer generated faces, rather than just making a 3D Mesh of the actor and their expressions.

RF Positioning

RF (radio frequency) positioning systems are becoming more viable as higher frequency RF devices allow greater precision than older RF technologies such as traditional radar. The speed of light is 30 centimeters per nanosecond (billionth of a second), so a 10 gigahertz (billion cycles per second) RF signal enables an accuracy of about 3 centimeters. By measuring amplitude to a quarter wavelength, it is possible to improve the resolution down to about 8 mm. To achieve the resolution of optical systems, frequencies of 50 gigahertz or higher are needed, which are almost as line of sight and as easy to block as optical systems. Multipath and reradiation of the signal are likely to cause additional problems, but these technologies will be ideal for tracking larger volumes with reasonable accuracy, since the required resolution at 100 meter distances is not likely to be as high. Many RF scientists believe that radio frequency will never produce the accuracy required for motion capture.

Non-traditional Systems

An alternative approach was developed where the actor is given an unlimited walking area through the use of a rotating sphere, similar to a hamster ball, which contains internal sensors recording the angular movements, removing the need for external cameras and other equipment. Even though this technology could potentially lead to much lower costs for motion capture, the basic sphere is only capable of recording a single continuous direction. Additional sensors worn on the person would be needed to record anything more.

Another alternative is using a 6DOF (Degrees of freedom) motion platform with an integrated omni-directional treadmill with high resolution optical motion capture to achieve the same effect. The captured person can walk in an unlimited area, negotiating different uneven terrains. Applications include medical rehabilitation for balance training, biomechanical research and virtual reality.

Crowd Simulation

Crowd simulation is the process of simulating the movement of a large number of entities or characters; this technique is now commonly used in 3D computer graphics for film. While simulating crowds, observed human behavior and interactions are taken into account to replicate collective behavior. It is a method of creating virtual cinematography.

The need for crowd simulation arises when a scene calls for more characters than can be practically animated using conventional systems, such as skeletons/bones. Simulating crowds offer the advantages of being cost effective as well as allow for total control of each simulated character or agent.

Animators typically create a library of motions, either for an entire character or for individual body parts. To simplify processing, these animations are sometimes *baked* as morphs. Alternately, the motions can be generated *procedurally* – i.e. choreographed automatically by software.

The actual movements and interactions of the crowd are typically implemented in one of two ways:

Particle Motion

The characters are attached to point particles, which are then animated by simulating wind, gravity, attractions, and collisions. The particle method is usually inexpensive to implement, and can be done in most 3D software packages. However, this method is not very realistic because it is difficult to direct individual entities when necessary. Also, motion is generally limited to flat surfaces.

Crowd AI

Entities – also called agents – are given artificial intelligence, which guides the entities based on one or more functions, such as sight, hearing, basic emotion, energy level, aggressiveness level, etc. Entities are given goals and then interact with each other just as members of a real crowd would. They are often programmed to respond to changes in their environment; for example, they may climb hills, jump over holes, scale ladders, etc. This system is much more realistic than particle motion, but it is very expensive to program and implement.

The most notable examples of AI simulation can be seen in New Line Cinema's *The Lord of the Rings* films, where AI armies of thousands of characters battle each other. This crowd simulation was done using Weta Digital's Massive software.

Sociology

Crowd simulation can also refer to simulations based on group dynamics and crowd psychology, often in public safety planning. In this case, the focus is just the behavior of the crowd, and not the visual realism of the simulation. Crowds have been studied as a scientific interest since the end of the 19th Century. A lot of research has focused on the collective social behavior of people at social gatherings, assemblies, protests, rebellions, concerts, sporting events and religious ceremonies. Gaining insight into natural human behavior under varying types of stressful situations will allow better models to be created which can be used to develop crowd controlling strategies.

Emergency response teams such as policemen, the National Guard, military and even volunteers must undergo some type of crowd control training. Using researched principles of human behavior in crowds can give disaster training designers more elements to incorporate to create realistic simulated disasters. Crowd behavior can be observed during panic and non-panic conditions. When natural and unnatural events toss social ideals into a twisting chaotic bind, such as the events of 9/11 and hurricane Katrina, humanity's social capabilities are truly put to the test. Military programs are looking more towards simulated training, involving emergency responses, due to their cost effective technology as well as how effective the learning can be transferred to the real world. Many events that may start out controlled can have a twisting event that turns them into catastrophic situations, where decisions need to be made on the spot. It is these situations in which crowd dynamical understanding would play a vital role in reducing the potential for anarchy.

Modeling techniques of crowds vary from holistic or network approaches to understanding individualistic or behavioral aspects of each agent. For example, the Social Force Model describes a need for individuals to find a balance between social interaction and physical interaction. An approach that incorporates both aspects, and is able to adapt depending on the situation, would better describe natural human behavior, always incorporating some measure of unpredictability. With the use of multi-agent models understanding these complex behaviors has become a much more comprehensible task. With the use of this type of software, systems can now be tested under extreme conditions, and simulate conditions over long periods of time in the matter of seconds.

Shader

In the field of computer graphics, a shader is a computer program that is used to do shading: the production of appropriate levels of color within an image, or, in the modern era, also to produce special effects or do video post-processing. A definition in layman's terms might be given as "a program that tells a computer how to draw something in a specific and unique way".

FLAT SHADING   PHONG SHADING

Shaders are most commonly used to produce lighting and shadow in 3D modeling. The image above illustrates Phong shading, one of the first computer shading models ever developed

Shaders calculate rendering effects on graphics hardware with a high degree of flexibility. Most shaders are coded for a graphics processing unit (GPU), though this is not a strict requirement. Shading languages are usually used to program the programmable GPU rendering pipeline, which has mostly superseded the fixed-function pipeline that allowed only common geometry transformation and pixel-shading functions; with shaders, customized effects can be used. The position, hue, saturation, brightness, and contrast of all pixels, vertices, or textures used to construct a final image can be altered on the fly, using algorithms defined in the shader, and can be modified by external variables or textures introduced by the program calling the shader.

Shaders can also be used for special effects. An example of a digital photograph from a webcam unshaded on the left, and the same image with a special effects shader applied on the right which replaces all light areas of the image with white and the dark areas with a brightly colored texture

Shaders are used widely in cinema postprocessing, computer-generated imagery, and video games to produce a seemingly infinite range of effects. Beyond just simple lighting models, more complex uses include altering the hue, saturation, brightness and/or contrast of an image, producing blur, light bloom, volumetric lighting, normal mapping for depth effects, bokeh, cel shading, posterization, bump mapping, distortion, chroma keying (so-called "bluescreen/ greenscreen" effects), edge detection and motion detection, psychedelic effects, and a wide range of others.

History

The modern use of "shader" was introduced to the public by Pixar with their "RenderMan Interface Specification, Version 3.0" originally published in May, 1988.

As graphics processing units evolved, major graphics software libraries such as OpenGL and Direct3D began to support shaders. The first shader-capable GPUs only supported pixel shading, but vertex shaders were quickly introduced once developers realized the power of shaders. Geometry shaders were recently introduced with Direct3D 10 and OpenGL 3.2. Eventually graphics hardware evolved toward a unified shader model.

Design

Shaders are simple programs that describe the traits of either a vertex or a pixel. Vertex shaders describe the traits (position, texture coordinates, colors, etc.) of a vertex, while pixel shaders describe the traits (color, z-depth and alpha value) of a pixel. A vertex shader is called for each vertex in a primitive (possibly after tessellation); thus one vertex in, one (updated) vertex out. Each vertex is then rendered as a series of pixels onto a surface (block of memory) that will eventually be sent to the screen.

Shaders replace a section of the graphics hardware typically called the Fixed Function Pipeline (FFP), so-called because it performs lighting and texture mapping in a hard-coded manner. Shaders provide a programmable alternative to this hard-coded approach.

The basic graphics pipeline is as follows:

- The CPU sends instructions (compiled shading language programs) and geometry data to the graphics processing unit, located on the graphics card.

- Within the vertex shader, the geometry is transformed.

- If a geometry shader is in the graphic processing unit and active, some changes of the geometries in the scene are performed.

- If a tessellation shader is in the graphic processing unit and active, the geometries in the scene can be subdivided.

- The calculated geometry is triangulated (subdivided into triangles).

- Triangles are broken down into fragment quads (one fragment quad is a 2 × 2 fragment primitive).

- Fragment quads are modified according to the fragment shader.

- The depth test is performed, fragments that pass will get written to the screen and might get blended into the frame buffer.

The graphic pipeline uses these steps in order to transform three-dimensional (and/or two-dimensional) data into useful two-dimensional data for displaying. In general, this is a large pixel matrix or "frame buffer".

Types

There are three types of shaders in common use, with one more recently added. While older graphics cards utilize separate processing units for each shader type, newer cards feature unified shaders which are capable of executing any type of shader. This allows graphics cards to make more efficient use of processing power.

2D Shaders

2D shaders act on digital images, also called textures in computer graphics work. They modify attributes of pixels. Currently the only 2D shader types are pixel shaders.

Pixel Shaders

Pixel shaders, also known as fragment shaders, compute color and other attributes of each "fragment" - a technical term usually meaning a single pixel. The simplest kinds of pixel shaders output one screen pixel as a color value; more complex shaders with multiple inputs/outputs are also possible. Pixel shaders range from always outputting the same color, to applying a lighting value, to doing bump mapping, shadows, specular highlights, translucency and other phenomena. They can alter the depth of the fragment (for Z-buffering), or output more than one color if multiple render targets are active. In 3D graphics, a pixel shader alone cannot produce very complex effects, because it operates only on a single fragment, without knowledge of a scene's geometry. However, pixel shaders do have knowledge of the screen coordinate being drawn, and can sample the screen and nearby pixels if the contents of the entire screen are passed as a texture to the shader. This technique can enable a wide variety of two-dimensional postprocessing effects, such as blur, or edge detection/enhancement for cartoon/cel shaders. Pixel shaders may also be applied in intermediate stages to any two-dimensional images—sprites or textures—in the pipeline, whereas vertex shaders always require a 3D scene. For instance, a pixel shader is the only kind of shader that can act as a postprocessor or filter for a video stream after it has been rasterized.

3D Shaders

3D shaders act on 3D models or other geometry but may also access the colors and textures used to draw the model or mesh. Vertex shaders are the oldest type of 3d shader, generally modifying on a per-vertex basis. Geometry shaders can generate new vertices from within the shader. Tessellation shaders are newer 3d shaders that act on batches of vertexes all at once to add detail - such as subdividing a model into smaller groups of triangles or other primitives at runtime, to improve things like curves and bumps, or change other attributes.

Vertex Shaders

Vertex shaders are the most established and common kind of 3d shader and are run once for each vertex given to the graphics processor. The purpose is to transform each vertex's 3D position in virtual space to the 2D coordinate at which it appears on the screen (as well as a depth value for the Z-buffer). Vertex shaders can manipulate properties such as position, color and texture coordinate, but cannot create new vertices.

The output of the vertex shader goes to the next stage in the pipeline, which is either a geometry shader if present, or the rasterizer. Vertex shaders can enable powerful control over the details of position, movement, lighting, and color in any scene involving 3D models.

Geometry Shaders

Geometry shaders are a relatively new type of shader, introduced in Direct3D 10 and OpenGL 3.2; formerly available in OpenGL 2.0+ with the use of extensions. This type of shader can generate new graphics primitives, such as points, lines, and triangles, from those primitives that were sent to the beginning of the graphics pipeline.

Geometry shader programs are executed after vertex shaders. They take as input a whole primitive, possibly with adjacency information. For example, when operating on triangles, the three vertices are the geometry shader's input. The shader can then emit zero or more primitives, which are rasterized and their fragments ultimately passed to a pixel shader.

Typical uses of a geometry shader include point sprite generation, geometry tessellation, shadow volume extrusion, and single pass rendering to a cube map. A typical real-world example of the benefits of geometry shaders would be automatic mesh complexity modification. A series of line strips representing control points for a curve are passed to the geometry shader and depending on the complexity required the shader can automatically generate extra lines each of which provides a better approximation of a curve.

Tessellation Shaders

As of OpenGL 4.0 and Direct3D 11, a new shader class called a tessellation shader has been added. It adds two new shader stages to the traditional model. Tessellation control shaders (also known as hull shaders) and tessellation evaluation shaders (also known as Domain Shaders), which together allow for simpler meshes to be subdivided into finer meshes at run-time according to a mathematical function. The function can be related to a variety of variables, most notably the distance from the viewing camera to allow active level-of-detail scaling. This allows objects close to the camera to have fine detail, while further away ones can have more coarse meshes, yet seem comparable in quality. It also can drastically reduce mesh bandwidth by allowing meshes to be refined once inside the shader units instead of downsampling very complex ones from memory. Some algorithms can upsample any arbitrary mesh, while others allow for "hinting" in meshes to dictate the most characteristic vertices and edges.

Other

Compute shaders are not limited to graphics applications, but use the same execution resources for GPGPU. They may be used in graphics pipelines e.g. for additional stages in animation or lighting algorithms, (e.g. tiled forward rendering). Some rendering APIs allow compute shaders to easily share data resources with the graphics pipeline.

Parallel Processing

Shaders are written to apply transformations to a large set of elements at a time, for example, to each pixel in an area of the screen, or for every vertex of a model. This is well suited to parallel processing, and most modern GPUs have multiple shader pipelines to facilitate this, vastly improving computation throughput.

A programming model with shaders is similar to a higher order function for rendering, taking the shaders as arguments, and providing a specific dataflow between intermediate results, enabling both data parallelism(across pixels, vertices etc.) and pipeline parallelism (between stages). (see also map reduce).

Programming

The language in which shaders are programmed depends on the target environment. The official OpenGL and OpenGL ES shading language is OpenGL Shading Language, also known as GLSL, and the official Direct3D shading language is High Level Shader Language, also known as HLSL. However, Cg is a deprecated third-party shading language developed by Nvidia that outputs both OpenGL and Direct3D shaders. Apple released its own shading language called Metal Shading Language as part of the Metal framework.

Rasterisation

Rasterisation (or rasterization) is the task of taking an image described in a vector graphics format (shapes) and converting it into a raster image (pixels or dots) for output on a video display or printer, or for storage in a bitmap file format. It refers to both rasterisation of models and 2D rendering primitives such as polygons, line segments, etc.

In normal usage, the term refers to the popular rendering algorithm for displaying 3D models on a computer. Rasterisation is currently the most popular technique for producing real-time 3D computer graphics. Real-time applications need to respond immediately to user input, and generally need to produce frame rates of at least 30 frames per second to achieve smooth animation.

Compared with other rendering techniques such as ray tracing, rasterisation is extremely fast. However, rasterization is simply the process of computing the mapping from scene geometry to pixels and does not prescribe a particular way to compute the color of those pixels. Shading, including programmable shading, may be based on physical light transport, or artistic intent.

Introduction

The term *"rasterisation"* in general can be applied to any process by which vector information (or other procedural description) can be converted into a raster format.

The process of rasterising 3D models onto a 2D plane for display on a computer screen ("screen space") is often carried out by fixed function hardware within the graphics pipeline. This is because there is no motivation for modifying the techniques for rasterisation used at render time and a special-purpose system allows for high efficiency.

Basic Approach for 3D Polygon Mesh Rendering

The most basic rasterization algorithm takes a 3D scene, described as polygons, and renders it onto a 2D surface, usually a computer monitor. Polygons are themselves represented as collections of triangles. Triangles are represented by 3 vertices in 3D-space. At a very basic level, rasterizers simply take a stream of vertices, transform them into corresponding 2-dimensional points on the viewer's monitor and fill in the transformed 2-dimensional triangles as appropriate.

Transformations

Transformations are usually performed by matrix multiplication. Quaternion math may also be used but that is outside the scope of this article. The main transformations are translation, scaling, rotation, and projection. A three-dimensional vertex may be transformed by augmenting an extra variable (known as a "homogeneous variable") and left multiplying the resulting 4-component vertex by a 4 x 4 transformation matrix.

A translation is simply the movement of a point from its original location to another location in 3-space by a constant offset. Translations can be represented by the following matrix:

$$\begin{bmatrix} 1 & 0 & 0 & X \\ 0 & 1 & 0 & Y \\ 0 & 0 & 1 & Z \\ 0 & 0 & 0 & 1 \end{bmatrix}$$

X, Y, and Z are the offsets in the 3 dimensions, respectively.

A scaling transformation is performed by multiplying the position of a vertex by a scalar value. This has the effect of scaling a vertex with respect to the origin. Scaling can be represented by the following matrix:

$$\begin{bmatrix} X & 0 & 0 & 0 \\ 0 & Y & 0 & 0 \\ 0 & 0 & Z & 0 \\ 0 & 0 & 0 & 1 \end{bmatrix}$$

X, Y, and Z are the values by which each of the 3-dimensions are multiplied. Asymmetric scaling can be accomplished by varying the values of X, Y, and Z.

Rotation matrices depend on the axis around which a point is to be rotated.

Rotation about the X-axis:

$$\begin{bmatrix} 1 & 0 & 0 & 0 \\ 0 & \cos\theta & -\sin\theta & 0 \\ 0 & \sin\theta & \cos\theta & 0 \\ 0 & 0 & 0 & 1 \end{bmatrix}$$

Rotation about the Y-axis:

$$\begin{bmatrix} \cos\theta & 0 & \sin\theta & 0 \\ 0 & 1 & 0 & 0 \\ -\sin\theta & 0 & \cos\theta & 0 \\ 0 & 0 & 0 & 1 \end{bmatrix}$$

Rotation about the Z-axis:

$$\begin{bmatrix} \cos\theta & -\sin\theta & 0 & 0 \\ \sin\theta & \cos\theta & 0 & 0 \\ 0 & 0 & 1 & 0 \\ 0 & 0 & 0 & 1 \end{bmatrix}$$

θ in all each of these cases represent the angle of rotation.

A series of translation, scaling, and rotation matrices can logically describe most transformations. Rasterization systems generally use a transformation stack to move the stream of input vertices into place. The transformation stack is a standard stack which stores matrices. Incoming vertices are multiplied by the matrix stack.

As an illustrative example of how the transformation stack is used, imagine a simple scene with a single model of a person. The person is standing upright, facing an arbitrary direction while his head is turned in another direction. The person is also located at a certain offset from the origin. A stream of vertices, the model, would be loaded to represent the person. First, a translation matrix would be pushed onto the stack to move the model to the correct location. A scaling matrix would be pushed onto the stack to size the model correctly. A rotation about the y-axis would be pushed onto the stack to orient the model properly. Then, the stream of vertices representing the body would be sent through the rasterizer. Since the head is facing a different direction, the rotation matrix would be popped off the top of the stack and a different rotation matrix about the y-axis with a different angle would be pushed. Finally the stream of vertices representing the head would be sent to the rasterizer.

After all points have been transformed to their desired locations in 3-space with respect to the viewer, they must be transformed to the 2-D image plane. The simplest projection, the orthographic projection, simply involves removing the z component from transformed 3d vertices. Orthographic projections have the property that all parallel lines in 3-space will remain parallel in the 2-D representation. However, real world images are perspective images, with distant objects appearing smaller than objects close to the viewer. A perspective projection transformation needs to be applied to these points.

Conceptually, the idea is to transform the perspective viewing volume into the orthogonal viewing volume. The perspective viewing volume is a frustum, that is, a truncated pyramid. The orthographic viewing volume is a rectangular box, where both the near and far viewing planes are parallel to the image plane.

A perspective projection transformation can be represented by the following matrix:

$$\begin{bmatrix} 1 & 0 & 0 & 0 \\ 0 & 1 & 0 & 0 \\ 0 & 0 & (N+F)/N & -F \\ 0 & 0 & 1/N & 0 \end{bmatrix}$$

F and N here are the distances of the far and near viewing planes, respectively. The resulting four vector will be a vector where the homogeneous variable is not 1. Homogenizing the vector, or multiplying it by the inverse of the homogeneous variable such that the homogeneous variable becomes unitary, gives us our resulting 2-D location in the x and y coordinates.

Clipping

Once triangle vertices are transformed to their proper 2D locations, some of these locations may be outside the viewing window, or the area on the screen to which pixels will actually be written. Clipping is the process of truncating triangles to fit them inside the viewing area.

The most common technique is the Sutherland-Hodgeman clipping algorithm. In this approach, each of the 4 edges of the image plane is tested at a time. For each edge, test all points to be rendered. If the point is outside the edge, the point is removed. For each triangle edge that is intersected by the image plane's edge, that is, one vertex of the edge is inside the image and another is outside, a point is inserted at the intersection and the outside point is removed.

Scan Conversion

The final step in the traditional rasterization process is to fill in the 2D triangles that are now in the image plane. This is also known as scan conversion.

The first problem to consider is whether or not to draw a pixel at all. For a pixel to be rendered, it must be within a triangle, and it must not be occluded, or blocked by another pixel. There are a number of algorithms to fill in pixels inside a triangle, the most popular of which is the scanline algorithm. Since it is difficult to know that the rasterization engine will draw all pixels from front to back, there must be some way of ensuring that pixels close to the viewer are not overwritten by pixels far away. A z buffer is the most common solution. The z buffer is a 2d array corresponding to the image plane which stores a depth value for each pixel. Whenever a pixel is drawn, it updates the z buffer with its depth value. Any new pixel must check its depth value against the z buffer value before it is drawn. Closer pixels are drawn and farther pixels are disregarded.

To find out a pixel's color, textures and shading calculations must be applied. A texture map is a bitmap that is applied to a triangle to define its look. Each triangle vertex is also associated with a texture and a texture coordinate (u,v) for normal 2-d textures in addition to its position coordinate. Every time a pixel on a triangle is rendered, the corresponding texel (or texture element) in the texture must be found. This is done by interpolating between the triangle's vertices' associated texture coordinates by the pixels on-screen distance from the vertices. In perspective projections, interpolation is performed on the texture coordinates divided by the depth of the vertex to avoid a problem known as perspective foreshortening (a process known as perspective texturing).

Before the final color of the pixel can be decided, a lighting calculation must be performed to shade the pixels based on any lights which may be present in the scene. There are generally three light types commonly used in scenes. Directional lights are lights which come from a single direction and have the same intensity throughout the entire scene. In real life, sunlight comes close to being a directional light, as the sun is so far away that rays from the sun appear parallel to Earth observers and the falloff is negligible. Point lights are lights with a definite position in space and radiate light evenly in all directions. Point lights are usually subject to some form of attenuation, or fall off in the intensity of light incident on objects farther away. Real life light sources experience quadratic falloff. Finally, spotlights are like real-life spotlights, with a definite point in space, a direction, and an angle defining the cone of the spotlight. There is also often an ambient light value that is added to all final lighting calculations to arbitrarily compensate for global illumination effects which rasterization can not calculate correctly.

There are a number of shading algorithms for rasterizers. All shading algorithms need to account for distance from light and the normal vector of the shaded object with respect to the incident direction of light. The fastest algorithms simply shade all pixels on any given triangle with a single lighting value, also known as flat shading. There is no way to create the illusion of smooth surfaces this way, except by subdividing into many small triangles. Algorithms can also separately shade vertices, and interpolate the lighting value of the vertices when drawing pixels. This is known as Gouraud shading. The slowest and most realistic approach is to calculate lighting separately for each pixel, also known as Phong shading. This performs bilinear interpolation of the normal vectors and uses the result to do local lighting calculation.

Acceleration Techniques

To extract the maximum performance out of any rasterization engine, a minimum number of polygons should be sent to the renderer. A number of acceleration techniques have been developed over time to cull out objects which can not be seen.

Backface Culling

The simplest way to cull polygons is to cull all polygons which face away from the viewer. This is known as backface culling. Since most 3d objects are fully enclosed, polygons facing away from a viewer are always blocked by polygons facing towards the viewer unless the viewer is inside the object. A polygon's facing is defined by its winding, or the order in which its vertices are sent to the renderer. A renderer can define either clockwise or counterclockwise winding as front or back facing. Once a polygon has been transformed to screen space, its winding can be checked and if it is in the opposite direction, it is not drawn at all. Of course, backface culling can not be used with degenerate and unclosed volumes.

Spatial Data Structures

More advanced techniques use data structures to cull out objects which are either outside the viewing volume or are occluded by other objects. The most common data structures are binary space partitions, octrees, and cell and portal culling.

Further Refinements

While the basic rasterization process has been known for decades, modern applications continue to make optimizations and additions to increase the range of possibilities for the rasterization rendering engine.

Texture Filtering

Textures are created at specific resolutions, but since the surface they are applied to may be at any distance from the viewer, they can show up at arbitrary sizes on the final image. As a result, one pixel on screen usually does not correspond directly to one texel. Some form of filtering technique needs to be applied to create clean images at any distance. A variety of methods are available, with different tradeoffs between image quality and computational complexity.

Environment Mapping

Environment mapping is a form of texture mapping in which the texture coordinates are view-dependent. One common application, for example, is to simulate reflection on a shiny object. One can environment map the interior of a room to a metal cup in a room. As the viewer moves about the cup, the texture coordinates of the cup's vertices move accordingly, providing the illusion of reflective metal.

Bump Mapping

Bump mapping is another form of texture mapping which does not provide pixels with color, but rather with depth. Especially with modern pixel shaders (see below), bump mapping creates the feel of view and lighting-dependent roughness on a surface to enhance realism greatly.

Level of Detail

In many modern applications, the number of polygons in any scene can be phenomenal. However, a viewer in a scene will only be able to discern details of close-by objects. Level of detail algorithms vary the complexity of geometry as a function of distance to the viewer. Objects right in front of the viewer can be rendered at full complexity while objects further away can be simplified dynamically, or even replaced completely with sprites.

Shadows

A shadow is an area where direct light from a light source cannot reach due to obstruction by an object. It occupies all of the space behind an opaque object with light in front of it. The cross section of a shadow is a two-dimensional silhouette, or reverse projection of the object blocking the light. The sun causes many objects to have shadows and at certain times of the day, when the sun is at certain heights, the lengths of shadows change.

Hardware Acceleration

Triangles

Starting in the mid 1990s, hardware acceleration of texture mapped triangle primitives for consumer desktop computers has become the norm. Whereas graphics programmers had earlier relied on hand-coded assembly to make their programs run fast, most modern programs are written to interface with one of the existing rendering APIs, which drives a dedicated GPU.

The unified shader model does calculations relating to different kinds of shader on the same hardware by iterating over the received data. Newer graphics APIs, such as e.g. the Vulkan (API), give further control.

Polygon Mesh

A polygon mesh is a collection of vertices, edges and faces that defines the shape of a polyhedral object in 3D computer graphics and solid modeling. The faces usually consist of triangles (triangle mesh), quadrilaterals, or other simple convex polygons, since this simplifies rendering, but may also be composed of more general concave polygons, or polygons with holes.

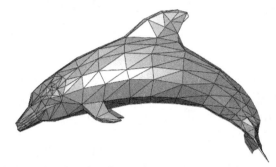

Example of a triangle mesh representing a dolphin.

The study of polygon meshes is a large sub-field of computer graphics and geometric modeling. Different representations of polygon meshes are used for different applications and goals. The variety of operations performed on meshes may include Boolean logic, smoothing, simplification, and many others. Volumetric meshes are distinct from polygon meshes in that they explicitly represent both the surface and volume of a structure, while polygon meshes only explicitly represent the surface (the volume is implicit). As polygonal meshes are extensively used in computer graphics, algorithms also exist for ray tracing, collision detection, and rigid-body dynamics of polygon meshes.

Elements of Mesh Modeling

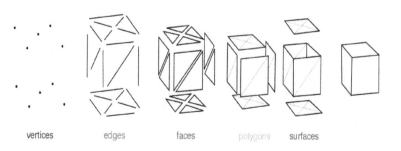

vertices   edges   faces   polygons   surfaces

Objects created with polygon meshes must store different types of elements. These include vertices, edges, faces, polygons and surfaces. In many applications, only vertices, edges and either faces or polygons are stored. A renderer may support only 3-sided faces, so polygons must be constructed of many of these, as shown above. However, many renderers either support quads and higher-sided polygons, or are able to convert polygons to triangles on the fly, making it unnecessary to store a mesh in a triangulated form. Also, in certain applications like head modeling, it is desirable to be able to create both 3- and 4-sided polygons.

vertex

A position (usually in 3D space) along with other information such as color, normal vector and texture coordinates.

edge

A connection between two vertices.

face

A closed set of edges, in which a *triangle face* has three edges, and a *quad face* has four edges. A polygon is a coplanar set of faces. In systems that support multi-sided faces, polygons and faces are equivalent. However, most rendering hardware supports only 3- or 4-sided faces, so polygons are represented as multiple faces. Mathematically a polygonal mesh may be considered an unstructured grid, or undirected graph, with additional properties of geometry, shape and topology.

Surfaces

More often called smoothing groups, are useful, but not required to group smooth regions. Consider a cylinder with caps, such as a soda can. For smooth shading of the sides, all surface normals must point horizontally away from the center, while the normals of the caps must point straight up and down. Rendered as a single, Phong-shaded surface, the crease vertices would have incorrect normals. Thus, some way of determining where to cease smoothing is needed to group smooth parts of a mesh, just as polygons group 3-sided faces. As an alternative to providing surfaces/smoothing groups, a mesh may contain other data for calculating the same data, such as a splitting angle (polygons with normals above this threshold are either automatically treated as separate smoothing groups or some technique such as splitting or chamfering is automatically applied to the edge between them). Additionally, very high resolution meshes are less subject to issues that would require smoothing groups, as their polygons are so small as to make the need irrelevant. Further, another alternative exists in the possibility of simply detaching the surfaces themselves from the rest of the mesh. Renderers do not attempt to smooth edges across noncontiguous polygons.

Groups

Some mesh formats contain Groups, which define separate elements of the mesh, and are useful for determining separate sub-objects for skeletal animation or separate actors for non-skeletal animation.

Materials

Generally materials will be defined, allowing different portions of the mesh to use different shaders when rendered.

UV coordinates

Most mesh formats also support some form of UV coordinates which are a separate 2d representation of the mesh "unfolded" to show what portion of a 2-dimensional texture map to apply to different polygons of the mesh. It is also possible for meshes to contain other such vertex *attribute* information such as colour, tangent vectors, weight maps to control animation, etc (sometimes also called *channels*).

Representations

Polygon meshes may be represented in a variety of ways, using different methods to store the vertex, edge and face data. These include:

Face-vertex meshes

A simple list of vertices, and a set of polygons that point to the vertices it uses.

Winged-edge

in which each edge points to two vertices, two faces, and the four (clockwise and counterclockwise) edges that touch them. Winged-edge meshes allow constant time traversal of the surface, but with higher storage requirements.

Half-edge meshes

Similar to winged-edge meshes except that only half the edge traversal information is used. (see OpenMesh)

Quad-edge meshes

which store edges, half-edges, and vertices without any reference to polygons. The polygons are implicit in the representation, and may be found by traversing the structure. Memory requirements are similar to half-edge meshes.

Corner-tables

which store vertices in a predefined table, such that traversing the table implicitly defines polygons. This is in essence the triangle fan used in hardware graphics rendering. The representation is more compact, and more efficient to retrieve polygons, but operations to change polygons are slow. Furthermore, corner-tables do not represent meshes completely. Multiple corner-tables (triangle fans) are needed to represent most meshes.

Vertex-vertex meshes

> A "VV" mesh represents only vertices, which point to other vertices. Both the edge and face information is implicit in the representation. However, the simplicity of the representation does not allow for many efficient operations to be performed on meshes.

Each of the representations above have particular advantages and drawbacks, further discussed in Smith (2006).

The choice of the data structure is governed by the application, the performance required, size of the data, and the operations to be performed. For example, it is easier to deal with triangles than general polygons, especially in computational geometry. For certain operations it is necessary to have a fast access to topological information such as edges or neighboring faces; this requires more complex structures such as the winged-edge representation. For hardware rendering, compact, simple structures are needed; thus the corner-table (triangle fan) is commonly incorporated into low-level rendering APIs such as DirectX and OpenGL.

Vertex-vertex Meshes

However, VV meshes benefit from small storage space and efficient morphing of shape. The above figure shows a four-sided box as represented by a VV mesh. Each vertex indexes its neighboring vertices. Notice that the last two vertices, 8 and 9 at the top and bottom center of the "box-cylinder", have four connected vertices rather than five. A general system must be able to handle an arbitrary number of vertices connected to any given vertex.

Vertex-Vertex Meshes (VV)

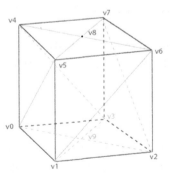

Vertex List		
v0	0,0,0	v1 v5 v4 v3 v9
v1	1,0,0	v2 v6 v5 v0 v9
v2	1,1,0	v3 v7 v6 v1 v9
v3	0,1,0	v2 v6 v7 v4 v9
v4	0,0,1	v5 v0 v3 v7 v8
v5	1,0,1	v6 v1 v0 v4 v8
v6	1,1,1	v7 v2 v1 v5 v8
v7	0,1,1	v4 v3 v2 v6 v8
v8	.5,.5,1	v4 v5 v6 v7
v9	.5,.5,0	v0 v1 v2 v3

Vertex-vertex meshes represent an object as a set of vertices connected to other vertices. This is the simplest representation, but not widely used since the face and edge information is implicit. Thus, it is necessary to traverse the data in order to generate a list of faces for rendering. In addition, operations on edges and faces are not easily accomplished.

Face-vertex Meshes

Face-vertex meshes improve on VV-mesh for modeling in that they allow explicit look-up of the vertices of a face, and the faces surrounding a vertex. The above figure shows the "box-cylinder" example as an FV mesh. Vertex v5 is highlighted to show the faces that surround it. Notice that, in this example, every face is required to have exactly 3 vertices. However, this does not mean every vertex has the same number of surrounding faces.

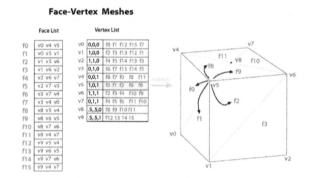

Face-vertex meshes represent an object as a set of faces and a set of vertices. This is the most widely used mesh representation, being the input typically accepted by modern graphics hardware.

For rendering, the face list is usually transmitted to the GPU as a set of indices to vertices, and the vertices are sent as position/color/normal structures (in the figure, only position is given). This has the benefit that changes in shape, but not geometry, can be dynamically updated by simply resending the vertex data without updating the face connectivity.

Modeling requires easy traversal of all structures. With face-vertex meshes it is easy to find the vertices of a face. Also, the vertex list contains a list of faces connected to each vertex. Unlike VV meshes, both faces and vertices are explicit, so locating neighboring faces and vertices is constant time. However, the edges are implicit, so a search is still needed to find all the faces surrounding a given face. Other dynamic operations, such as splitting or merging a face, are also difficult with face-vertex meshes.

Winged-edge Meshes

Winged-edge meshes address the issue of traversing from edge to edge, and providing an ordered set of faces around an edge. For any given edge, the number of outgoing edges may be arbitrary. To simplify this, winged-edge meshes provide only four, the nearest clockwise and counter-clockwise edges at each end. The other edges may be traversed incrementally. The information for each edge therefore resembles a butterfly, hence "winged-edge" meshes. The above figure shows the "box-cylinder" as a winged-edge mesh. The total data for an edge consists of 2 vertices (endpoints), 2 faces (on each side), and 4 edges (winged-edge).

Rendering of winged-edge meshes for graphics hardware requires generating a Face index list. This is usually done only when the geometry changes. Winged-edge meshes are ideally suited for dynamic geometry, such as subdivision surfaces and interactive modeling, since changes to the mesh can occur locally. Traversal across the mesh, as might be needed for collision detection, can be accomplished efficiently.

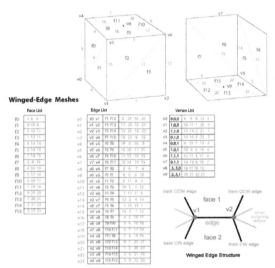

Introduced by Baumgart 1975, winged-edge meshes explicitly represent the vertices, faces, and edges of a mesh. This representation is widely used in modeling programs to provide the greatest flexibility in dynamically changing the mesh geometry, because split and merge operations can be done quickly. Their primary drawback is large storage requirements and increased complexity due to maintaining many indices. A good discussion of implementation issues of Winged-edge meshes may be found in the book *Graphics Gems II*.

See Baumgart (1975) for more details.

Render Dynamic Meshes

Winged-edge meshes are not the only representation which allows for dynamic changes to geometry. A new representation which combines winged-edge meshes and face-vertex meshes is the render dynamic mesh, which explicitly stores both, the vertices of a face and faces of a vertex (like FV meshes), and the faces and vertices of an edge (like winged-edge).

Render dynamic meshes require slightly less storage space than standard winged-edge meshes, and can be directly rendered by graphics hardware since the face list contains an index of vertices. In addition, traversal from vertex to face is explicit (constant time), as is from face to vertex. RD meshes do not require the four outgoing edges since these can be found by traversing from edge to face, then face to neighboring edge.

RD meshes benefit from the features of winged-edge meshes by allowing for geometry to be dynamically updated.

See Tobler & Maierhofer (WSCG 2006) for more details.

Summary of Mesh Representation

Operation		Vertex-vertex	Face-vertex	Winged-edge	Render dynamic
V-V	All vertices around vertex	Explicit	V → f1, f2, f3, ... → v1, v2, v3, ...	V → e1, e2, e3, ... → v1, v2, v3, ...	V → e1, e2, e3, ... → v1, v2, v3, ...
E-F	All edges of a face	F(a,b,c) → {a,b}, {b,c}, {a,c}	F → {a,b}, {b,c}, {a,c}	Explicit	Explicit
V-F	All vertices of a face	F(a,b,c) → {a,b,c}	Explicit	F → e1, e2, e3 → a, b, c	Explicit
F-V	All faces around a vertex	Pair search	Explicit	V → e1, e2, e3 → f1, f2, f3, ...	Explicit
E-V	All edges around a vertex	V → {v,v1}, {v,v2}, {v,v3}, ...	V → f1, f2, f3, ... → v1, v2, v3, ...	Explicit	Explicit
F-E	Both faces of an edge	List compare	List compare	Explicit	Explicit
V-E	Both vertices of an edge	E(a,b) → {a,b}	E(a,b) → {a,b}	Explicit	Explicit
Flook	Find face with given vertices	F(a,b,c) → {a,b,c}	Set intersection of v1,v2,v3	Set intersection of v1,v2,v3	Set intersection of v1,v2,v3
Storage size		V*avg(V,V)	3F + V*avg(F,V)	3F + 8E + V*avg(E,V)	6F + 4E + V*avg(E,V)
Example with 10 vertices, 16 faces, 24 edges:					
	10 * 5 = 50	3*16 + 10*5 = 98	3*16 + 8*24 + 10*5 = 290	6*16 + 4*24 + 10*5 = 242	

Figure 6: summary of mesh representation operations

In the above table, *explicit* indicates that the operation can be performed in constant time, as the data is directly stored; *list compare* indicates that a list comparison between two lists must be performed to accomplish the operation; and *pair search* indicates a search must be done on two indices. The notation $avg(V,V)$ means the average number of vertices connected to a given vertex; $avg(E,V)$ means the average number of edges connected to a given vertex, and $avg(F,V)$ is the average number of faces connected to a given vertex.

The notation "$V \rightarrow f_1, f_2, f_3, ... \rightarrow v_1, v_2, v_3, ...$" describes that a traversal across multiple elements is required to perform the operation. For example, to get "all vertices around a given vertex V" using the face-vertex mesh, it is necessary to first find the faces around the given vertex V using the vertex list. Then, from those faces, use the face list to find the vertices around them. Notice that winged-edge meshes explicitly store nearly all information, and other operations always traverse to the edge first to get additional info. Vertex-vertex meshes are the only representation that explicitly stores the neighboring vertices of a given vertex.

As the mesh representations become more complex (from left to right in the summary), the amount of information explicitly stored increases. This gives more direct, constant time, access to traversal and topology of various elements but at the cost of increased overhead and space in maintaining indices properly.

Figure 7 shows the connectivity information for each of the four technique described in this article. Other representations also exist, such as half-edge and corner tables. These are all variants of how vertices, faces and edges index one another.

As a general rule, face-vertex meshes are used whenever an object must be rendered on graphics hardware that does not change geometry (connectivity), but may deform or morph shape (vertex positions) such as real-time rendering of static or morphing objects. Winged-edge or render dynamic meshes are used when the geometry changes, such as in interactive modeling packages or for computing subdivision surfaces. Vertex-vertex meshes are ideal for efficient, complex changes in geometry or topology so long as hardware rendering is not of concern.

Other Representations

Streaming meshes

store faces in an ordered, yet independent, way so that the mesh can be transmitted in pieces. The order of faces may be spatial, spectral, or based on other properties of the mesh. Streaming meshes allow a very large mesh to be rendered even while it is still being loaded.

Progressive meshes

transmit the vertex and face data with increasing levels of detail. Unlike *streaming meshes*, progressive meshes give the overall shape of the entire object, but at a low level of detail. Additional data, new edges and faces, progressively increase the detail of the mesh.

Normal meshes

transmit progressive changes to a mesh as a set of normal displacements from a base mesh. With this technique, a series of textures represent the desired incremental modifications. Normal meshes are compact, since only a single scalar value is needed to express displacement. However, the technique requires a complex series of transformations to create the displacement textures.

File Formats

There exist many different file formats for storing polygon mesh data. Each format is most effective when used for the purpose intended by its creator. Some of these formats are presented below:

File suffix	Format name	Organization(s)	Program(s)	Description
.raw	Raw mesh	Unknown	Various	Open, ASCII-only format. Each line contains 3 vertices, separated by spaces, to form a triangle, like so: X1 Y1 Z1 X2 Y2 Z2 X3 Y3 Z3
.blend	Blender File Format	Blender Foundation	Blender 3D	Open source, binary-only format
.fbx	Autodesk FBX Format	Autodesk	Various	Proprietary. Binary and ASCII specifications exist.
.3ds	3ds Max File	Autodesk	3ds Max	A common but outdated format with hard 16-bit limits on the number of vertices and faces. Neither standardised nor well documented, but used to be a "de facto standard" for data exchange.
.dae	Digital Asset Exchange (COLLADA)	Sony Computer Entertainment, Khronos Group	N/A	Stands for "**COLLA**borative **D**esign **A**ctivity". A universal format designed to prevent incompatibility.
.dgn	MicroStation File	Bentley Systems	MicroStation	There are two dgn file formats: pre-version 8 and version 8 (V8)
.3dm	Rhino File	Robert McNeel & Associates	Rhinoceros 3D	

File suffix	Format name	Organization(s)	Program(s)	Description
.dxf	Drawing Exchange Format	Autodesk	AutoCAD	
.obj	Wavefront OBJ	Wavefront Technologies	Various	ASCII format describing 3D geometry. All faces' vertices are ordered counter-clockwise, making facet normals implicit. Smooth normals are specified per vertex.
.ply	Polygon File Format	Stanford University	Unknown	Binary and ASCII
.pmd	Polygon Movie Maker data	Yu Higuchi	MikuMiku-Dance	Proprietary binary file format for storing humanoid model geometry with rigging, material, and physics information.
.stl	Stereolithography Format	3D Systems	Many	Binary and ASCII format originally designed to aid in "3D printing".
.amf	Additive Manufacturing File Format	ASTM International	N/A	Like the STL format, but with added native color, material, and constellation support.
.wrl	Virtual Reality Modeling Language	Web3D Consortium	Web Browsers	ISO Standard 14772-1:1997
.wrz	VRML Compressed	Web3D Consortium	Web Browsers	
.x3d, .x3db, .x3dv	Extensible 3D	Web3D Consortium	Web Browsers	XML-based, open source, royalty-free, extensible, and interoperable; also supports color, texture, and scene information. ISO Standard 19775/19776/19777
.x3dz, .x3dbz, .x3dvz	X3D Compressed Binary	Web3D Consortium	Web Browsers	
.c4d	Cinema 4D File	MAXON	CINEMA 4D	
.lwo	LightWave 3D object File	NewTek	LightWave 3D	
.smb	SCOREC apf	RPI SCOREC	PUMI	Open source parallel adaptive unstructured 3D meshes for PDE based simulation workflows.
.msh	Gmsh Mesh	GMsh Developers	GMsh Project	Open source, providing an ASCII mesh description for linear and polynomially interpolated elements in 1 to 3 dimensions.

File suffix	Format name	Organiza-tion(s)	Program(s)	Description
.mesh	OGRE XML	OGRE De-velopment Team	OGRE, pure-basic	Open Source. Binary (.mesh) and ASCII (.mesh.xml) format available. Includes data for vertex animation and Morph target animation (blendshape). Skeletal animation data in separate file (.skeleton).
.veg	Vega FEM tetrahedral mesh	Jernej Barbič	Vega FEM	Open Source. Stores a tetrahedral mesh and its material properties for FEM sim-ulation. ASCII (.veg) and binary (.vegb) formats available.
.z3d	Z3d	Oleg Me-lashenko	Zanoza Mod-eler	-
.vtk	VTK mesh	VTK, Kit-ware	VTK, Paraview	Open, ASCII or binary format that con-tains many different data fields, including point data, cell data, and field data.

Feathering

Feathering is a technique used in computer graphics software to smooth or blur the edges of a feature. The term is inherited from a technique of fine retouching using fine feathers.

An example of a photograph with feathered edges

Paintbrush Feathering

Feathering is most commonly used on a paintbrush tool in computer graphics software. This form of feathering makes the painted area appear smooth. It may give the effect of an airbrush or spraypaint. Color is concentrated at the center of the brush area, and it blends out toward the edges.

Selection Feathering

Feathering is not only used on paintbrushes in computer graphics software. Feathering may also blend the edges of a selected feature into the background of the image. When composing an image from pieces of other images, feathering helps make added features look "in place" with the background image. For instance, if someone were to want to add a leaf to a photograph of grass using computer graphics software, he or she might use feathering on the leaf to make it blend in with the grassy background.

Clone Tool Feathering

The "Clone" tool is very important in photograph manipulation on computer graphics software. The clone tool is used to actively copy and offset pixels from one area of an image to another while the artist moves the clone tool around the area to be copied. A good example is the use of the clone tool to cover a skin blemish by copying skin from one area of an image and placing it over the blemish. An important aspect of making a clone tool blend well in an image is to use feathering on the clone tool. This makes the pixels being copied have more effect on the area they are copied to closer to where the artist is dragging his or her mouse or stylus, and makes the pixels have less effect the farther they are from the clone tool (and where the artist is using it). Thus, with the skin example, skin pixels copied directly over the blemish will have strong effect on the blemish, thus hiding it, but skin pixels copied to the area around the blemish will not affect this area much, and will keep the natural look of the skin (wrinkles etc.) intact as much as possible.

Visual Effects

In filmmaking, visual effects (abbreviated VFX) are the processes by which imagery is created and/or manipulated outside the context of a live action shot.

Visual effects involve the integration of live-action footage and generated imagery to create environments which look realistic, but would be dangerous, expensive, impractical, or impossible to capture on film. Visual effects using computer generated imagery have recently become accessible to the independent filmmaker with the introduction of affordable and easy-to-use animation and compositing software.

Timing

Visual effects are often integral to a movie's story and appeal. Although most visual effects work is completed during post-production, it usually must be carefully planned and choreographed in pre-production and production. Visual effects primarily executed in Post-Production with the use of multiple tools and technologies such as graphic design, modeling, animation and similar software, while special effects such as explosions and car chases are made on set. A visual effects supervisor is usually involved with the production from an early stage to work closely with production and the film's director design, guide and lead the teams required to achieve the desired effects.

Categories

Visual effects may be divided into at least four categories:

- Matte paintings and stills: digital or traditional paintings or photographs which serve as background plates for keyed or rotoscoped elements.

- Live-action effects: keying actors or models through bluescreening and greenscreening.

- Digital animation: modeling, computer graphics lighting, texturing, rigging, animating, and rendering computer-generated 3D characters, particle effects, digital sets, backgrounds.

- Digital effects (commonly shortened to digital FX or FX) are the various processes by which imagery is created and/or manipulated with or from photographic assets. Digital effects often involve the integration of still photography and computer-generated imagery (CGI) to create environments which look realistic, but would be dangerous, costly, or impossible to capture in camera. FX is usually associated with the still photography world in contrast to visual effects which is associated with motion film production.

Types

VFX can be categorized into:

- Simulation FX

- Matte painting

- Compositing

Global Illumination

Global illumination (shortened as GI) or indirect illumination is a general name for a group of algorithms used in 3D computer graphics that are meant to add more realistic lighting to 3D scenes. Such algorithms take into account not only the light which comes directly from a light source (*direct illumination*), but also subsequent cases in which light rays from the same source are reflected by other surfaces in the scene, whether reflective or not (*indirect illumination*).

Rendering without global illumination. Areas that lie outside of the ceiling lamp's direct light lack definition. For example, the lamp's housing appears completely uniform. Without the ambient light added into the render, it would appear uniformly black.

Rendering with global illumination. Light is reflected by surfaces, and colored light transfers from one surface to another. Notice how color from the red wall and green wall (not visible) reflects onto other surfaces in the scene. Also notable is the caustic projected onto the red wall from light passing through the glass sphere.

Theoretically reflections, refractions, and shadows are all examples of global illumination, because when simulating them, one object affects the rendering of another object (as opposed to an object being affected only by a direct light). In practice, however, only the simulation of diffuse inter-reflection or caustics is called global illumination.

Images rendered using global illumination algorithms often appear more photorealistic than images rendered using only direct illumination algorithms. However, such images are computationally more expensive and consequently much slower to generate. One common approach is to compute the global illumination of a scene and store that information with the geometry, e.g., radiosity. That stored data can then be used to generate images from different viewpoints for generating walkthroughs of a scene without having to go through expensive lighting calculations repeatedly.

Radiosity, ray tracing, beam tracing, cone tracing, path tracing, Metropolis light transport, ambient occlusion, photon mapping, and image based lighting are examples of algorithms used in global illumination, some of which may be used together to yield results that are not fast, but accurate.

These algorithms model diffuse inter-reflection which is a very important part of global illumination; however most of these (excluding radiosity) also model specular reflection, which makes them more accurate algorithms to solve the lighting equation and provide a more realistically illuminated scene.

The algorithms used to calculate the distribution of light energy between surfaces of a scene are closely related to heat transfer simulations performed using finite-element methods in engineering design.

In real-time 3D graphics, the diffuse inter-reflection component of global illumination is sometimes approximated by an "ambient" term in the lighting equation, which is also called "ambient lighting" or "ambient color" in 3D software packages. Though this method of approximation (also known as a "cheat" because it's not really a global illumination method) is easy to perform computationally, when used alone it does not provide an adequately realistic effect. Ambient lighting is known to "flatten" shadows in 3D scenes, making the overall visual effect more bland. However, used properly, ambient lighting can be an efficient way to make up for a lack of processing power.

Procedure

More and more specialized algorithms are used in 3D programs that can effectively simulate the global illumination. These algorithms are numerical approximations to the rendering equation. Well known algorithms for computing global illumination include path tracing, photon mapping and radiosity. The following approaches can be distinguished here:

- Inversion: $L = (1-T)^{-1} L^e$

    o   is not applied in practice

- Expansion: $L = \sum_{i=0}^{\infty} T^i L^e$

    o   bi-directional approach: Photon mapping + Distributed ray tracing, Bi-directional path tracing, Metropolis light transport

- Iteration: $L_n tl_e += L^{(n-1)}$

    o   Radiosity

In Light path notation global lighting the paths of the type L (D | S) corresponds * E.

A full treatment can be found in

Image-based Lighting

Another way to simulate real global illumination is the use of High dynamic range images (HDRIs), also known as environment maps, which encircle and illuminate the scene. This process is known as image-based lighting.

List of Methods

Method	Description/Notes
Ray tracing	Several enhanced variants exist for solving problems related to sampling, aliasing, soft shadows: Distributed ray tracing, Cone tracing, Beam tracing.
Path tracing	Unbiased, Variant: Bi-directional Path Tracing, Energy Redistriution Path Tracing
Photon mapping	Consistent, biased; enhanced variants: Progressive Photon Mapping, Stochastic Progressive Photon Mapping ()
Lightcuts	enhanced variants: Multidimensional Lightcuts, Bidirectional Lightcuts
Point Based Global Illumination	Extensively used in movie animations
Radiosity	Finite element method, very good for precomputations. Improved versions Instant Radiosity and Bidirectional Instant Radiosity
Metropolis light transport	Builds upon bi-directional path tracing, unbiased, Multiplexed
Spherical harmonic lighting	Encodes global illumination results for real-time rendering of static scenes
Ambient occlusion	Not a physically correct method, but gives good results in general. Good for precomputation.
Voxel-based Global Illumination	Several variants exist including Voxel Cone Tracing Global Illumination, Sparse Voxel Octree Global Illumination and Voxel Global Illumination (VXGI)
Light Propagation Volumes Global Illumination	Light propagation volumes is a technique to approximately achieve global illumination (GI) in Real-time. It uses lattices and spherical harmonics (SH) to represent the spatial and angular distribution of light in the scene. Variant Cascaded Light Propagation Volumes.
Deferred Radiance Transfer Global Illumination	
Deep G-Buffer based Global Illumination	

References

- Philip Dutre; Philippe Bekaert; Kavita Bala (August 30, 2006). Advanced Global Illumination, Second Edition. ISBN 978-1568813073.
- "Fast Global Illumination Approximations on Deep G-Buffers". graphics.cs.williams.edu. Retrieved 2016-05-14.
- "Realtime Global Illumination techniques collection | extremeistan". extremeistan.wordpress.com. Retrieved 2016-05-14.
- "Interactive Simulation of Dynamic Crowd Behaviors using General Adaptation Syndrome Theory" (PDF). Retrieved 6 October 2016.

Animation: An Integrated Study

Animation is the process of creating an illusion of movement with the help of drawings. Computer animation helps in this process by generating these images. Traditional animation, stop motion, skeletal animation and animation database are some of the aspects of animation that have been elaborately explained in the following section.

Animation

Animation is the process of making the illusion of motion and change by means of the rapid display of a sequence of static images that minimally differ from each other. The illusion—as in motion pictures in general—is thought to rely on the phi phenomenon. Animators are artists who specialize in the creation of animation.

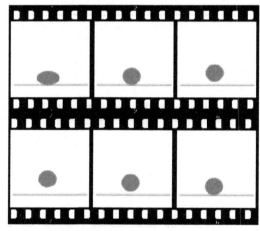

The bouncing ball animation (below) consists of these six frames.

Animation can be recorded with either analogue media, a flip book, motion picture film, video tape, digital media, including formats with animated GIF, Flash animation and digital video. To display animation, a digital camera, computer, or projector are used along with new technologies that are produced.

Animation creation methods include the traditional animation creation method and those involving stop motion animation of two and three-dimensional objects, paper cutouts, puppets and clay figures. Images are displayed in a rapid succession, usually 24, 25, 30, or 60 frames per second.

History

Early examples of attempts to capture the phenomenon of motion into a still drawing can be found in paleolithic cave paintings, where animals are often depicted with multiple legs in superimposed positions, clearly attempting to convey the perception of motion.

Reproduction of drawing on a pottery vessel found in Shahr-e Sūkhté, Iran.

An earthen goblet discovered at the site of the 5,200-year-old Shahr-e Sūkhté (Burnt City) in southeastern Iran, depicts what could possibly be the world's oldest example of animation. The artifact bears five sequential images depicting a Persian Desert Ibex jumping up to eat the leaves of a tree.

A phenakistoscope disc by Eadweard Muybridge (1893)

Ancient Chinese records contain several mentions of devices that were said to "give an impression of movement" to human or animal figures, these accounts are unclear and may only refer to the actual movement of the figures through space.

In the 19th century, the phenakistoscope (1832), zoetrope (1834) and praxinoscope (1877) were introduced. A thaumatrope (1824) is a simple toy with a small disk with different pictures on each side; a bird in a cage, and is attached to two pieces of strings. The phenakistoscope was invented simultaneously by Belgian Joseph Plateau and Austrian Simon von Stampfer in 1831. The phenakistoscope consists of a disk with a series of images, drawn on radi evenly space around the center of the disk.

John Barnes Linnett patented the first flip book in 1868 as the *kineograph*. The common flip book were early animation devices that produced an illusion of movement from a series of sequential drawings, animation did not develop further until the advent of motion picture film and cinematography in the 1890s.

The cinématographe was a projector, printer, and camera in one machine that allowed moving pictures to be shown successfully on a screen which was invented by history's earliest film makers, Auguste and Louis Lumière, in 1894. The first animated projection (screening) was created in France, by Charles-Émile Reynaud, who was a French science teacher. Reynaud created the Praxinoscope in 1877 and the Théâtre Optique in December 1888. On 28 October 1892, he projected the first animation in public, *Pauvre Pierrot*, at the Musée Grévin in Paris. This film is also notable as the first known instance of film perforations being used. His films were not photographed, they were drawn directly onto the transparent strip. In 1900, more than 500,000 people had attended these screenings.

A projecting praxinoscope, 1882, here shown superimposing an animated figure on a separately projected background scene

The first film that was recorded on standard picture film and included animated sequences was the 1900 *Enchanted Drawing*, which was followed by the first entirely animated film - the 1906 *Humorous Phases of Funny Faces* by J. Stuart Blackton, who, because of that, is considered the father of American animation.

The first animated film created by using what came to be known as traditional (hand-drawn) animation - the 1908 *Fantasmagorie* by Émile Cohl

In Europe, the French artist, Émile Cohl, created the first animated film using what came to be known as traditional animation creation methods - the 1908 *Fantasmagorie*. The film largely consisted of a stick figure moving about and encountering all manner of morphing objects, a wine bottle that transforms into a flower. There were also sections of live action in which the animator's hands would enter the scene. The film was created by drawing each frame on paper and then shooting each frame onto negative film, which gave the picture a blackboard look.

Charlie in Turkey (1916), an animated film by Pat Sullivan for Keen Cartoon Corporation.

The author of the first puppet-animated film (*The Beautiful Lukanida* (1912)) was the Russian-born (ethnically Polish) director Wladyslaw Starewicz, known as Ladislas Starevich.

More detailed hand-drawn animation, requiring a team of animators drawing each frame manually with detailed backgrounds and characters, were those directed by Winsor McCay, a successful newspaper cartoonist, including the 1911 *Little Nemo*, the 1914 *Gertie the Dinosaur*, and the 1918 *The Sinking of the Lusitania*.

During the 1910s, the production of animated short films, typically referred to as "cartoons", became an industry of its own and cartoon shorts were produced for showing in movie theaters. The most successful producer at the time was John Randolph Bray, who, along with animator Earl Hurd, patented the cel animation process which dominated the animation industry for the rest of the decade.

El Apóstol (Spanish: "The Apostle") was a 1917 Argentine animated film utilizing cutout animation, and the world's first animated feature film. Unfortunately, a fire that destroyed producer Federico Valle's film studio incinerated the only known copy of *El Apóstol*, and it is now considered a lost film.

In 1958, Hanna-Barbara released *Huckleberry Hound*, the first half hour television program to feature only in animation. Terrytoons released *Tom Terrific* that same year. Television significantly decreased public attention to the animated shorts being shown in theaters.

Computer animation has become popular since *Toy Story* (1995), the first feature-length animated film completely made using this technique.

Italian-Argentine cartoonist Quirino Cristiani showing the cut and articulated figure of his satirical character El Peludo (based on President Yrigoyen) patented in 1916 for the realization of his movies, including the world's first animated feature film El Apóstol.

In 2008, the animation market was worth US$68.4 billion. Animation as an art and industry continues to thrive as of the mid-2010s, because well-made animated projects can find audiences across borders and in all four quadrants. Animated feature-length films returned the highest gross margins (around 52%) of all film genres in the 2004–2013 timeframe.

Techniques

Traditional Animation

An example of traditional animation, a horse animated by rotoscoping from Eadweard Muybridge's 19th century photos

Traditional animation (also called cel animation or hand-drawn animation) was the process used for most animated films of the 20th century. The individual frames of a traditionally animated film are photographs of drawings, first drawn on paper. To create the illusion of movement, each drawing differs slightly from the one before it. The animators' drawings are traced or photocopied onto transparent acetate sheets called cels, which are filled in with paints in assigned colors or tones on the side opposite the line drawings. The completed character cels are photographed one-by-one against a painted background by a rostrum camera onto motion picture film.

The traditional cel animation process became obsolete by the beginning of the 21st century. Today, animators' drawings and the backgrounds are either scanned into or drawn directly into a computer system. Various software programs are used to color the drawings and simulate camera movement and effects. The final animated piece is output to one of several delivery media, including traditional 35 mm film and newer media with digital video. The "look" of traditional cel animation is still preserved, and the character animators' work has remained essentially the same over the past 70 years. Some animation producers have used the term "tradigital" (a play on the words "traditional" and "digital") to describe cel animation which makes extensive use of computer technologies.

Examples of traditionally animated feature films include *Pinocchio* (United States, 1940), *Animal Farm* (United Kingdom, 1954), and *The Illusionist* (British-French, 2010). Traditionally animated films which were produced with the aid of computer technology include *The Lion King* (US, 1994), *The Prince of Egypt* (US, 1998), *Akira* (Japan, 1988), *Spirited Away* (Japan, 2001), *The Triplets of Belleville* (France, 2003), and *The Secret of Kells* (Irish-French-Belgian, 2009).

- Full animation refers to the process of producing high-quality traditionally animated films that regularly use detailed drawings and plausible movement, having a smooth animation. Fully animated films can be made in a variety of styles, from more realistically animated works those produced by the Walt Disney studio (*The Little Mermaid, Beauty and the Beast, Aladdin, The Lion King*) to the more 'cartoon' styles of the Warner Bros. animation studio. Many of the Disney animated features are examples of full animation, as are non-Disney works, *The Secret of NIMH* (US, 1982), *The Iron Giant* (US, 1999), and *Nocturna* (Spain, 2007). Fully animated films are animated at 24 frames per second, with a combination of animation on ones and twos, meaning that drawings can be held for one frame out of 24 or two frames out of 24.

- Limited animation involves the use of less detailed or more stylized drawings and methods of movement usually a choppy or "skippy" movement animation. Limited animation uses fewer drawings per second, thereby limiting the fluidity of the animation. This is a more economic technique. Pioneered by the artists at the American studio United Productions of America, limited animation can be used as a method of stylized artistic expression, as in *Gerald McBoing-Boing* (US, 1951), *Yellow Submarine* (UK, 1968), and certain anime produced in Japan. Its primary use, however, has been in producing cost-effective animated content for media for television (the work of Hanna-Barbera, Filmation, and other TV animation studios) and later the Internet (web cartoons).

- Rotoscoping is a technique patented by Max Fleischer in 1917 where animators trace live-action movement, frame by frame. The source film can be direct-ly copied from actors' outlines into animated drawings, as in *The Lord of the Rings* (US, 1978), or used in a stylized and expressive manner, as in *Waking Life* (US, 2001) and *A Scanner Darkly* (US, 2006). Some other examples are: *Fire and Ice* (US, 1983), *Heavy Metal* (1981), and *Aku no Hana* (2013).

- Live-action/animation is a technique combining hand-drawn characters into live action shots or live action actors into animated shots. One of the earlier uses was in Koko the Clown when Koko was drawn over live action footage. Other ex-amples include *Who Framed Roger Rabbit* (US, 1988), *Space Jam* (US, 1996) and *Osmosis Jones* (US, 2001).

Stop Motion Animation

Stop-motion animation is used to describe animation created by physically manipulat-ing real-world objects and photographing them one frame of film at a time to create the illusion of movement. There are many different types of stop-motion animation, usual-ly named after the medium used to create the animation. Computer software is widely available to create this type of animation; however, traditional stop motion animation is usually less expensive and time-consuming to produce than current computer animation.

- Puppet animation typically involves stop-motion puppet figures interacting in a constructed environment, in contrast to real-world interaction in model animation. The puppets generally have an armature inside of them to keep them still and steady to constrain their motion to particular joints. Examples include *The Tale of the Fox* (France, 1937), *The Nightmare Before Christmas* (US, 1993), *Corpse Bride* (US, 2005), *Coraline* (US, 2009), the films of Jiří Trnka and the adult animated sketch-comedy television series *Robot Chicken* (US, 2005–present).

    o Puppetoon, created using techniques developed by George Pal, are pup-pet-animated films which typically use a different version of a puppet for different frames, rather than simply manipulating one existing puppet.

A clay animation scene from a Finnish television commercial

- Clay animation, or Plasticine animation (often called *claymation*, which, however, is a trademarked name), uses figures made of clay or a similar malleable material to create stop-motion animation. The figures may have an armature or wire frame inside, similar to the related puppet animation (below), that can be manipulated to pose the figures. Alternatively, the figures may be made entirely of clay, in the films of Bruce Bickford, where clay creatures morph into a variety of different shapes. Examples of clay-animated works include *The Gumby Show* (US, 1957–1967) *Morph* shorts (UK, 1977–2000), *Wallace and Gromit* shorts (UK, as of 1989), Jan Švankmajer's *Dimensions of Dialogue* (Czechoslovakia, 1982), *The Trap Door* (UK, 1984). Films include *Wallace & Gromit: The Curse of the Were-Rabbit*, *Chicken Run* and *The Adventures of Mark Twain*.

  o Strata-cut animation, Strata-cut animation is most commonly a form of clay animation in which a long bread-like "loaf" of clay, internally packed tight and loaded with varying imagery, is sliced into thin sheets, with the animation camera taking a frame of the end of the loaf for each cut, eventually revealing the movement of the internal images within.

- Cutout animation is a type of stop-motion animation produced by moving two-dimensional pieces of material paper or cloth. Examples include Terry Gilliam's animated sequences from *Monty Python's Flying Circus* (UK, 1969–1974); *Fantastic Planet* (France/Czechoslovakia, 1973) ; *Tale of Tales* (Russia, 1979), The pilot episode of the adult television sitcom series (and sometimes in episodes) of *South Park* (US, 1997) and the music video Live for the moment, from Verona Riots band (produced by Alberto Serrano and Nívola Uyá, Spain 2014).

  o Silhouette animation is a variant of cutout animation in which the characters are backlit and only visible as silhouettes. Examples include *The Adventures of Prince Achmed* (Weimar Republic, 1926) and *Princes et princesses* (France, 2000).

- Model animation refers to stop-motion animation created to interact with and exist as a part of a live-action world. Intercutting, matte effects, and split screens are often employed to blend stop-motion characters or objects with live actors and settings. Examples include the work of Ray Harryhausen, as seen in films, *Jason and the Argonauts* (1963), and the work of Willis H. O'Brien on films, *King Kong* (1933).

  o Go motion is a variant of model animation that uses various techniques to create motion blur between frames of film, which is not present in traditional stop-motion. The technique was invented by Industrial Light & Magic and Phil Tippett to create special effects scenes for the film *The Empire Strikes Back* (1980). Another example is the dragon named "Vermithrax" from *Dragonslayer* (1981 film).

- Object animation refers to the use of regular inanimate objects in stop-motion animation, as opposed to specially created items.

    o Graphic animation uses non-drawn flat visual graphic material (photographs, newspaper clippings, magazines, etc.), which are sometimes manipulated frame-by-frame to create movement. At other times, the graphics remain stationary, while the stop-motion camera is moved to create on-screen action.

    o Brickfilm A subgenre of object animation involving using Lego or other similar brick toys to make an animation. These have had a recent boost in popularity with the advent of video sharing sites, YouTube and the availability of cheap cameras and animation software.

- Pixilation involves the use of live humans as stop motion characters. This allows for a number of surreal effects, including disappearances and reappearances, allowing people to appear to slide across the ground, and other effects. Examples of pixilation include *The Secret Adventures of Tom Thumb* and *Angry Kid* shorts.

Computer Animation

Computer animation encompasses a variety of techniques, the unifying factor being that the animation is created digitally on a computer. 2D animation techniques tend to focus on image manipulation while 3D techniques usually build virtual worlds in which characters and objects move and interact. 3D animation can create images that seem real to the viewer.

2D Animation

2D animation figures are created or edited on the computer using 2D bitmap graphics or created and edited using 2D vector graphics. This includes automated computerized versions of traditional animation techniques, interpolated morphing, onion skinning and interpolated rotoscoping.

A 2D animation of two circles joined by a chain

2D animation has many applications, including analog computer animation, Flash animation and PowerPoint animation. Cinemagraphs are still photographs in the form of an animated GIF file of which part is animated.

Final line advection animation is a technique used in 2d animation, to give artists and animators more influence and control over the final product as everything is done within the same department. Speaking about using this approach in *Paperman*, John Kahrs said that "Our animators can change things, actually erase away the CG underlayer if they want, and change the profile of the arm."

3D Animation

3D animation is digitally modeled and manipulated by an animator. The animator usually starts by creating a 3D polygon mesh to manipulate. A mesh typically includes many vertices that are connected by edges and faces, which give the visual appearance of form to a 3D object or 3D environment. Sometimes, the mesh is given an internal digital skeletal structure called an armature that can be used to control the mesh by weighting the vertices. This process is called rigging and can be used in conjunction with keyframes to create movement.

Other techniques can be applied, mathematical functions (e.g., gravity, particle simulations), simulated fur or hair, and effects, fire and water simulations. These techniques fall under the category of 3D dynamics.

3D Terms

- Cel-shaded animation is used to mimic traditional animation using computer software. Shading looks stark, with less blending of colors. Examples include, *Skyland* (2007, France), *The Iron Giant* (1999, United States), *Futurama* (Fox, 1999) *Appleseed Ex Machina* (2007, Japan), *The Legend of Zelda: The Wind Waker* (2002, Japan)

- Machinima – Films created by screen capturing in video games and virtual worlds.

- Motion capture is used when live-action actors wear special suits that allow computers to copy their movements into CG characters. Examples include *Polar Express* (2004, US), *Beowulf* (2007, US), *A Christmas Carol* (2009, US), *The Adventures of Tintin (film)* (2011, US) *kochadiiyan* (2014, India).

- Photo-realistic animation is used primarily for animation that attempts to resemble real life, using advanced rendering that mimics in detail skin, plants, water, fire, clouds, etc. Examples include *Up* (2009, US), *How to Train Your Dragon* (2010, US), *Ice Age* (2002, US).

Mechanical Animation

- Animatronics is the use of mechatronics to create machines which seem animate rather than robotic.

    o   Audio-Animatronics and Autonomatronics is a form of robotics animation, combined with 3-D animation, created by Walt Disney Imagineering for shows and attractions at Disney theme parks move and make noise (generally a recorded speech or song). They are fixed to whatever supports them. They can sit and stand, and they cannot walk. An Audio-Animatron is different from an android-type robot in that it uses prerecorded movements and sounds, rather than responding to external stimuli. In 2009, Disney created an interactive version of the technology called Autonomatronics.

o   Linear Animation Generator is a form of animation by using static picture frames installed in a tunnel or a shaft. The animation illusion is created by putting the viewer in a linear motion, parallel to the installed picture frames. The concept and the technical solution, were invented in 2007 by Mihai Girlovan in Romania.

- Chuckimation is a type of animation created by the makers of the television series *Action League Now!* in which characters/props are thrown, or chucked from off camera or wiggled around to simulate talking by unseen hands.

- Puppetry is a form of theatre or performance animation that involves the manipulation of puppets. It is very ancient, and is believed to have originated 3000 years BC. Puppetry takes many forms, they all share the process of animating inanimate performing objects. Puppetry is used in almost all human societies both as entertainment – in performance – and ceremonially in rituals, celebrations and carnivals. Most puppetry involves storytelling.

Toy Story zoetrope at Disney California Adventure creates illusion of motion using figures, rather than static pictures.

- Zoetrope is a device that produces the illusion of motion from a rapid succession of static pictures. The term zoetrope is from the Greek words ζωή (*zoē*), meaning "alive, active", and τρόπος (*tropos*), meaning "turn", with "zoetrope" taken to mean "active turn" or "wheel of life".

Other Animation Styles, Techniques and Approaches

World of Color hydrotechnics at Disney California Adventure creates illusion of motion using 1200 fountains with high-definition projections on mist screens.

- Hydrotechnics: a technique that includes lights, water, fire, fog, and lasers, with high-definition projections on mist screens.

- Drawn on film animation: a technique where footage is produced by creating the images directly on film stock, for example by Norman McLaren, Len Lye and Stan Brakhage.

- Paint-on-glass animation: a technique for making animated films by manipulating slow drying oil paints on sheets of glass, for example by Aleksandr Petrov.

- Erasure animation: a technique using traditional 2D media, photographed over time as the artist manipulates the image. For example, William Kentridge is famous for his charcoal erasure films, and Piotr Dumała for his auteur technique of animating scratches on plaster.

- Pinscreen animation: makes use of a screen filled with movable pins that can be moved in or out by pressing an object onto the screen. The screen is lit from the side so that the pins cast shadows. The technique has been used to create animated films with a range of textural effects difficult to achieve with traditional cel animation.

- Sand animation: sand is moved around on a back- or front-lighted piece of glass to create each frame for an animated film. This creates an interesting effect when animated because of the light contrast.

- Flip book: a flip book (sometimes, especially in British English, called a flick book) is a book with a series of pictures that vary gradually from one page to the next, so that when the pages are turned rapidly, the pictures appear to animate by simulating motion or some other change. Flip books are often illustrated books for children, they also be geared towards adults and employ a series of photographs rather than drawings. Flip books are not always separate books, they appear as an added feature in ordinary books or magazines, often in the page corners. Software packages and websites are also available that convert digital video files into custom-made flip books.

- Character animation

- Multi-sketching

- Special effects animation

Production

The creation of non-trivial animation works (i.e., longer than a few seconds) has developed as a form of filmmaking, with certain unique aspects. One thing live-action and animated feature-length films do have in common is that they are both extremely labor-intensive and have high production costs.

The most important difference is that once a film is in the production phase, the marginal cost of one more shot is higher for animated films than live-action films. It is relatively easy for a director to ask for one more take during principal photography of a live-action film, but every take on an animated film must be manually rendered by animators (although the task of rendering slightly different takes has been made less tedious by modern computer animation). It is pointless for a studio to pay the salaries of dozens of animators to spend weeks creating a visually dazzling five-minute scene, if that scene fails to effectively advance the plot of the film. Thus, animation studios starting with Disney began the practice in the 1930s of maintaining story departments where storyboard artists develop every single scene through storyboards, then handing the film over to the animators only after the production team is satisfied that all the scenes will make sense as a whole. While live-action films are now also storyboarded, they enjoy more latitude to depart from storyboards (i.e., real-time improvisation).

Another problem unique to animation is the necessity of ensuring that the style of an animated film is consistent from start to finish, even as films have grown longer and teams have grown larger. Animators, like all artists, necessarily have their own individual styles, but must subordinate their individuality in a consistent way to whatever style was selected for a particular film. Since the early 1980s, feature-length animated films have been created by teams of about 500 to 600 people, of whom 50 to 70 are animators. It is relatively easy for two or three artists to match each other's styles; it is harder to keep dozens of artists synchronized with one another.

This problem is usually solved by having a separate group of visual development artists develop an overall look and palette for each film before animation begins. Character designers on the visual development team draw model sheets to show how each character should look like with different facial expressions, posed in different positions, and viewed from different angles. On traditionally animated projects, maquettes were often sculpted to further help the animators see how characters would look from different angles.

Unlike live-action films, animated films were traditionally developed beyond the synopsis stage through the storyboard format; the storyboard artists would then receive credit for writing the film. In the early 1960s, animation studios began hiring professional screenwriters to write screenplays (while also continuing to use story departments) and screenplays had become commonplace for animated films by the late 1980s.

Criticism

Criticism of animation has become a domineering force in media and cinema since its inception. With its popularity, a large amount of criticism has arisen, especially animated feature-length films. Many concerns of cultural representation, psychological effects on children have been brought up around the animation industry, which has remained rather politically unchanged and stagnant since its inception into mainstream culture.

Certain under-representation of women has been criticized in animation films and the industry.

Awards

As with any other form of media, animation too has instituted awards for excellence in the field. The original awards for animation were presented by the Academy of Motion Picture Arts and Sciences for animated shorts from the year 1932, during the 5th Academy Awards function. The first winner of the Academy Award was the short *Flowers and Trees*, a production by Walt Disney Productions. The Academy Award for a feature-length animated motion picture was only instituted for the year 2001, and awarded during the 74th Academy Awards in 2002. It was won by the film *Shrek*, produced by DreamWorks and Pacific Data Images. Disney/Pixar have produced the most films either to win or be nominated for the award. The list of both awards can be obtained here:

- Academy Award for Best Animated Feature

- Academy Award for Best Animated Short Film

Several other countries have instituted an award for best animated feature film as part of their national film awards: Africa Movie Academy Award for Best Animation (since 2008), BAFTA Award for Best Animated Film (since 2006), César Award for Best Animated Film (since 2011), Golden Rooster Award for Best Animation (since 1981), Goya Award for Best Animated Film (since 1989), Japan Academy Prize for Animation of the Year (since 2007), National Film Award for Best Animated Film (since 2006). Also since 2007, the Asia Pacific Screen Award for Best Animated Feature Film has been awarded at the Asia Pacific Screen Awards. Since 2009, the European Film Awards have awarded the European Film Award for Best Animated Film.

The Annie Award is another award presented for excellence in the field of animation. Unlike the Academy Awards, the Annie Awards are only received for achievements in the field of animation and not for any other field of technical and artistic endeavor. They were re-organized in 1992 to create a new field for Best Animated feature. The 1990s winners were dominated by Walt Disney, however newer studios, led by Pixar & DreamWorks, have now begun to consistently vie for this award. The list of awardees is as follows:

- Annie Award for Best Animated Feature

- Annie Award for Best Animated Short Subject

- Annie Award for Best Animated Television Production

Computer Animation

Computer animation, or CGI animation, is the process used for generating animated images. The more general term computer-generated imagery encompasses both static scenes and dynamic images, while computer animation *only* refers to the moving images. Modern computer animation usually uses 3D computer graphics, although 2D computer graphics are still used for stylistic, low bandwidth, and faster real-time renderings. Sometimes, the target of the animation is the computer itself, but sometimes film as well.

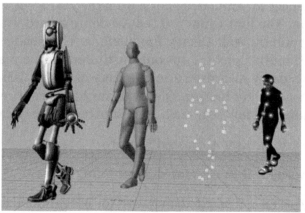

An example of computer animation which is produced in the "motion capture" technique

Computer animation is essentially a digital successor to the stop motion techniques used in traditional animation with 3D models and frame-by-frame animation of 2D illustrations. Computer-generated animations are more controllable than other more physically based processes, constructing miniatures for effects shots or hiring extras for crowd scenes, and because it allows the creation of images that would not be feasible using any other technology. It can also allow a single graphic artist to produce such content without the use of actors, expensive set pieces, or props. To create the illusion of movement, an image is displayed on the computer monitor and repeatedly replaced by a new image that is similar to it, but advanced slightly in time (usually at a rate of 24 or 30 frames/second). This technique is identical to how the illusion of movement is achieved with television and motion pictures.

For 3D animations, objects (models) are built on the computer monitor (modeled) and 3D figures are rigged with a virtual skeleton. For 2D figure animations, separate objects (illustrations) and separate transparent layers are used with or without that virtual skeleton. Then the limbs, eyes, mouth, clothes, etc. of the figure are moved by the animator on key frames. The differences in appearance between key frames are automatically calculated by the computer in a process known as tweening or morphing. Finally, the animation is rendered.

For 3D animations, all frames must be rendered after the modeling is complete. For 2D vector animations, the rendering process is the key frame illustration process, while tweened frames are rendered as needed. For pre-recorded presentations, the rendered frames are transferred to a different format or medium, like digital video. The frames may also be rendered in real time as they are presented to the end-user audience. Low bandwidth animations transmitted via the internet (e.g. Adobe Flash, X3D) often use software on the end-users computer to render in real time as an alternative to streaming or pre-loaded high bandwidth animations.

Explanation

To trick the eye and the brain into thinking they are seeing a smoothly moving object, the pictures should be drawn at around 12 frames per second or faster. (A frame is one complete image.) With rates above 75-120 frames per second, no improvement in realism or smoothness is perceivable due to the way the eye and the brain both process images. At rates below 12 frames per second, most people can detect jerkiness associated with the drawing of new images that detracts from the illusion of realistic movement. Conventional hand-drawn cartoon animation often uses 15 frames per second in order to save on the number of drawings needed, but this is usually accepted because of the stylized nature of cartoons. To produce more realistic imagery, computer animation demands higher frame rates.

Films seen in theaters in the United States run at 24 frames per second, which is sufficient to create the illusion of continuous movement. For high resolution, adapters are used.

History

Early digital computer animation was developed at Bell Telephone Laboratories in the 1960s by Edward E. Zajac, Frank W. Sinden, Kenneth C. Knowlton, and A. Michael Noll. Other digital animation was also practiced at the Lawrence Livermore National Laboratory.

An early step in the history of computer animation was the sequel to the 1973 film *Westworld*, a science-fiction film about a society in which robots live and work among humans. The sequel, *Futureworld* (1976), used the 3D wire-frame imagery, which featured a computer-animated hand and face both created by University of Utah graduates Edwin Catmull and Fred Parke. This imagery originally appeared in their student film *A Computer Animated Hand*, which they completed in 1971.

Developments in CGI technologies are reported each year at SIGGRAPH, an annual conference on computer graphics and interactive techniques that is attended by thousands of computer professionals each year. Developers of computer games and 3D video cards strive to achieve the same visual quality on personal computers in real-time as is possible for CGI films and animation. With the rapid advancement of real-time rendering quality, artists began to use game engines to render non-interactive movies, which led to the art form Machinima.

The very first full length computer animated television series was *ReBoot*, which debuted in September 1994; the series followed the adventures of characters who lived inside a computer. The first feature-length computer animated film was *Toy Story* (1995), which was made by Pixar. It followed an adventure centered around toys and their owners. This groundbreaking film was also the first of many fully computer-animated movies.

Computer animation helped to create blockbuster films, *Toy Story 3* (2010), *Avatar* (2009), *Shrek 2* (2004), *Cars 2* (2011), *Life of Pi* (2012), *Frozen* (2013), and *Inside Out* (2015).

Animation Methods

In most 3D computer animation systems, an animator creates a simplified representation of a character's anatomy, which is analogous to a skeleton or stick figure. The position of each segment of the skeletal model is defined by animation variables, or Avars for short. In human and animal characters, many parts of the skeletal model correspond to the actual bones, but skeletal animation is also used to animate other things, with facial features (though other methods for facial animation exist). The character "Woody" in *Toy Story*, for example, uses 700 Avars (100 in the face alone). The computer doesn't usually render the skeletal model directly (it is invisible), but it does use the skeletal model to compute the exact position and orientation of that certain character, which is eventually rendered into an image. Thus by changing the values of Avars over time, the animator creates motion by making the character move from frame to frame.

There are several methods for generating the Avar values to obtain realistic motion. Traditionally, animators manipulate the Avars directly. Rather than set Avars for every frame, they usually set Avars at strategic points (frames) in time and let the computer interpolate or tween between them in a process called keyframing. Keyframing puts control in the hands of the animator and has roots in hand-drawn traditional animation.

In contrast, a newer method called motion capture makes use of live action footage. When computer animation is driven by motion capture, a real performer acts out the scene as if they were the character to be animated. His/her motion is recorded to a computer using video cameras and markers and that performance is then applied to the animated character.

Each method has its advantages and as of 2007, games and films are using either or both of these methods in productions. Keyframe animation can produce motions that would be difficult or impossible to act out, while motion capture can reproduce the subtleties of a particular actor. For example, in the 2006 film *Pirates of the Caribbean: Dead Man's Chest*, Bill Nighy provided the performance for the character Davy Jones. Even though Nighy doesn't appear in the movie himself, the movie benefited from his performance by recording the nuances of his body language, posture, facial expressions, etc. Thus motion capture is appropriate in situations where believable, realistic behavior and action is required, but the types of characters required exceed what can be done throughout the conventional costuming.

Modeling

3D computer animation combines 3D models of objects and programmed or hand "keyframed" movement. These models are constructed out of geometrical vertices, faces, and edges in a 3D coordinate system. Objects are sculpted much like real clay or plaster, working from general forms to specific details with various sculpting tools. Unless a 3D model is intended to be a solid color, it must be painted with "textures" for realism. A bone/joint animation system is set up to deform the CGI model (e.g., to make a humanoid model walk). In a process known as rigging, the virtual marionette is given various controllers and handles for controlling movement. Animation data can be created using motion capture, or keyframing by a human animator, or a combination of the two.

3D models rigged for animation may contain thousands of control points — for example, "Woody" from *Toy Story* uses 700 specialized animation controllers. Rhythm and Hues Studios labored for two years to create Aslan in the movie *The Chronicles of Narnia: The Lion, the Witch and the Wardrobe*, which had about 1,851 controllers (742 in the face alone). In the 2004 film *The Day After Tomorrow*, designers had to design forces of extreme weather with the help of video references and accurate meteorological facts. For the 2005 remake of *King Kong*, actor Andy Serkis was used to help designers pinpoint the gorilla's prime location in the shots and used his expressions to model "human" characteristics onto the creature. Serkis had earlier provided the voice and performance for Gollum in J. R. R. Tolkien's *The Lord of the Rings* trilogy.

Equipment

Computer animation can be created with a computer and an animation software. Some impressive animation can be achieved even with basic programs; however, the rendering can take a lot of time on an ordinary home computer. Professional animators of movies, television and video games could make photorealistic animation with high detail. This level of quality for movie animation would take hundreds of years to create on a home computer. Instead, many powerful workstation computers are used. Graphics workstation computers use two to four processors, and they are a lot more powerful than an actual home computer and are specialized for rendering. A large number of workstations (known as a "render farm") are networked together to effectively act as a giant computer. The result is a computer-animated movie that can be completed in about one to five years (however, this process is not composed solely of rendering). A workstation typically costs $2,000-16,000 with the more expensive stations being able to render much faster due to the more technologically-advanced hardware that they contain. Professionals also use digital movie cameras, motion/performance capture, bluescreens, film editing software, props, and other tools used for movie animation.

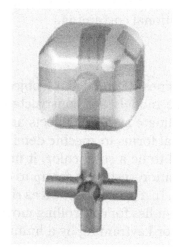

A ray-traced 3-D model of a jack inside a cube, and the jack alone below.

Facial Animation

The realistic modeling of human facial features is both one of the most challenging and sought after elements in computer-generated imagery. Computer facial animation is a highly complex field where models typically include a very large number of animation variables. Historically speaking, the first SIGGRAPH tutorials on *State of the art in Facial Animation* in 1989 and 1990 proved to be a turning point in the field by bringing together and consolidating multiple research elements and sparked interest among a number of researchers.

The Facial Action Coding System (with 46 "action units", "lip bite" or "squint"), which had been developed in 1976, became a popular basis for many systems. As early as 2001, MPEG-4 included 68 Face Animation Parameters (FAPs) for lips, jaws, etc., and the field has made significant progress since then and the use of facial microexpression has increased.

In some cases, an affective space, the PAD emotional state model, can be used to assign specific emotions to the faces of avatars. In this approach, the PAD model is used as a high level emotional space and the lower level space is the MPEG-4 Facial Animation Parameters (FAP). A mid-level Partial Expression Parameters (PEP) space is then used to in a two-level structure – the PAD-PEP mapping and the PEP-FAP translation model.

Realism

Realism in computer animation can mean making each frame look photorealistic, in the sense that the scene is rendered to resemble a photograph or make the characters' animation believable and lifelike. Computer animation can also be realistic with or without the photorealistic rendering.

One of the greatest challenges in computer animation has been creating human characters that look and move with the highest degree of realism. Part of the difficulty in making pleasing, realistic human characters is the uncanny valley, the concept where the human audience (up to a point) tends to have an increasingly negative, emotional response as a human replica looks and acts more and more human. Films that have attempted photorealistic human characters, such as *The Polar Express, Beowulf*, and *A Christmas Carol* have been criticized as "creepy" and "disconcerting".

The goal of computer animation is not always to emulate live action as closely as possible, so many animated films instead feature characters who are anthropomorphic animals (*The Angry Birds Movie, Horton Hears a Who!, Shark Tale, Ratatouille, The Secret Life of Pets, Finding Nemo, The Nut Job, Ice Age, Bolt, Madagascar, Over the Hedge, Rio, Kung Fu Panda, Alpha and Omega, Zootopia, The Wild, Surf's Up, Happy Feet*), machines (*Cars, WALL-E, Robots*), insects (*Antz, A Bug's Life, The Ant Bully, Bee Movie*), fantasy creatures and characters (*Monsters, Inc., Shrek, TMNT, Brave, Epic*), superheroes (*The Incredibles, Megamind, Big Hero 6*), or humans with non-realistic, cartoon-like proportions (*Toy Story, The Book of Life, Despicable Me, Home, Mr. Peabody & Sherman , The Peanuts Movie, Inside Out, Hotel Transylvania, Cloudy with a Chance of Meatballs, Escape from Planet Earth, Arthur Christmas, Wreck-It Ralph*). Computer animation can also be tailored to mimic or substitute for other kinds of animation, traditional stop-motion animation (as shown in *Flushed Away* or *The*

Lego Movie). Some of the long-standing basic principles of animation, like squash & stretch, call for movement that is not strictly realistic, and such principles still see widespread application in computer animation.

Notable Examples

- *Final Fantasy: The Spirits Within*: often cited as the first computer-generated movie to attempt to show realistic-looking humans

- *The Polar Express*

- *Mars Needs Moms*

- *L.A. Noire*: received attention for its use of MotionScan technology

- *The Adventures of Tintin: The Secret of the Unicorn*

- *Heavy Rain*

- *Beyond: Two Souls*

- *Beowulf*

Films

CGI short films have been produced as independent animation since 1976, although the popularity of computer animation (especially in the field of special effects) skyrocketed during the modern era of U.S. animation. The first completely computer-animated television series was *ReBoot* in 1994, and the first completely computer-animated movie was *Toy Story* (1995), but *VeggieTales* is the 1st American fully 3-D Computer Animated Christian direct-to-video series that started all in 1993.

CGI film made using Machinima

Animation Studios

- Pixar Animation Studios - Notable for *Toy Story* (1995), *A Bug's Life* (1998), *Monsters, Inc.* (2001), *Finding Nemo* (2003), *The Incredibles* (2004), *Cars*

(2006), *Ratatouille* (2007), *WALL-E* (2008), *Up* (2009), *Brave* (2012), *Inside Out* (2015), and *The Good Dinosaur* (2015)

- Walt Disney Animation Studios - Notable for *Dinosaur* (2000), *Chicken Little* (2005), *Meet the Robinsons* (2007), *Bolt* (2008), *Tangled* (2010), *Wreck-It Ralph* (2012), *Frozen* (2013), *Big Hero 6* (2014), and *Zootopia* (2016)

- DreamWorks Animation - Notable for *Antz* (1998), *Shrek* (2001), *Shark Tale* (2004), *Madagascar* (2005), *Over the Hedge* (2006), *Flushed Away* (2006) - with Aardman Animations, *Bee Movie* (2007), *Kung Fu Panda* (2008), *Monsters vs. Aliens* (2009), *How to Train Your Dragon* (2010), *Megamind* (2010), *Puss in Boots* (2011), *Rise of the Guardians* (2012) *The Croods* (2013), *Turbo* (2013), *Mr. Peabody & Sherman* (2014), and *Home* (2015)

- Blue Sky Studios - Notable for *Ice Age* (2002), *Robots* (2005), *Horton Hears a Who!* (2008), *Rio* (2011), *Epic* (2013), and *The Peanuts Movie* (2015)

- Sony Pictures Animation - Notable for *Open Season* (2006), *Surf's Up* (2007), *Cloudy with a Chance of Meatballs* (2009), *The Smurfs* (2011), *Arthur Christmas* (2011) - with Aardman Animations, *Hotel Transylvania* (2012), and *Goosebumps* (2015)

- Illumination Entertainment - Notable for *Despicable Me* (2010), *Hop* (2011), *The Lorax* (2012), *Minions* (2015) and *The Secret Life of Pets* (2016)

- Reel FX Animation Studios - Notable for *Free Birds* (2013) and *The Book of Life* (2014)

- Sony Pictures Imageworks - Notable for *The Angry Birds Movie* (2016) and for visual effects on live action films like *Pixels* (2015), *Alice in Wonderland* (2010), *The Amazing Spider-Man* (2012), *Oz: The Great and Powerful* (2013), *Guardians of the Galaxy* (2014) and *Ghostbusters* (2016)

- Industrial Light & Magic - Notable for *Rango* (2011) and *Strange Magic* (2015), Notable for visual effects on live action films like *Star Wars* (1977) and *Pirates of the Caribbean* (2003)

- Weta Digital - Notable for *The Adventures of Tintin* (2011) Notable for visual effects on live action films like *The Lord of the Rings* film series, *The Hobbit* film series, *King Kong* (2005), *Rise of the Planet of the Apes* (2011), and *Avatar* (2009)

- Animal Logic - Notable for *Happy Feet* (2006), *Legend of the Guardians: The Owls of Ga'Hoole* (2010), and *The Lego Movie* (2014) Notable for visual effects on live action films like *Moulin Rouge!* (2001), *The Great Gatsby* (2013), and *Walking with Dinosaurs* (2013)

Amateur Animation

The popularity of websites that allow members to upload their own movies for others to view has created a growing community of amateur computer animators. With utilities and programs often included free with modern operating systems, many users can make their own animated movies and shorts. Several free and open source animation software applications exist as well. A popular amateur approach to animation is via the animated GIF format, which can be uploaded and seen on the web easily.

Detailed Examples and Pseudocode

In 2D computer animation, moving objects are often referred to as "sprites." A sprite is an image that has a location associated with it. The location of the sprite is changed slightly, between each displayed frame, to make the sprite appear to move. The following pseudocode makes a sprite move from left to right:

var *int* x := 0, y := screenHeight / 2;

while x < screenWidth

drawBackground()

drawSpriteAtXY (x, y) *// draw on top of the background*

x := x + 5 *// move to the right*

Computer animation uses different techniques to produce animations. Most frequently, sophisticated mathematics is used to manipulate complex three-dimensional polygons, apply "textures", lighting and other effects to the polygons and finally rendering the complete image. A sophisticated graphical user interface may be used to create the animation and arrange its choreography. Another technique called constructive solid geometry defines objects by conducting boolean operations on regular shapes, and has the advantage that animations may be accurately produced at any resolution.

Computer-assisted Vs Computer-generated

Computer-assisted animation is usually classed as two-dimensional (2D) animation. Creators drawings either hand drawn (pencil to paper) or interactively drawn(drawn on the computer) using different assisting appliances and are positioned into specific software packages. Within the software package the creator will place drawings into different key frames which fundamentally create an outline of the most important movements. The computer will then fill in all the " in-between frames", commonly known as Tweening. Computer-assisted animation is basically using new technologies to cut down the time scale that traditional animation could take, but still having the elements of traditional drawings of characters or objects.

Two examples of films using computer-assisted animation are *Beauty and the Beast* and *Antz*.

Computer-generated animation is known as 3-dimensional (3D) animation. Creators will design an object or character with an X,Y and Z axis. Unlike the traditional way of animation no pencil to paper drawings create the way computer generated animation works. The object or character created will then be taken into a software, key framing and tweening are also carried out in computer generated animation but are also a lot of techniques used that do not relate to traditional animation. Animators can break physical laws by using mathematical algorithms to cheat, mass, force and gravity rulings. Fundamentally, time scale and quality could be said to be a preferred way to produce animation as they are two major things that are enhanced by using computer generated animation. Another great aspect of CGA is the fact you can create a flock of creatures to act independently when created as a group. An animal's fur can be programmed to wave in the wind and lie flat when it rains instead of programming each strand of hair separately.

A few examples of computer-generated animation movies are *Toy Story, Tangled, Frozen, Inside Out, Shrek, Finding Nemo, Ice Age, Despicable Me* and *Zootopia* .

Traditional Animation

Traditional animation (or classical animation, cel animation or hand-drawn animation) is an animation technique where each frame is drawn by hand. The technique was the dominant form of animation in cinema until the advent of computer animation.

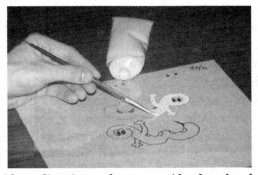

Painting with acrylic paint on the reverse side of an already inked cel.

Process

Animation productions begin by deciding on a story. The oral or literary source material must then be converted into an animation film script, from which the storyboard is derived. The storyboard has an appearance somewhat similar to a comic book, and it shows the sequence of shots as consecutive sketches that also indicate transitions, camera angles and framing. The images allow the animation team to plan the flow of the plot and the composition of the imagery. The *storyboard artists* will have regular meetings with the director, and may have to redraw or "re-board" a sequence many times before it meets final approval.

Voice Recording

Before true animation begins, a preliminary soundtrack or "scratch track" is recorded, so that the animation may be more precisely synchronized to the soundtrack. Given the slow, methodical manner in which traditional animation is produced, it is almost always easier to synchronize animation to a pre-existing soundtrack than it is to synchronize a soundtrack to pre-existing animation. A completed cartoon soundtrack will feature music, sound effects, and dialogue performed by voice actors. However, the scratch track used during animation typically contains only the voices, any vocal songs to which characters must sing along, and temporary musical score tracks; the final score and sound effects are added during post-production.

In the case of Japanese anime, as well as most pre-1930 sound animated cartoons, the sound was *post-synched*; that is, the sound track was recorded after the film elements were finished by watching the film and performing the dialogue, music, and sound effects required. Some studios, most notably Fleischer Studios, continued to post-synch their cartoons through most of the 1930s, which allowed for the presence of the "muttered ad-libs" present in many *Popeye the Sailor* and *Betty Boop* cartoons.

Animatic

Often, an *animatic* or *story reel* is made after the soundtrack is created, but before full animation begins. An animatic typically consists of pictures of the storyboard synchronized with the soundtrack. This allows the animators and directors to work out any script and timing issues that may exist with the current storyboard. The storyboard and soundtrack are amended if necessary, and a new animatic may be created and reviewed with the director until the storyboard is perfected. Editing the film at the animatic stage prevents the animation of scenes that would be edited out of the film; as traditional animation is a very expensive and time-consuming process, creating scenes that will eventually be edited out of the completed cartoon is strictly avoided.

Advertising agencies today employ the use of animatics to test their commercials before they are made into full up spots. Animatics use drawn artwork, with moving pieces (for example, an arm that reaches for a product, or a head that turns). Video storyboards are similar to animatics, but do not have moving pieces. Photomatics are another option when creating test spots, but instead of using drawn artwork, there is a shoot in which hundreds of digital photographs are taken. The large amount of images to choose from may make the process of creating a test commercial a bit easier, as opposed to creating an animatic, because changes to drawn art take time and money. Photomatics generally cost more than animatics, as they may require a shoot and on-camera talent. However, the emergence of affordable stock photography and image editing software permits the inexpensive creation of photomatics using stock elements and photo composites.

Design and Timing

Once the animatic has been approved, it and the storyboards are sent to the design departments. Character designers prepare model sheets for all important characters and props in the film; these are used to help standardize appearance, poses, and gestures. These model sheets will show how a character or object looks from a variety of angles with a variety of poses and expressions, so that all artists working on the project can deliver consistent work. Sometimes, small statues known as *maquettes* may be produced, so that an animator can see what a character looks like in three dimensions. At the same time, the *background stylists* will do similar work for the settings and locations in the project, and the art directors and *color stylists* will determine the art style and color schemes to be used.

While design is going on, the *timing director* (who in many cases will be the main director) takes the animatic and analyzes exactly what poses, drawings, and lip movements will be needed on what frames. An *exposure sheet* (or *X-sheet* for short) is created; this is a printed table that breaks down the action, dialogue, and sound frame-by-frame as a guide for the animators. If a film is based more strongly in music, a *bar sheet* may be prepared in addition to or instead of an X-sheet. Bar sheets show the relationship between the on-screen action, the dialogue, and the actual musical notation used in the score.

Layout

Layout begins after the designs are completed and approved by the director. The layout process is the same as the blocking out of shots by a cinematographer on a live-action film. It is here that the background layout artists determine the camera angles, camera paths, lighting, and shading of the scene. Character layout artists will determine the major poses for the characters in the scene, and will make a drawing to indicate each pose. For short films, character layouts are often the responsibility of the director.

The layout drawings and storyboards are then spliced, along with the audio and an animatic is formed (not to be confused with its predecessor, the leica reel). The term "animatic" was originally coined by Disney animation studios.

Animation

Once the animatic is finally approved by the director, animation begins.

In the traditional animation process, animators will begin by drawing sequences of animation on sheets of transparent paper perforated to fit the peg bars in their desks, often using colored pencils, one picture or "frame" at a time. A peg bar is an animation tool used in traditional (cel) animation to keep the drawings in place. The pins in the peg bar match the holes in the paper. It is attached to the animation desk or light table, depending on which is being used. A *key animator* or *lead animator* will draw the key drawings in a scene, using the character layouts as a guide. The key animator draws enough of the frames to get across the major points of the action; in a sequence of a character jumping across a gap, the key animator may draw a frame of the character as he is about to leap, two or more frames as the character is flying through the air, and the frame for the character landing on the other side of the gap.

Timing is important for the animators drawing these frames; each frame must match exactly what is going on in the soundtrack at the moment the frame will appear, or else the discrepancy between sound and visual will be distracting to the audience. For example, in high-budget productions, extensive effort is given in making sure a speaking character's mouth matches in shape the sound that character's actor is producing as he or she speaks.

While working on a scene, a key animator will usually prepare a *pencil test* of the scene. A pencil test is a preliminary version of the final animated scene; the pencil drawings are quickly photographed or scanned and synced with the necessary soundtracks. This allows the animation to be reviewed and improved upon before passing the work on to his *assistant animators,* who will add details and some of the missing frames in the scene. The work of the assistant animators is reviewed, pencil-tested, and corrected until the lead animator is ready to meet with the director and have his scene *sweatboxed,* or reviewed by the director, producer, and other key creative team members. Similar to the storyboarding stage, an animator may be required to redo a scene many times before the director will approve it.

In high-budget animated productions, often each major character will have an animator or group of animators solely dedicated to drawing that character. The group will be made up of one supervising animator, a small group of key animators, and a larger group of assistant animators. For scenes where two characters interact, the key animators for both characters will decide which character is "leading" the scene, and that character will be drawn first. The second character will be animated to react to and support the actions of the "leading" character.

Once the key animation is approved, the lead animator forwards the scene on to the *clean-up department,* made up of the *clean-up animators* and the *inbetweeners.* The clean-up animators take the lead and assistant animators' drawings and trace them onto a new sheet of paper, taking care in including all of the details present on the original model sheets, so that it appears that one person animated the entire film. The *inbetweeners* will draw in whatever frames are still missing *in between* the other animators' drawings. This procedure is called tweening. The resulting drawings are again pencil-tested and sweatboxed until they meet approval.

At each stage during pencil animation, approved artwork is spliced into the Leica reel.

This process is the same for both *character animation* and *special effects animation*, which on most high-budget productions are done in separate departments. Effects animators animate anything that moves and is not a character, including props, vehicles, machinery and phenomena such as fire, rain, and explosions. Sometimes, instead of drawings, a number of special processes are used to produce special effects in animated films; rain, for example, has been created in Disney animated films since the late 1930s by filming slow-motion footage of water in front of a black background, with the resulting film superimposed over the animation.

Pencil Test

After all the drawings are cleaned up, they are then photographed on an animation camera, usually on black and white film stock. Nowadays, pencil tests can be made using a video camera and computer software.

Backgrounds

While the animation is being done, the *background artists* will paint the sets over which the action of each animated sequence will take place. These backgrounds are generally done in gouache or acrylic paint, although some animated productions have used backgrounds done in watercolor or oil paint. Background artists follow very closely the work of the background layout artists and color stylists (which is usually compiled into a workbook for their use), so that the resulting backgrounds are harmonious in tone with the character designs.

Traditional Ink-and-Paint And Camera

Once the clean-ups and in-between drawings for a sequence are completed, they are prepared for photography, a process known as *ink-and-paint*. Each drawing is then transferred from paper to a thin, clear sheet of plastic called a *cel*, a contraction of the material name celluloid (the original flammable cellulose nitrate was later replaced with the more stable cellulose acetate). The outline of the drawing is inked or photocopied onto the cel, and gouache, acrylic or a similar type of paint is used on the reverse sides of the cels to add colors in the appropriate shades. In many cases, characters will have more than one color palette assigned to them; the usage of each one depends upon the mood and lighting of each scene. The transparent quality of the cel allows for each character or object in a frame to be animated on different cels, as the cel of one character can be seen underneath the cel of another; and the opaque background will be seen beneath all of the cels.

When an entire sequence has been transferred to cels, the photography process begins. Each cel involved in a frame of a sequence is laid on top of each other, with the background at the bottom of the stack. A piece of glass is lowered onto the artwork in order to flatten any irregularities, and the composite image is then photographed by a special animation camera, also called rostrum camera. The cels are removed, and the process repeats for the next frame until each frame in the sequence has been photographed. Each cel has *registration holes,* small holes along the top or bottom edge of the cel, which allow the cel to be placed on corresponding peg bars before the camera to ensure that each cel aligns with the one before it; if the cels are not aligned in such a manner, the animation, when played at full speed, will appear "jittery." Sometimes, frames may need to be photographed more than once, in order to implement superimpositions and other camera effects. Pans are created by either moving the cels or backgrounds one step at a time over a succession of frames (the camera does not pan; it only zooms in and out).

A camera used for shooting traditional animation. See also Aerial image.

As the scenes come out of final photography, they are spliced into the Leica reel, taking the place of the pencil animation. Once every sequence in the production has been photographed, the final film is sent for development and processing, while the final music and sound effects are added to the soundtrack. Again, editing in the traditional live-action sense is generally not done in animation, but if it is required it is done at this time, before the final print of the film is ready for duplication or broadcast.

Among the most common types of animation rostrum cameras was the Oxberry. Such cameras were always made of black anodized aluminum, and commonly had two pegbars, one at the top and one at the bottom of the lightbox. The Oxberry Master Series had four pegbars, two above and two below, and sometimes used a "floating pegbar" as well. The height of the column on which the camera was mounted determined the amount of zoom achievable on a piece of artwork. Such cameras were massive mechanical affairs which might weigh close to a ton and take hours to break down or set up.

In the later years of the animation rostrum camera, stepper motors controlled by computers were attached to the various axes of movement of the camera, thus saving many hours of hand cranking by human operators. A notable early use of computerized cameras was in *Star Wars* (1977), using the Dykstra system at Lucas' Sun Valley facility. Gradually, motion control techniques were adopted throughout the industry. While several computer camera software packages became available in the early 1980s, the Tondreau System became one of the most widely adopted.

Digital ink and paint processes gradually made these traditional animation techniques and equipment obsolete.

Digital Ink and Paint

The current process, termed "digital ink and paint", is the same as traditional ink and paint until after the animation drawings are completed; instead of being transferred to cels, the animators' drawings are either scanned into a computer or drawn directly onto a computer monitor (such as a Wacom Cintiq tablet), where they are colored and processed using one or more of a variety of software packages. The resulting drawings are composited in the computer over their respective backgrounds, which have also been scanned into the computer (if not digitally painted), and the computer outputs the final film by either exporting a digital video file, using a video cassette recorder, or printing to film using a high-resolution output device. Use of computers allows for easier exchange of artwork between departments, studios, and even countries and continents (in most low-budget animated productions, the bulk of the animation is actually done by animators working in other countries, including South Korea, Japan, Singapore, Mexico and India). As the cost of both inking and painting new cels for animated films and TV programs and the repeated usage of older cels for newer animated TV programs and films went up and the cost of doing the same thing digitally went down, eventually, the digital ink-and-paint process became the standard for future animated movies and TV programs. Digital ink and paint has been in use at Walt Disney Feature Animation since 1989, where it was used for the final rainbow shot in *The Little Mermaid*. All subsequent Disney animated features were digitally inked-and-painted (starting with *The Rescuers Down Under*, which was also the first major feature film to entirely use digital ink and paint), using Disney's proprietary CAPS (Computer Animation Production System) technology, developed primarily by Pixar.

While Disney was the first to switch to digital inking and painting, it took the rest of the industry longer to adapt. Many filmmakers and studios didn't want to shift to the digital ink-and-paint process because they felt that the digitally-colored animation would look too synthetic and would lose the aesthetic appeal of the non-computerized cel for their projects. Many animated television series were still animated in foreign countries by using the traditionally inked-and-painted cel process as late as 2004; though most of them switched over to the digital process at some point during their run. For example, *Hey Arnold!* and *SpongeBob SquarePants* made the switch in 1999 and 2000, respectively. Other shows, such as *The Powerpuff Girls*, *The Simpsons*, and *King of the Hill*, tested the digital ink process for a few episodes but didn't fully upgrade until later on.

The last major feature film to use traditional ink and paint was Studio Ghibli's *Princess Mononoke* (1997); the last major animation production to use the traditional process was Cartoon Network's *Ed, Edd n Eddy*, which switched to digital paint in 2004. Minor productions such as *Hair High* (2004) by Bill Plympton have used traditional cels long after the introduction of digital techniques. Most studios today use one of a number of other high-end software packages, such as Toon Boom Harmony, Toonz Bravo!, Animo, and RETAS, or even consumer-level applications such as Adobe Flash, Toon Boom Studio, TVPaint, and Toonz Harlequin.

Computers and Digital Video Cameras

Computers and digital video cameras can also be used as tools in traditional cel animation without affecting the film directly, assisting the animators in their work and making the whole process faster and easier. Doing the layouts on a computer is much more effective than doing it by traditional methods. Additionally, video cameras give the opportunity to see a "preview" of the scenes and how they will look when finished, enabling the animators to correct and improve upon them without having to complete them first. This can be considered a digital form of *pencil testing*.

Techniques

Cels

The cel is an important innovation to traditional animation, as it allows some parts of each frame to be repeated from frame to frame, thus saving labor. A simple example would be a scene with two characters on screen, one of which is talking and the other standing silently. Since the latter character is not moving, it can be displayed in this scene using only one drawing, on one cel, while multiple drawings on multiple cels are used to animate the speaking character.

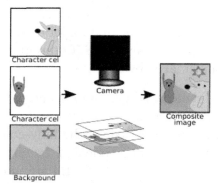

This image shows how two transparent cels, each with a different character drawn on them, and an opaque background are photographed together to form the composite image.

For a more complex example, consider a sequence in which a boy sets a plate upon a table. The table stays still for the entire sequence, so it can be drawn as part of the background. The plate can be drawn along with the character as the character places it on the table. However, after the plate is on the table, the plate no longer moves, although the boy continues to move as he draws his arm away from the plate. In this example, after the boy puts the plate down, the plate can then be drawn on a separate cel from the boy. Further frames feature new cels of the boy, but the plate does not have to be redrawn as it is not moving; the same cel of the plate can be used in each remaining frame that it is still upon the table. The cel paints were actually manufactured in shaded versions of each color to compensate for the extra layer of cel added between the image and the camera; in this example the still plate would be painted slightly brighter to compensate for being moved one layer down. In TV and other low-budget productions, cels were often "cycled" (i.e., a sequence of cels was repeated several times), and even archived and reused in other episodes. After the film was completed, the cels were either thrown out or, especially in the early days of animation, washed clean and reused for the next film. Also, after the completion of the film, some of the cels were put into the "archive" to be used again and again for future purposes in order to save money. Some studios saved a portion of the cels and either sold them in studio stores or presented them as gifts to visitors.

In very early cartoons made before the use of the cel, such as *Gertie the Dinosaur* (1914), the entire frame, including the background and all characters and items, were drawn on a single sheet of paper, then photographed. Everything had to be redrawn for each frame containing movements. This led to a "jittery" appearance; imagine seeing a sequence of drawings of a mountain, each one slightly different from the one preceding it. The pre-cel animation was later improved by using techniques like the slash and tear system invented by Raoul Barre; the background and the animated objects were drawn on separate papers. A frame was made by removing all the blank parts of the papers where the objects were drawn before being placed on top of the backgrounds and finally photographed. The cel animation process was invented by Earl Hurd and John Bray in 1915.

Limited Animation

In lower-budget productions, shortcuts available through the cel technique are used extensively. For example, in a scene in which a man is sitting in a chair and talking, the chair and the body of the man may be the same in every frame; only his head is redrawn, or perhaps even his head stays the same while only his mouth moves. This is known as *limited animation*. The process was popularized in theatrical cartoons by United Productions of America and used in most television animation, especially that of Hanna-Barbera. The end result does not look very lifelike, but is inexpensive to produce, and therefore allows cartoons to be made on small television budgets.

"Shooting on Twos"

Moving characters are often shot "on twos", that is to say, one drawing is shown for every two frames of film (which usually runs at 24 frames per second), meaning there are only 12 drawings per second. Even though the image update rate is low, the fluidity is satisfactory for most subjects. However, when a character is required to perform a quick movement, it is usually necessary to revert to animating "on ones", as "twos" are too slow to convey the motion adequately. A blend of the two techniques keeps the eye fooled without unnecessary production cost.

Academy Award-nominated animator Bill Plympton is noted for his style of animation that uses very few inbetweens and sequences that are done on threes or on fours, holding each drawing on the screen from an eighth to a sixth of a second. While Plympton uses near-constant three-frame holds, sometimes animation that simply averages eight drawings per second is also termed "on threes" and is usually done to meet budget constraints, along with other cost-cutting measures like holding the same drawing of a character for a prolonged time or panning over a still image, techniques often used in low-budget TV productions. It is also common in anime, where fluidity is sacrificed in lieu of a shift towards complexity in the designs and shading (in contrast with the more functional and optimized designs in the western tradition); even high-budget theatrical features such as Studio Ghibli's employ the full range: from smooth animation "on ones" in selected shots (usually quick action accents) to common animation "on threes" for regular dialogue and slow-paced shots.

Animation Loops

Creating *animation loops* or *animation cycles* is a labor-saving technique for animating repetitive motions, such as a character walking or a breeze blowing through the trees. In the case of walking, the character is animated taking a step with his right foot, then a step with his left foot. The loop is created so that, when the sequence repeats, the motion is seamless. However, since an animation loop essentially uses the same bit of animation over and over again, it is easily detected and can in fact become distracting to an audience. In general, they are used only sparingly by productions with moderate or high budgets.

Ryan Larkin's 1969 Academy Award-nominated National Film Board of Canada short *Walking* makes creative use of loops. In addition, a promotional music video from Cartoon Network's Groovies featuring the Soul Coughing song "Circles" poked fun at animation loops as they are often seen in *The Flintstones*, in which Fred and Barney (along with various Hanna-Barbera characters that aired on Cartoon Network), supposedly walking in a house, wonder why they keep passing the same table and vase over and over again.

Multiplane Camera

The multiplane camera is a tool used to add depth to scenes in 2D animated movies, called the multiplane effect or the parallax process. The art is placed on different layers of glass plates, and as the camera moves vertically towards or away from the artwork levels, the camera's viewpoint appears to move through the various layers of artwork in 3D space. The panorama views in *Pinocchio* are examples of the effects a multiplane camera can achieve. Different versions of the camera have been made through time, but the most famous is the one developed by the Walt Disney studio beginning with their 1937 short *The Old Mill*. Another one, the "Tabletop", was developed by Fleischer Studios. The Tabletop, first used in 1934's *Poor Cinderella*, used miniature sets made of paper cutouts placed in front of the camera on a rotating platform, with the cels between them. By rotating the entire setup one frame at a time in accordance with the cel animation, realistic panoramas could be created. Ub Iwerks and Don Bluth also built multiplane cameras for their studios.

Xerography

Applied to animation by Ub Iwerks at the Walt Disney studio during the late 1950s, the electrostatic copying technique called xerography allowed the drawings to be copied directly onto the cels, eliminating much of the "inking" portion of the ink-and-paint process. This saved time and money, and it also made it possible to put in more details and to control the size of the xeroxed objects and characters (this replaced the little known, and seldom used, photographic lines technique at Disney, used to reduce the size of animation when needed). At first it resulted in a more sketchy look, but the technique was improved upon over time.

Disney animator and engineer Bill Justice had patented a forerunner of the Xerox process in 1944, where drawings made with a special pencil would be transferred to a cel by pressure, and then fixing it. It is not known if the process was ever used in animation.

The xerographic method was first tested by Disney in a few scenes of *Sleeping Beauty*, and was first fully used in the short film *Goliath II*, while the first feature entirely using this process was *One Hundred and One Dalmatians* (1961). The graphic style of this film was strongly influenced by the process. Some hand inking was still used together with xerography in this and subsequent films when distinct colored lines were needed. Later, colored toners became available, and several distinct line colors could be used, even simultaneously. For instance, in *The Rescuers* the characters' outlines are gray. White and blue toners were used for special effects, such as snow and water.

The APT Process

Invented by Dave Spencer for the 1985 Disney film *The Black Cauldron*, the APT (Animation Photo Transfer) process was a technique for transferring the animators' art onto cels. Basically, the process was a modification of a repro-photographic process; the artists' work were photographed on high-contrast "litho" film, and the image on the resulting negative was then transferred to a cel covered with a layer of light sensitive dye. The cel was exposed through the negative. Chemicals were then used to remove the unexposed portion. Small and delicate details were still inked by hand if needed. Spencer received an Academy Award for Technical Achievement for developing this process.

Cel Overlay

A *cel overlay* is a cel with inanimate objects used to give the impression of a foreground when laid on top of a ready frame. This creates the illusion of depth, but not as much as a multiplane camera would. A special version of cel overlay is called *line overlay*, made to complete the background instead of making the foreground, and was invented to deal with the sketchy appearance of xeroxed drawings. The background was first painted as shapes and figures in flat colors, containing rather few details. Next, a cel with detailed black lines was laid directly over it, each line drawn to add more information to the underlying shape or figure and give the background the complexity it needed. In this way, the visual style of the background will match that of the xeroxed character cels. As the xerographic process evolved, line overlay was left behind.

Computers and Traditional Animation

The methods mentioned above describe the techniques of an animation process that originally depended on cels in its final stages, but painted cels are rare today as the computer moves into the animation studio, and the outline drawings are usually scanned into the computer and filled with digital paint instead of being transferred to cels and then colored by hand. The drawings are composited in a computer program on many transparent "layers" much the same way as they are with cels, and made into a sequence of images which may then be transferred onto film or converted to a digital video format.

It is now also possible for animators to draw directly into a computer using a graphics tablet, Cintiq or a similar device, where the outline drawings are done in a similar manner as they would be on paper. The Goofy short *How To Hook Up Your Home Theater* (2007) represented Disney's first project based on the paperless technology available today. Some of the advantages are the possibility and potential of controlling the size of the drawings while working on them, drawing directly on a multiplane background and eliminating the need of photographing line tests and scanning.

Though traditional animation is now commonly done with computers, it is important to differentiate computer-assisted traditional animation from 3D computer animation, such as *Toy Story* and *Ice Age*. However, often traditional animation and 3D computer animation will be used together, as in Don Bluth's *Titan A.E.* and Disney's *Tarzan* and *Treasure Planet*. Most anime still use traditional animation today. DreamWorks executive Jeffrey Katzenberg coined the term "tradigital animation" to describe animated films produced by his studio which incorporated elements of traditional and computer animation equally, such as *Spirit: Stallion of the Cimarron* and *Sinbad: Legend of the Seven Seas*.

Many video games such as *Viewtiful Joe, The Legend of Zelda: The Wind Waker* and others use "cel-shading" animation filters or lighting systems to make their full 3D animation appear as though it were drawn in a traditional cel style. This technique was also used in the animated movie *Appleseed,* and cel-shaded 3D animation is typically integrated with cel animation in Disney films and in many television shows, such as the Fox animated series *Futurama*. In one scene of the 2007 Pixar movie *Ratatouille*, an illustration of Gusteau (in his cook-book), speaks to Remy (who, in that scene, was lost in the sewers of Paris) as a figment of Remy's imagination; this scene is also considered an example of cel-shading in an animated feature. More recently, animated shorts such as *Paperman, Feast* and *The Dam Keeper* have used a more distinctive style of cel-shaded 3D animation, capturing a look and feel similar to a 'moving painting'.

Rotoscoping

Rotoscoping is a method of traditional animation invented by Max Fleischer in 1915, in which animation is "traced" over actual film footage of actors and scenery. Traditionally, the live action will be printed out frame by frame and registered. Another piece of paper is then placed over the live action printouts and the action is traced frame by frame using a lightbox. The end result still looks hand drawn but the motion will be remarkably lifelike. The films *Waking Life* and *American Pop* are full-length rotoscoped films. Rotoscoped animation also appears in the music videos for A-ha's song "Take On Me" and Kanye West's "Heartless". In most cases, rotoscoping is mainly used to aid the animation of realistically rendered human beings, as in *Snow White and the Seven Dwarfs, Peter Pan*, and *Sleeping Beauty*.

A method related to conventional rotoscoping was later invented for the animation of solid inanimate objects, such as cars, boats, or doors. A small live action model of the required object was built and painted white, while the edges of the model were painted with thin black lines. The object was then filmed as required for the animated scene by moving the model, the camera, or a combination of both, in real time or using stop-motion animation. The film frames were then printed on paper, showing a model made up of the painted black lines. After the artists had added details to the object not present in the live-action photography of the model, it was xeroxed onto cels. A notable example is Cruella de Vil's car in Disney's *One Hundred and One Dalmatians*. The process of transferring 3D objects to cels was greatly improved in the 1980s when computer graphics advanced enough to allow the creation of 3D computer generated objects that could be manipulated in any way the animators wanted, and then printed as outlines on paper before being copied onto cels using Xerography or the APT process. This technique was used in Disney films such as *Oliver and Company* (1988) and *The Little Mermaid* (1989). This process has more or less been superseded by the use of cel-shading.

Related to rotoscoping are the methods of vectorizing live-action footage, in order to achieve a very graphical look, like in Richard Linklater's film *A Scanner Darkly*.

Live-action Hybrids

Similar to the computer animation and traditional animation hybrids described above, occasionally a production will combine both live-action and animated footage. The live-action parts of these productions are usually filmed first, the actors pretending that they are interacting with the animated characters, props, or scenery; animation will then be added into the footage later to make it appear as if it has always been there. Like rotoscoping, this method is rarely used, but when it is, it can be done to terrific effect, immersing the audience in a fantasy world where humans and cartoons co-exist. Early examples include the silent *Out of the Inkwell* (begun in 1919) cartoons by Max Fleischer and Walt Disney's *Alice Comedies* (begun in 1923). Live-action and animation were later combined in features such as *Mary Poppins* (1964), *Who Framed Roger Rabbit* (1988), *Space Jam* (1996), and *Enchanted* (2007), among many others. The technique has also seen significant use in television commercials, especially for breakfast cereals marketed to children.

Special Effects Animation

Besides traditional animated characters, objects and backgrounds, many other techniques are used to create special elements such as smoke, lightning and "magic", and to give the animation in general a distinct visual appearance. Today special effects are mostly done with computers, but earlier they had to be done by hand. To produce these effects, the animators used different techniques, such as drybrush, airbrush, charcoal, grease pencil, backlit animation, diffusing screens, filters, or gels. For instance, the *Nutcracker Suite* segment in *Fantasia* has a fairy sequence where stippled cels are used, creating a soft pastel look.

Stop Motion

Stop motion (hyphenated stop-motion when used as an adjective) is an animation technique that physically manipulates an object so that it appears to move on its own. The object is moved in small increments between individually photographed frames, creating the illusion of movement when the series of frames is played as a continuous sequence. Dolls with movable joints or clay figures are often used in stop motion for their ease of repositioning. Stop motion animation using plasticine is called clay animation or "clay-mation". Not all stop motion requires figures or models; many stop motion films can involve using humans, household appliances and other things for comedic effect. Stop motion using objects is sometimes referred to as object animation.

Terminology

The term "stop motion", related to the animation technique, is often spelled with a hyphen, "stop-motion". Both orthographical variants, with and without the hyphen, are correct, but the hyphenated one has, in addition, a second meaning, not related to animation or cinema: "a device for automatically stopping a machine or engine when something has gone wrong" (*The New Shorter Oxford English Dictionary*, 1993 edition).

Stop motion is often confused with the time lapse technique, where still photographs of a live surrounding are taken at regular intervals and combined into a continuous film. Time lapse is a technique whereby the frequency at which film frames are captured is much lower than that used to view the sequence. When played at normal speed, time appears to be moving faster and thus lapsing.

History

Stop motion animation has a long history in film. It was often used to show objects moving as if by magic. The first instance of the stop motion technique can be credited to Albert E. Smith and J. Stuart Blackton for Vitagraph's *The Humpty Dumpty Circus* (1898), in which a toy circus of acrobats and animals comes to life. In 1902, the film *Fun in a Bakery Shop* used the stop trick technique in the "lightning sculpting" sequence. French trick film maestro Georges Méliès used stop motion animation once to produce moving title-card letters in one of his short films, and a number of his special effects are based on stop motion photography. In 1907, *The Haunted Hotel* is a new stop motion film by J. Stuart Blackton, and was a resounding success when released. Segundo de Chomón (1871–1929), from Spain, released *El Hotel Eléctrico* later that same year, and used similar techniques as the Blackton film. In 1908, *A Sculptor's Welsh Rarebit Nightmare* was released, as was *The Sculptor's Nightmare*, a film by Billy Bitzer. Italian animator Roméo Bossetti impressed audiences with his object animation tour-de-force, *The Automatic Moving Company* in 1912. The great European stop motion pioneer was Wladyslaw Starewicz (1892–1965), who animated *The Beautiful Lukanida* (1910), *The Battle of the Stag Beetles* (1910), *The Ant and the Grasshopper* (1911).

One of the earliest clay animation films was *Modelling Extraordinary*, which impressed audiences in 1912. December 1916 brought the first of Willie Hopkins' 54 episodes of "Miracles in Mud" to the big screen. Also in December 1916, the first woman animator, Helena Smith Dayton, began experimenting with clay stop motion. She would release her first film in 1917, an adaptation of William Shakespeare's *Romeo and Juliet*.

In the turn of the century, there was another well known animator known as Willis O' Brien (known by others as O'bie). His work on *The Lost World* (1925) is well known, but he is most admired for his work on *King Kong* (1933), a milestone of his films made possible by stop motion animation.

O'Brien's protege and eventual successor in Hollywood was Ray Harryhausen. After learning under O'Brien on the film *Mighty Joe Young* (1949), Harryhausen would go on to create the effects for a string of successful and memorable films over the next three decades. These included *The Beast from 20,000 Fathoms* (1953), *It Came from*

Beneath the Sea (1955), *Jason and the Argonauts* (1963), *The Golden Voyage of Sinbad* (1973) and *Clash of the Titans* (1981).

In a 1940 promotional film, Autolite, an automotive parts supplier, featured stop motion animation of its products marching past Autolite factories to the tune of Franz Schubert's *Military March*. An abbreviated version of this sequence was later used in television ads for Autolite, especially those on the 1950s CBS program *Suspense*, which Autolite sponsored.

1960s and 1970s

In the 1960s and 1970s, independent clay animator Eliot Noyes Jr. refined the technique of "free-form" clay animation with his Oscar-nominated 1965 film *Clay (or the Origin of Species)*. Noyes also used stop motion to animate sand lying on glass for his musical animated film *Sandman* (1975).

Stop motion was used by Rankin/Bass on some of their Christmas specials, most notably *Rudolph the Red-Nosed Reindeer* (1964)

In 1975, filmmaker and clay animation experimenter Will Vinton joined with sculptor Bob Gardiner to create an experimental film called *Closed Mondays* which became the world's first stop motion film to win an Oscar. Will Vinton followed with several other successful short film experiments including *The Great Cognito*, *Creation*, and *Rip Van Winkle* which were each nominated for Academy Awards. In 1977, Vinton made a documentary about this process and his style of animation which he dubbed "claymation"; he titled the documentary *Claymation*. Soon after this documentary, the term was trademarked by Vinton to differentiate his team's work from others who had been, or were beginning to do, "clay animation". While the word has stuck and is often used to describe clay animation and stop motion, it remains a trademark owned currently by Laika Entertainment, Inc. Twenty clay-animation episodes featuring the clown Mr. Bill were a feature of *Saturday Night Live*, starting from a first appearance in February 1976.

At very much the same time in the UK, Peter Lord and David Sproxton formed Aardman Animations. In 1976 they created the character Morph who appeared as an animated side-kick to the TV presenter Tony Hart on his BBC TV programme Take Hart. The five-inch-high presenter was made from a traditional British modelling clay called Plasticine. In 1977 they started on a series of animated films, again using modelling clay, but this time made for a more adult audience. The soundtrack for Down and Out was recorded in a Salvation Army Hostel and Plasticine puppets were animated to dramatise the dialogue. A second film, also for the BBC followed in 1978. A TV series The Amazing Adventures of Morph was aired in 1980.

Sand-coated puppet animation was used in the Oscar-winning 1977 film *The Sand Castle*, produced by Dutch-Canadian animator Co Hoedeman. Hoedeman was one of dozens of animators sheltered by the National Film Board of Canada, a Canadian government film arts agency that had supported animators for decades. A pioneer of refined multiple stop motion films under the NFB banner was Norman McLaren, who brought in many other animators to create their own creatively controlled films. Notable among these are the pinscreen animation films of Jacques Drouin, made with the original pinscreen donated by Alexandre Alexeieff and Claire Parker.

Italian stop motion films include *Quaq Quao* (1978), by Francesco Misseri, which was stop motion with origami, *The Red and the Blue* and the clay animation kittens *Mio and Mao*. Other European productions included a stop motion-animated series of Tove Jansson's *The Moomins* (from 1979, often referred to as "The Fuzzy Felt Moomins"), produced by Film Polski and Jupiter Films.

One of the main British Animation teams, John Hardwick and Bob Bura, were the main animators in many early British TV shows, and are famous for their work on the *Trumptonshire* trilogy.

Disney experimented with several stop motion techniques by hiring independent animator-director Mike Jittlov to do the first stop motion animation of Mickey Mouse toys ever produced for a short sequence called *Mouse Mania*, part of a TV special commemorating Mickey Mouse's 50th Anniversary called *Mickey's 50* in 1978. Jittlov again produced some impressive multi-technique stop motion animation a year later for a 1979 Disney special promoting their release of the feature film *The Black Hole*. Titled *Major Effects*, Jittlov's work stood out as the best part of the special. Jittlov released his footage the following year to 16mm film collectors as a short film titled *The Wizard of Speed and Time*, along with four of his other short multi-technique animated films, most of which eventually evolved into his own feature-length film of the same title. Effectively demonstrating almost all animation techniques, as well as how he produced them, the film was released to theaters in 1987 and to video in 1989.

1980s to Present

In the 1970s and 1980s, Industrial Light & Magic often used stop motion model animation for films such as the original *Star Wars* trilogy: the chess sequence in *Star Wars*, the Tauntauns and AT-AT walkers in *The Empire Strikes Back*, and the AT-ST walkers in *Return of the Jedi* were all stop motion animation, some of it using the Go films. The many shots including the ghosts in *Raiders of the Lost Ark* and the first two feature films in the *RoboCop* series use Phil Tippett's go motion version of stop motion.

In the UK, Aardman Animations continued to grow. Channel 4 funded a new series of clay animated films Conversation Pieces based on real recorded soundtracks. A further series in 1986 called Lip Sync premiered the work of Richard Goleszowski - Ident, Barry Purves - Next and Nick Park - Creature Comforts as well as further films by Sproxton and Lord. Creature Comforts won the Oscar for Best Animated Short in 1990.

In 1980, Marc Paul Chinoy directed the 1st feature-length clay animated film; a film based on the famous *Pogo* comic strip. Titled *I go Pogo*, it was aired a few times on American cable channels, but has yet to be commercially released. Primarily clay, some characters required armatures, and walk cycles used pre-sculpted hard bases legs.

Stefano Bessoni, Italian filmmaker, illustrator and stop-motion animator working on
Gallows Songs (2014)

Stop motion was also used for some shots of the final sequence of *Terminator* movie, also for the scenes of the small alien ships in Spielberg's *Batteries Not Included* in 1987, animated by David W. Allen. Allen's stop motion work can also be seen in such feature films as *The Crater Lake Monster* (1977), *Q - The Winged Serpent* (1982), *The Gate* (1986) and *Freaked* (1993). Allen's King Kong Volkswagen commercial from the 1970s is now legendary among model animation enthusiasts.

In 1985, Will Vinton and his team released an ambitious feature film in stop motion called "The Adventures Of Mark Twain" based on the life and works of the famous American author. While the film may have been a little sophisticated for young audiences at the time, it got rave reviews from critics and adults in general. Vinton's team also created the Nomes and the Nome King for Disney's "Return to Oz" feature, for which they received an Academy Award Nomination for Special Visual Effects. In the 80's and early 90's, Will Vinton became very well known for his commercial work as well with stop motion campaigns including The California Raisins.

Of note are the films of Czech filmmaker Jan Švankmajer, which mix stop motion and live actors. These include *Alice*, an adaptation of Lewis Carroll's *Alice's Adventures in Wonderland*, and *Faust*, a rendition of the legend of the German scholar. The Czech school is also illustrated by the series *Pat & Mat* (1979–present). Created by Lubomír Beneš and Vladimír Jiránek, and it was wildly popular in a number of countries.

Since the general animation renaissance headlined by the likes of *Who Framed Roger Rabbit* and *The Little Mermaid* at the end of the 1980s and the beginning of the 1990s, there have been an increasing number of traditional stop motion feature films, despite advancements with computer animation. *The Nightmare Before Christmas*, directed by Henry Selick and produced by Tim Burton, was one of the more widely released stop motion features and become the highest grossing stop motion animated movie of its time, grossing over $50 million domestic. Henry Selick also went on to direct *James and the Giant Peach* and *Coraline*, and Tim Burton went on to direct *Corpse Bride* and *Frankenweenie*.

Toward the end of the 90's, Will Vinton launched the first prime-time stop motion television series called The PJs, with creator Eddie Murphy. The Emmy winning show aired on Fox then UPN for 3 seasons.

Another individual who found fame in clay animation is Nick Park, who created the characters Wallace and Gromit. In addition to a series of award-winning shorts and featurettes, he won the Academy Award for Best Animated Feature for the feature-length outing *Wallace & Gromit: The Curse of the Were-Rabbit. Chicken Run*, to date, is the highest grossing stop motion animated movie ever grossing nearly $225 million worldwide.

Other notable stop motion feature films released since 1990 include *The Secret Adventures of Tom Thumb* (1993), *Fantastic Mr. Fox* and *$9.99*, both released in 2009, and *Anomalisa* (2015).

Variations of Stop Motion

Stereoscopic Stop Motion

Stop motion has very rarely been shot in stereoscopic 3D throughout film history. The first 3D stop motion short was *In Tune With Tomorrow* (also known as *Motor Rhythm*) in 1939 by John Norling. The second stereoscopic stop motion release was *The Adventures of Sam Space* in 1955 by Paul Sprunck. The third and latest stop motion short in stereo 3D was *The Incredible Invasion of the 20,000 Giant Robots from Outer Space* in 2000 by Elmer Kaan and Alexander Lentjes. This is also the first ever 3D stereoscopic stop motion and CGI short in the history of film. The first all stop motion 3D feature is *Coraline* (2009), based on Neil Gaiman's best-selling novel and directed by Henry Selick. Another recent example is the Nintendo 3DS video software which comes with the option for Stop Motion videos. This has been released December 8, 2011 as a 3DS system update. Also, the movie ParaNorman is in 3D stop motion.

Go Motion

Another more-complicated variation on stop motion is go motion, co-developed by Phil Tippett and first used on the films *The Empire Strikes Back* (1980), *Dragonslayer* (1981), and the *RoboCop* films. Go motion involved programming a computer to move parts of a model slightly during each exposure of each frame of film, combined with traditional hand manipulation of the model in between frames, to produce a more realistic motion blurring effect. Tippett also used the process extensively in his 1984 short film *Prehistoric Beast*, a 10 minutes long sequence depicting a herbivorous dinosaur

(*Monoclonius*), being chased by a carnivorous one (*Tyrannosaurus*). With new footage *Prehistoric Beast* became *Dinosaur!* in 1985, a full-length dinosaurs documentary hosted by Christopher Reeve. Those Phil Tippett's go motion tests acted as motion models for his first photo-realistic use of computers to depict dinosaurs in *Jurassic Park* in 1993. A lo-tech, manual version of this blurring technique was originally pioneered by Wladyslaw Starewicz in the silent era, and was used in his feature film *The Tale of the Fox* (1931).

Comparison to Computer-Generated Imagery

Reasons for using stop motion instead of the more advanced computer-generated imagery (CGI) include the low entry price and the appeal of its distinct look. It is now mostly used in children's programming, in commercials and some comic shows such as *Robot Chicken*. Another merit of stop motion is that it is superior in displaying textures. This is appreciated by a number of movie makers, such as Tim Burton, who produced the puppet-animated 2005 film *Corpse Bride*.

Stop Motion in Television and Movies

Dominating children's TV stop motion programming for three decades in America was Art Clokey's *Gumby* series—which spawned a feature film, *Gumby I* in 1995—using both freeform and character clay animation. Clokey started his adventures in clay with a 1953 freeform clay short film called *Gumbasia* (1953) which shortly thereafter propelled him into his more structured *Gumby* TV series.

In November 1959 the first episode of *Sandmännchen* was shown on East German television, a children's show that had Cold War propaganda as its primary function. New episodes, minus any propaganda, are still being produced in the now-reunified Germany, making it one of the longest running animated series in the world.

In the 1960s, the French animator Serge Danot created the well-known *The Magic Roundabout* (1965) which played for many years on the BBC. Another French/Polish stop motion animated series was *Colargol* (*Barnaby the Bear* in the UK, *Jeremy* in Canada), by Olga Pouchine and Tadeusz Wilkosz.

A British TV-series *Clangers* (1969) became popular on television. The British artists Brian Cosgrove and Mark Hall (Cosgrove Hall Films) produced a full-length film *The Wind in the Willows* (1983) and later a multi-season TV series *The Wind in the Willows* based on Kenneth Grahame's classic children's book of the same title. They also produced a documentary of their production techniques, *Making Frog and Toad*. Since the 1970s and continuing into the 21st century, Aardman Animations, a British studio, has produced short films, television series, commercials and feature films, starring plasticine characters such as Wallace and Gromit; they also produced a notable music video for "Sledgehammer", a song by Peter Gabriel.

During 1986 to 1991, Churchill Films produced *The Mouse and the Motorcycle*, *Runaway Ralph*, and *Ralph S. Mouse* for ABC television. The shows featured stop-motion characters combined with live action, based on the books of Beverly Cleary. John Clark Matthews was animation director, with Justin Kohn, Joel Fletcher, and Gail Van Der Merwe providing character animation.

From 1986 to 2000, over 150 five-minute episodes of *Pingu*, a Swiss children's comedy were produced by Trickfilmstudio. In the 1990s Trey Parker and Matt Stone made two shorts and the pilot of *South Park* almost entirely out of construction paper.

In 1999, Tsuneo Gōda directed an official 30-second sketches of the character Domo. With the shorts animated by stop-motion studio dwarf is still currently produced in Japan and has then received universal critical acclaim from fans and critics. Gōda also directed the stop-motion movie series *Komaneko* in 2004.

In 2003, the pilot film for the series *Curucuru and Friends*, produced by Korean studio Ffango Entertoyment is greenlighted into a children's animated series in 2004 after an approval with the Gyeonggi Digital Contents Agency. It was aired in KBS1 on November 24, 2006 and won the 13th Korean Animation Awards in 2007 for Best Animation. Ffango Entertoyment also worked with Frontier Works in Japan to produce the 2010 film remake of *Cheburashka*.

Since 2005, *Robot Chicken* has mostly utilized stop motion animation, using custom made action figures and other toys as principal characters.

Since 2009 Laika, the stop-motion successor to Will Vinton Studios, has released four feature films, all of which earned over $100 million at the box office.

Stop Motion in Other Media

Many younger people begin their experiments in movie making with stop motion, thanks to the ease of modern stop motion software and online video publishing. Many new stop motion shorts use clay animation into a new form.

Singer-songwriter Oren Lavie's music video for the song Her Morning Elegance was posted on YouTube on January 19, 2009. The video, directed by Lavie and Yuval and Merav Nathan, uses stop motion and has achieved great success with over 25.4 million views, also earning a 2010 Grammy Award nomination for "Best Short Form Music Video".

Stop motion has occasionally been used to create the characters for computer games, as an alternative to CGI. The Virgin Interactive Entertainment Mythos game Magic and Mayhem (1998) featured creatures built by stop motion specialist Alan Friswell, who made the miniature figures from modelling clay and latex rubber, over armatures of wire and ball-and-socket joints. The models were then animated one frame at a time, and incorporated into the CGI elements of the game through digital photography. "ClayFighter" for the Super NES and The Neverhood for the PC are other examples.

Stop motion is a prominent production method on Vine due to its six-second time constraint, a contemporary digital mass revival of a technique which dates back almost to the beginning to cinema itself.

Skeletal Animation

Skeletal animation is a technique in computer animation in which a character (or other articulated object) is represented in two parts: a surface representation used to draw the character (called *skin* or *mesh*) and a hierarchical set of interconnected bones (called the *skeleton* or *rig*) used to animate (*pose* and *keyframe*) the mesh. While this technique is often used to animate humans or more generally for organic modeling, it only serves to make the animation process more intuitive and the same technique can be used to control the deformation of any object — a door, a spoon, a building, or a galaxy. When the animated object is more general than for example a humanoid character the set of bones may not be hierarchical or interconnected, but it just represents a higher level description of the motion of the part of mesh or skin it is influencing.

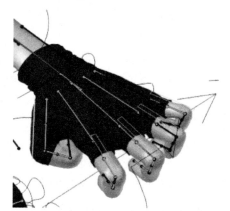

'Bones' (in green) used to pose a hand. In practice, the 'bones' themselves are often hidden and replaced by more user-friendly objects. In this example from the open source project Blender, these 'handles' (in blue) have been scaled down to bend the fingers. The bones are still controlling the deformation, but the animator only sees the 'handles'.

The technique was introduced in 1988 by Nadia Magnenat Thalmann, Richard Laperrière, and Daniel Thalmann. This technique is used in virtually all animation systems where simplified user interfaces allows animators to control often complex algorithms and a huge amount of geometry; most notably through inverse kinematics and other "goal-oriented" techniques. In principle, however, the intention of the technique is never to imitate real anatomy or physical processes, but only to control the deformation of the mesh data.

Technique

"Rigging is making our characters able to move. The process of rigging is we take that digital sculpture, and we start building the skeleton, the muscles, and we attach the skin to the character, and we also create a set of animation controls, which our animators use to push and pull the body around."

— *Frank Hanner, character CG supervisor of the Walt Disney Animation Studios, provided a basic understanding on the technique of character rigging.*

This technique is used by constructing a series of 'bones,' sometimes referred to as *rigging*. Each bone has a three-dimensional transformation (which includes its position, scale and orientation), and an optional parent bone. The bones therefore form a hierarchy. The full transform of a child node is the product of its parent transform and its own transform. So moving a thigh-bone will move the lower leg too. As the character is animated, the bones change their transformation over time, under the influence of some animation controller. A rig is generally composed of both forward kinematics and inverse kinematics parts that may interact with each other. Skeletal animation is referring to the forward kinematics part of the rig, where a complete set of bones configurations identifies a unique pose.

Each bone in the skeleton is associated with some portion of the character's visual representation. *Skinning* is the process of creating this association. In the most common case of a polygonal mesh character, the bone is associated with a group of vertices; for example, in a model of a human being, the 'thigh' bone would be associated with the vertices making up the polygons in the model's thigh. Portions of the character's skin can normally be associated with multiple bones, each one having a scaling factors called vertex weights, or blend weights. The movement of skin near the joints of two bones, can therefore be influenced by both bones. In most state-of-the-art graphical engines, the skinning process is done on the GPU thanks to a shader program.

For a polygonal mesh, each vertex can have a blend weight for each bone. To calculate the final position of the vertex, a transformation matrix is created for each bone which, when applied to the vertex, first puts the vertex in bone space then puts it back into mesh space, the vertex. After applying a matrix to the vertex, it is scaled by its corresponding weight. This algorithm is called matrix palette skinning, because the set of bone transformations (stored as transform matrices) form a palette for the skin vertex to choose from.

Benefits And Drawbacks

Strengths

- Bone represent set of vertices (or some other objects, which represent for example a leg).
    - Animator controls fewer characteristics of the model

- ▪ Animator can focus on the large scale motion.
  - o Bones are independently movable.

An animation can be defined by simple movements of the bones, instead of vertex by vertex (in the case of a polygonal mesh).

Weaknesses

- • Bone represents set of vertices (or some other object).
  - o Does not provide realistic muscle movement and skin motion
  - o Possible solutions to this problem:
    - ▪ Special muscle controllers attached to the bones
    - ▪ Consultation with physiology experts (increase accuracy of musculoskeletal realism with more thorough virtual anatomy simulations)

Applications

Skeletal animation is the standard way to animate characters or mechanical objects for a prolonged period of time (usually over 100 frames). It is commonly used by video game artists and in the movie industry, and can also be applied to mechanical objects and any other object made up of rigid elements and joints.

Performance capture (or motion capture) can speed up development time of skeletal animation, as well as increasing the level of realism.

For motion that is too dangerous for performance capture, there are computer simulations that automatically calculate physics of motion and resistance with skeletal frames. Virtual anatomy properties such as weight of limbs, muscle reaction, bone strength and joint constraints may be added for realistic bouncing, buckling, fracture and tumbling effects known as virtual stunts. However, there are other applications of virtual anatomy simulations such as military and emergency response. Virtual soldiers, rescue workers, patients, passengers and pedestrians can be used for training, virtual engineering and virtual testing of equipment. Virtual anatomy technology may be combined with artificial intelligence for further enhancement of animation and simulation technology.

Animation Database

A dancer's movements, captured via optical motion capture can be stored in an *animation database*, then analyzed and reused.

An animation database is a database which stores fragments of animations or human movements and which can be accessed, analyzed and queried to develop and assemble new animations. Given that the manual generation of a large amount of animation can be time consuming and expensive, an animation database can assist users in building animations by using existing components, and sharing animation fragments.

Early examples of animation databases include the system MOVE which used an object oriented database. Modern animation databases can be populated via the extraction of skeletal animations from motion capture data.

Other examples include crowd simulation in which a number of people are simulated as a crowd. Given that in some applications the people need to be walking at different speeds, say on a sidewalk, the animation database can be used to retrieve and merge different animated figures. The method is mainly known as "motion graphs".

Animation databases can also be used for "interactive storytelling" in which fragments of animations are retrieved from the animation database and are *recycled* to combine into new stories. For instance, the animation database called *Animebase* is used within the system *Words Anime* to help generate animations using recycled components. In this approach, the user may input words which form parts of a story and queries against the database help select suitable animation fragments. This type of system may indeed use two databases: an animation database, as well as a story knowledge database. The story knowledge database may use subjects, predicates and objects to refer to story fragments. The system then assists the user in matching between story fragments and animation fragments.

Animation databases can also be used for the generation of visual scenes using humanoid models. An example application has been the development of an animated humanoid-based sign language system to help the disabled.

Another application of an animation database is in the synthesis of *idle motion* for human characters. Human beings move all the time and in unique ways, and the presentation of a consistent and realistic set of idle motions for each character between different animation segments has been a challenge, e.g. each person has a unique way of standing and this needs to be represented in a realistic way throughout an animation. One of the problems is that idle motion affects all joints and simply showing statistical movements at each joint results in less than realistic portrayals. One approach to solving this problem is to use an animation database with a large set of pre-recorded human movements, and obtain the suitable patterns of motion from the database through statistical analysis.

References

- S. Kuroki, "Walkthrough using Animation database MOVE" in Database and expert systems applications, Volume 4 edited by Vladimír Marík, 1994 ISBN 3-540-57234-1.

- O'Keefe, Matt (November 11, 2014). "6 Major Innovations That Sprung from the Heads of Disney Imagineers". Theme Park Tourist. Retrieved 9 March 2016.

- Kenyon, Heather (February 1, 1998). "How'd They Do That?: Stop-Motion Secrets Revealed". Animation World Network. Retrieved 2 March 2016.

- Carbone, Ken (February 24, 2010). "Stone-Age Animation in a Digital World: William Kentridge at MoMA". Fast Company. Retrieved 7 March 2016.

- Amidi, Amid (2 December 2011). "NY Film Critics Didn't like a Single Animated Film This Year". Cartoon Brew. Retrieved 19 February 2016.

- Herman, Barbara (2013-10-30). "The 10 Scariest Movies and Why They Creep Us Out". Newsweek. Retrieved 2015-06-08.

- Neumaier, Joe (November 5, 2009). "Blah, humbug! 'A Christmas Carol's 3-D spin on Dickens well done in parts but lacks spirit". New York Daily News. Retrieved October 10, 2015.

- Williams, Mary Elizabeth (November 5, 2009). "Disney's 'A Christmas Carol': Bah, humbug!". Salon.com. Archived from the original on January 11, 2010. Retrieved October 10, 2015.

- Wloszczyna, Susan (November 26, 2013). "With Frozen, Director Jennifer Lee Breaks the Ice for Women Directors". Indiewire. Retrieved 8 January 2014.

- McDuling, John (3 July 2014). "Hollywood Is Giving Up on Comedy". The Atlantic. The Atlantic Monthly Group. Retrieved 20 July 2014.

- Watercutter, Angela (May 24, 2012). "35 Years After Star Wars, Effects Whiz Phil Tippett Is Slowly Crafting a Mad God". Wired. Retrieved 2016-02-06.

Various Computer Graphics Software

Amira is a software used for 3D and 4D management and visualization. The other software used for computer graphics are Amira, iClone, Indigo Renderer and CityEngine. This chapter helps the reader in understanding the various computer graphics software.

Amira (Software)

Amira (pronounce: Ah-meer-ah) is a software platform for 3D and 4D data visualization, processing, and analysis. It is being actively developed by Visualization Sciences Group, Bordeaux, France and the Zuse Institute Berlin (ZIB), Germany.

Overview

Amira is an extendable software system for scientific visualization, data analysis, and presentation of 3D and 4D data. Amira is being developed and commercially distributed by FEI in cooperation with the Zuse Institute Berlin (ZIB). It is used by several thousand researchers and engineers in academia and industry around the world. Amira's flexible user interface and its modular architecture make it a universal tool for processing and analysis of data from various modalities; e.g. micro-CT, PET, Ultrasound. Its ever expanding functionality has made it a versatile data analysis and visualization solution, applicable to and being used in many fields, such as microscopy in biology and materials science, molecular biology, quantum physics, astrophysics, computational fluid dynamics (CFD), finite element modeling (FEM), non-destructive testing (NDT), and many more. One of the key features, besides data visualization, is Amira's set of tools for image segmentation and geometry reconstruction. This allows the user to mark (or segment) structures and regions of interest in 3D image volumes using automatic, semi-automatic, and manual tools. The segmentation can then be used for a variety of subsequent tasks, such as volumetric analysis, density analysis, shape analysis, or the generation of 3D computer models for visualization, numerical simulations, or rapid prototyping or 3D printing, to name a few. Other key Amira features are multi-planar and volume visualization, image registration, filament tracing, cell separation and analysis, tetrahedral mesh generation, fiber-tracking from diffusion tensor imaging (DTI) data, skeletonization, spatial graph analysis, and stereoscopic rendering of 3D data over multiple displays including CAVEs (Cave automatic virtual environments).

As a commercial product Amira requires the purchase of a license or an academic subscription. A time-limited, but full-featured evaluation version is available for download free of charge.

History

1994–1998 Research Software

Amira's roots go back to 1994 and the Department for Scientific Visualization, headed by Hans-Christian Hege at the Zuse Institute Berlin (ZIB). The ZIB is a research institute for mathematics and informatics. The Scientific Visualization department's mission is to help solve computationally and scientifically challenging tasks in medicine, biology, and engineering. For this purpose, it develops algorithms and software for 2D, 3D, and 4D data visualization and visually supported exploration and analysis. At that time, the young visualization group at the ZIB had experience with the extendable, data flow-oriented visualization environments apE, IRIS Explorer, and Advanced Visualization Studio (AVS), but was not satisfied with these products' interactivity, flexibility, and ease-of-use for non-computer scientists.

Therefore, in a subproject within a medically oriented, multi-disciplinary collaborative research center the development of a new software system was started in early 1994. The initial development was performed by Detlev Stalling, who later became the chief software architect. The software system was called "HyperPlan", highlighting its initial target application – a planning system for hyperthermia cancer treatment. The system was being developed on Silicon Graphics (SGI) computers, which at the time were the standard workstations used for high-end graphics computing. Software development was based on libraries such as OpenGL, SGI Open Inventor, and the graphical user interface libraries X11, Motif (software), and ViewKit. In 1998, X11/Motif/Viewkit were replaced by the Qt toolkit.

The HyperPlan framework served as the base for more and more projects at the ZIB and was used by a growing number of researchers in collaborating institutions. The projects included applications in neurobiology, confocal microscopy, flow visualization, molecule visualization and analysis and computational astrophysics.

1998–today Commercially Supported Product

The growing number of users of the system started to exceed the capacities that ZIB could spare for software distribution and support, as ZIB's primary mission was algorithmic research. Therefore, the spin-off company Indeed, – Visual Concepts GmbH was founded by Hans-Christian Hege, Detlev Stalling, and Malte Westerhoff with the vision of making the extensive capabilities of the software available to researchers in industry and academia worldwide and to provide the product support and robustness needed in today's fast-paced and competitive world.

In Feb 1998 the HyperPlan software was given the new, less application-specific name "Amira". This name is not an acronym but was chosen for being pronounceable in different languages, starting with an 'A', and having an appropriate connotation: the Latin verb "admirare" (to admire), meaning "to look at" and "to wonder at", describes a typical situation in data visualization.

A major re-design of the software was undertaken by Detlev Stalling and Malte Westerhoff in order to make it a commercially supportable product and to make it available on non-SGI computers as well. In March 1999, the first version of the commercial Amira was shown at the CeBIT tradeshow in Hannover, Germany on SGI IRIX and Hewlett-Packard UniX (HP-UX). Versions for Linux and Microsoft Windows followed within the following twelve months. Later Mac OS X support was added. Indeed, – Visual Concepts selected the Bordeaux, France and San Diego, United States based company TGS, Inc. as the worldwide distributor for Amira and completed five major releases (up to version 3.1) in the subsequent four years.

In 2003 both Indeed, as well as TGS were acquired by Massachusetts-based Mercury Computer Systems, Inc. (NASDAQ:MRCY) and became part of Mercury's newly formed life sciences business unit, later branded Visage Imaging. In 2009, Mercury Computer Systems, Inc. spun off Visage Imaging again and sold it to Melbourne, Australia based Promedicus Ltd (ASX:PME), a leading provider of radiology information systems and medical IT solutions. During this time, Amira continued to be developed in Berlin, Germany and in close collaboration with the ZIB, still headed by the original creators of Amira. TGS, located in Bordeaux, France was sold by Mercury Computer systems to a French investor and renamed to Visualization Sciences Group (VSG). VSG continued the work on a complementary product named Avizo, based on the same source code but customized for material sciences.

In August 2012, FEI, to that date the largest OEM reseller of Amira, purchased VSG and the Amira business from Promedicus. In August 2013, Visualization Sciences Group (VSG) became a business unit of FEI. Amira and Avizo are still being marketed as two different products; Amira for life sciences and Avizo for materials science, but the development efforts are now joined once again. As in the beginning, the Amira roadmap continues to be driven by the interesting and challenging scientific questions that Amira users around the world are trying to answer, often at the leading edge in their fields.

Amira Options

Microscopy Option

- Specific readers for microscopy data

- Image deconvolution

- Exploration of 3D imagery obtained from virtually any microscope

- Extraction and editing of filament networks from microscopy images

DICOM Reader

- Import of clinical and preclinical data in DICOM format

Mesh Option

- Generation of 3D finite element (FE) meshes from segmented image data

- Support for many state-of-the-art FE solver formats

- High-quality visualization of simulation mesh-based results, using scalar, vector, and tensor field display modules

Skeletonization Option

- Reconstruction and analysis of neural and vascular networks

- Visualization of skeletonized networks

- Length and diameter quantification of network segments

- Ordering of segments in a tree graph

- Skeletonization of very large image stacks

Molecular Option

- Advanced tools for the visualization of molecule models

- Hardware-accelerated volume rendering

- Powerful molecule editor

- Specific tools for complex molecular visualization

Developer Option

- Creation of new custom components for visualizing or data processing

- Implementation of new file readers or writers

- C++ programming language

- Development wizard for getting started quickly

Neuro Option

- Medical image analysis for DTI and brain perfusion
- Fiber tracking supporting several stream-line based algorithms
- Fiber separation into fiber bundles based on user defined source and destination regions
- Computation of tensor fields, diffusion weighted maps
- Eigenvalue decomposition of tensor fields
- Computation of mean transit time, cerebral blood flow, and cerebral blood volume

VR Option

- Visualization of data on large tiled displays or in immersive Virtual Reality (VR) environments
- Support of 3D navigation devices
- Fast multi-threaded and distributed rendering

Very Large Data Option

- Support for visualization of image data exceeding the available main memory, using efficient out-of-core data management
- Extensions of many standard modules, such as orthogonal and oblique slicing, volume rendering, and isosurface rendering, to work on out-of-core data

Editors

- CameraPath Editor: create a camera path using key-frames for animations and movies
- Color Dialog: define a color value using a graphical interface
- 2 Colormap Editors: modify the RGBA values of a discrete colormap
- Curve Editor: create and edit curves
- Demo Manager: manage and control demos using a graphical interface
- Digital Image Filters: apply standard image processing filters
- Filament Editor: skeletonize image data and modify spatial graphs
- Grid Editor: edit and simplify tetrahedral grids

- Image Crop Editor: crop 3D images, change bounding box, and voxel size

- Landmark Editor: add, move, or delete markers in a landmark set

- LineSet Editor: select, create, modify, and delete polylines

- Multi-planar Viewer: view up to two data sets simultaneously in a 3+1 MPR viewer

- Parameter Editor: add, change, or delete attributes of a data object

- Plot Tool: display 2D plots

- Segmentation Editor: 3D image segmentation using interactive and semi-automatic tools

- Surface Simplification Editor: reduce the number of triangles of a triangulated surface

- Surface Editor: modify triangles, remove intersections, assign boundary ids in triangulated surfaces

- Transform Editor: translate, rotate, or scale any 3D data object

Application Areas

- Anatomy
- Biochemistry
- Biophysics
- Cellular microbiology
- Computational fluid dynamics
- Cryo-electron tomography
- Diffusion MR^I/Fiber Tracking
- Embryology
- Endocrinology
- Finite Element Modelling
- Histology
- Medical imaging research
- Microscopy in life and material sciences
- Molecular biology

- Neuroscience

- Orthopedics

- Otolaryngology

- Preclinical imaging

- Urology

Processing and Data Analysis

- Surface and grid generation

- 3D image segmentation

- Image registration and slice alignment

- Skeletonization and deconvolution

- Multitude of quantification tools

- Arithmetic operations

- MATLAB integration

- 2D and 3D image filtering

- Surface generation

- Finite element model (FEM) grid generation

- Interactive and automatic segmentation

- Interactive and automatic slice alignment

- Image registration and morphing

- Tensor computation

- Skeletonization and tracing of neural and vascular networks

- Deconvolution and z-drop correction

- Powerful scripting interface

- Dedicated editors for segmentation, tracing, and fusion

Visualization

- Orthogonal and oblique slicing

- Volume rendering
- Surface rendering
- Isolines and isosurfaces
- Multi-channel imaging and fusion
- Vector and tensor visualization
- Support of structured / unstructured grids
- Molecular simulation and visualization
- Structured workflow visualization
- Active and passive stereo support
- Tiled screen support
- Virtual reality navigation and tools

Presentation

- Easy-to-use interactive 3D navigation
- Tools for designing animated demos
- Automation of complex animations and demonstrations
- Embedded tools for movie generation
- Active and passive 3D stereo vision
- 2D and 3D annotation
- Support for stereoscopic and auto-stereoscopic displays
- Virtual reality navigation tools
    - Single and tiled screen display
    - Single or multi-pipe rendering
    - Support for "trackd" input devices
- Geometry data
- Scalar fields and all types of multidimensional images
- Vector and flow data

- Tensor fields

- Molecular models

- Simulation data on finite element models

Supported File Formats

File Formats		
Format Name	**Access Type**	**Description**
Amira Script	read/write	Amira Tcl script
Amira Script Object	read/write	Amira custom module written in Tcl
AmiraMesh Format	read/write	Amira's native general purpose format
AmiraMesh as LargeDiskData	read/write	access image data blockwise
Analyze 7.5	read/write	3D image data with separate header file
AnalyzeAVW	read/write	contains 2D and 3D medical image data
BMP Image Format	read/write	uncompressed Windows bitmap format
AutoCAD DXF	read/write	Drawing Interchange Format for AutoCAD 3D models
Encapsulated PostScript	write	for 2D raster images only
HTML	read	Hypertext document format
Hoc	read/write	Hoc file reader of morphometric models for NEURON environment
HxSurface	read/write	Amira's native format for triangular surfaces
Icol	read/write	ASCII format for colormaps with alpha channel
Interfile	read	Interfile file reader
JPEG Image Format	read/write	2D image format with lossy compression
MATLAB Binary Format (.mat)	read/write	MATLAB matrices
MATLAB M-files Format (.m)	read/write	MATLAB script
Nifti	read/write	Nifti file reader
Open Inventor	read/write	standard file format for 3D models
PNG Image Format	read/write	portable network graphics format for 2D images
PNM Image Format	read/write	simple uncompressed 2D image format
PSI format	read/write	ASCII format for 3D points and associated data values
PLY Format	read/write	Stanford triangle format for points and surfaces
Raw Data	read/write	binary data as a 3D uniform field
Raw Data as LargeDiskData	read/write	access image data blockwise
SGI-RGB Image Format	read/write	2D image format with run-length encoding

STL	read/write	simple format for triangular surfaces, no connectivity
SWC	read/write	interchange-file reader of morphometric models for neuroscience
Stacked-Slices	read	info file grouping together 2D images
TIFF Image Format	read/write	standard format for 2D and 3D image data
Tecplot	read	Tecplot ASCII and Binary file reader
VRML	read/write	virtual reality markup language for 3D models
Vevo Mode Raw Images	read	2D and 3D ultrasound images from VisualSonics' Vevo 770
Wavefront Technologies 3D Geometry (.obj)	write	3D geometries such as surfaces
AMBER	read	Assisted Model Building with Energy Refinement format
AMF	read/write	Amira Molecule Format
DX	read	APBS DX electrostatic field file
GROMACS	read/write	Groningen Machine for Chemical Simulations format
MAP	read	Autogrid interaction field file
MDL	read/write	MDL file format saving chemical structures
PDB	read/write	protein data base file format
PHI	read	Congen PHI Electrostatic field file (r)
PSF/DCD (CHARMM)	read	file format used by CHARMM
Tripos	read/write	file format used to save Tripos Sybyl mol2 molecules
UniChem	read/write	file format used by the UniChem molecular software
ZIB Molecular File Format	read/write	structured molecular file format
Amira Virtual Reality Option Config File	read	Amira Virtual Reality Option Config File (.cfg)
LDA	read	VolumeViz native file format
LargeDiskData	read/write	access image data blockwise
Stacked-Slices as LargeDiskData	read	access image data blockwise
AVS Field	read/write	stores data defined on regular grid
AVS UCD Format	read/write	stores unstructured cell data
Abaqus format	write	describes FEM grids and density data
FIDAP NEUTRAL	read	stores FEM meshes and solution data
Fluent / UNS	read/write	contains FEM meshes, boundary ids, solution data
HyperMesh	read/write	used by Altair HyperWorks FEM software
I-DEAS universal format	read/write	describes FEM grids and simulation data
Plot 3D Single Structured	read/write	stores curvilinear grids and associated data
Bio-Rad Confocal Format	read	simple uncompressed format for 3D image stacks

FEIStackedScalarField3	read	scalar fields consisting of parallel slices (MRC format)
FEIUniformScalarField3	read	scalar fields defined on a uniform lattice (MRC format)
Leica 3D TIFF	read	contains 3D image data with voxel sizes
Leica Binary Format (.lei)	read	3D image stacks, time series, and meta information
Leica Image Format (.lif)	read	3D image stacks, time series, and meta information
Leica Slice Series (.info)	read	contains list of 2D TIFF files and meta information
MRC	read/write	MRC file format for electron microscopy
Metamorph STK Format	read	special TIFF variant for 3D image stacks
Olympus (.oib/.oif)	read	file formats used by the Olympus FluoView 1000F
Zeiss LSM	read	3D raster image format
ACR-NEMA	read	predecessor of the DICOM format for medical images
DICOM export	write	medical image export
DICOM import	read	standard file format for medical images

Release History

Amira versions		
Version	**Release Date**	**Supported Platforms**
public BETA	Dec 1998	SGI Irix 6.x
public BETA	Mar 1999	SGI Irix 6.x HP-UX 10.20 32-bit Linux: Red Hat 5.2, SuSE 6.0 (Linux: software rendering only)
2.0.0	Oct 1999	SGI Irix 6.5.x HP-UX 10.20 32-bit Linux: Red Hat 6.0, SuSE 6.1
2.1.0	Mar 2000	Microsoft Windows 9x/NT4 32-bit Linux: Red Hat 6.x, SuSE 6.3 SGI Irix 6.5.x HP-UX 10.20 Sun Solaris 7 (SunOS 5.7)
2.1.1	May 2000	Microsoft Windows 9x/NT4 32-bit Linux: Red Hat 6.x, SuSE 6.3 SGI Irix 6.5.x HP-UX 10.20 Sun Solaris 7 (SunOS 5.7)
2.2.0	Sep 2000	Microsoft Windows 9x/NT4/2000 32-bit Linux: Red Hat 6.2, SuSE 6.3 SGI Irix 6.5.x HP-UX 10.20 Sun Solaris 7 (SunOS 5.7)

2.3.0	Aug 2001	Microsoft Windows 9x/ME/NT4/2000, 32-bit Linux: Red Hat 7.x, SuSE 7.x SGI Irix 6.5.x HP-UX 11.0 Sun Solaris 7 (SunOS 5.7)
3.0.0	Jul 2002	Microsoft Windows 98/ME/NT4/2000/XP, 32-bit Linux: Red Hat 8.0 SGI Irix 6.5.x Sun Solaris 8 HP-UX 11.0
3.1.0	Dec 2003	Microsoft Windows 98/ME/NT4/2000/XP, 32-bit Linux IA64 (Red Hat AW 2.1), 64-bit Linux Red Hat 8.0 (<=glibc-2.3.2), 32-bit Linux SUSE 9.0 (x86-64), 64-bit Sun Solaris 8/9, 32/64-bit SGI Irix 6.5.x, 32/64-bit HP-UX 11.0, 32/64-bit
3.1.1	Jun 2004	Microsoft Windows 98/ME/NT4/2000/XP, 32-bit Linux IA64 (Red Hat AW 2.1), 64-bit Linux Red Hat 8.0 (<=glibc-2.3.2), 32-bit Linux SUSE 9.0 (x86-64), 64-bit Sun Solaris 8/9, 32/64-bit SGI Irix 6.5.x, 32/64-bit HP-UX 11.0, 32/64-bit
4.0.0	Dec 2005	Microsoft Windows XP 2003 (x86-64), 64-bit Microsoft Windows 2000/XP, 32-bit Linux IA64 (RHEL 3.0, Itanium 2), 64-bit Linux x86-64 (RHEL 3.0), 64-bit Linux x86 (RHEL 3.0), 32-bit Mac OS X 10.4(Tiger), 32-bit Sun Solaris 8, 32/64-bit SGI Irix 6.5.x, 32/64-bit HP-UX 11.0, 32/64-bit
4.1.0	May 2006	Microsoft Windows XP 2003 (x86-64), 64-bit Microsoft Windows 2000/XP, 32-bit Linux IA64 (RHEL 3.0, Itanium 2), 64-bit Linux x86-64 (RHEL 3.0), 64-bit Linux x86 (RHEL 3.0), 32-bit Sun Solaris 8, 32/64-bit SGI Irix 6.5.x, 32/64-bit HP-UX 11.0, 32/64-bit
4.1.1	Oct 2006	Microsoft Windows XP 2003 (x86-64), 64-bit Microsoft Windows 2000/XP, 32-bit Linux IA64 (RHEL 3.0, Itanium 2), 64-bit Linux x86-64 (RHEL 3.0), 64-bit Linux x86 (RHEL 3.0), 32-bit Mac OS X 10.4 (Tiger), 32-bit Sun Solaris 8, 32/64-bit SGI Irix 6.5.x, 32/64-bit HP-UX 11.0, 32/64-bit

4.1.2	Feb 2007	Microsoft Windows XP 2003 (x86-64), 64-bit Microsoft Windows 2000/XP, 32-bit Linux IA64 (RHEL 3.0, Itanium 2), 64-bit Linux x86-64 (RHEL 3.0), 64-bit Linux x86 (RHEL 3.0), 32-bit Mac OS X 10.4 (Tiger), 32-bit Sun Solaris 8, 32/64-bit SGI Irix 6.5.x, 32/64-bit HP-UX 11.0, 32/64-bit
5.0.0	May 2008	Microsoft Windows 2000/XP/Vista (x86-64), 64-bit Microsoft Windows 2000/XP/Vista, 32-bit
5.0.1	Jun 2008	Microsoft Windows 2000/XP/Vista (x86-64), 64-bit Microsoft Windows 2000/XP/Vista, 32-bit
5.2.0	Nov 2008	Microsoft Windows 2000/XP/Vista (x86-64), 64-bit Microsoft Windows 2000/XP/Vista, 32-bit Mac OS X 10.5 (Leopard), 32-bit Linux x86-64 (RHEL 5.2), 64-bit
5.2.1	Mar 2009	Microsoft Windows 2000/XP/Vista (x86-64), 64-bit Microsoft Windows 2000/XP/Vista, 32-bit Mac OS X 10.5 (Leopard), 32-bit Linux x86-64 (RHEL 5.2), 64-bit
5.2.2	Jul 2009	Microsoft Windows 2000/XP/Vista (x86-64), 64-bit Microsoft Windows 2000/XP/Vista, 32-bit Mac OS X 10.5 (Leopard), 32-bit Linux x86-64 (RHEL 5.2), 64-bit
5.3.0	Jun 2010	Microsoft Windows 2000/XP/Vista (x86-64), 64-bit Microsoft Windows 2000/XP/Vista, 32-bit Mac OS X 10.5 (Leopard), 32-bit Mac OS X 10.6 (Snow Leopard), 32-bit Linux x86-64 (RHEL 5.5), 64-bit
5.3.1	Jul 2010	Microsoft Windows 2000/XP/Vista (x86-64), 64-bit Microsoft Windows 2000/XP/Vista, 32-bit Mac OS X 10.5 (Leopard), 32-bit Mac OS X 10.6 (Snow Leopard), 32-bit Linux x86-64 (RHEL 5.5), 64-bit
5.3.2	Oct 2010	Microsoft Windows 2000/XP/Vista (x86-64), 64-bit Microsoft Windows 2000/XP/Vista, 32-bit Mac OS X 10.5 (Leopard), 32-bit Mac OS X 10.6 (Snow Leopard), 32-bit Linux x86-64 (RHEL 5.5), 64-bit
5.3.3	Dec 2010	Microsoft Windows 2000/XP/Vista (x86-64), 64-bit Microsoft Windows 2000/XP/Vista, 32-bit Mac OS X 10.5 (Leopard), 32-bit Mac OS X 10.6 (Snow Leopard), 32-bit Linux x86-64 (RHEL 5.5), 64-bit

5.4.0	Oct 2011	Microsoft Windows XP/Vista/7 (x86-64), 64-bit Microsoft Windows XP/Vista/7, 32-bit Mac OS X 10.5 (Leopard), 32-bit Mac OS X 10.6 (Snow Leopard), 32-bit Mac OS X 10.7 (Lion), 32-bit Linux x86-64 (RHEL 5.5), 64-bit
5.4.1	Dec 2011	Microsoft Windows XP/Vista/7 (x86-64), 64-bit Microsoft Windows XP/Vista/7, 32-bit Mac OS X 10.5 (Leopard), 32-bit Mac OS X 10.6 (Snow Leopard), 32-bit Mac OS X 10.7 (Lion), 32-bit Linux x86-64 (RHEL 5.5), 64-bit
5.4.2	Mar 2012	Microsoft Windows XP/Vista/7 (x86-64), 64-bit Microsoft Windows XP/Vista/7, 32-bit Mac OS X 10.5 (Leopard), 32-bit Mac OS X 10.6 (Snow Leopard), 32-bit Mac OS X 10.7 (Lion), 32-bit Linux x86-64 (RHEL 5.5), 64-bit
5.4.3	Oct 2012	Microsoft Windows XP/Vista/7 (x86-64), 64-bit Microsoft Windows XP/Vista/7, 32-bit Mac OS X 10.5 (Leopard), 32-bit Mac OS X 10.6 (Snow Leopard), 32-bit Mac OS X 10.7 (Lion), 32-bit Linux x86-64 (RHEL 5.5), 64-bit
5.4.4	Mar 2013	Microsoft Windows XP/Vista/7 (x86-64), 64-bit Microsoft Windows XP/Vista/7, 32-bit Mac OS X 10.5 (Leopard), 32-bit Mac OS X 10.6 (Snow Leopard), 32-bit Mac OS X 10.7 (Lion), 32-bit Linux x86-64 (RHEL 5.5), 64-bit
5.4.5	Mar 2013	Microsoft Windows XP/Vista/7 (x86-64), 64-bit Microsoft Windows XP/Vista/7, 32-bit Mac OS X 10.5 (Leopard), 32-bit Mac OS X 10.6 (Snow Leopard), 32-bit Mac OS X 10.7 (Lion), 32-bit Linux x86-64 (RHEL 5.5), 64-bit
5.5.0	Oct 2013	Microsoft Windows XP/Vista/7 (x86-64), 64-bit Microsoft Windows XP/Vista/7, 32-bit Mac OS X 10.7 (Lion), 64-bit Mac OS X 10.8 (Mountain Lion), 64-bit Linux x86-64 (RHEL 5.5), 64-bit
5.6.0	Apr 2014	Microsoft Windows XP/Vista/7/8 (x86-64), 64-bit Microsoft Windows XP/Vista/7/8, 32-bit Mac OS X 10.7/10.8 (Lion), 64-bit Mac OS X 10.8 (Mountain Lion), 64-bit Linux x86-64 (RHEL 5.5), 64-bit

6.0	Jan 2015	Microsoft Windows 7/8 (x86-64), 64-bit Microsoft Windows 7/8, 32-bit Mac OS X 10.7 (Lion), 64-bit Mac OS X 10.8 (Mountain Lion), 64-bit Mac OS X 10.9 (Mavericks), 64-bit Linux x86-64 (RHEL 6), 64-bit
6.0.1	Jul 2015	Microsoft Windows 7/8 (x86-64), 64-bit Microsoft Windows 7/8, 32-bit Mac OS X 10.7 (Lion), 64-bit Mac OS X 10.8 (Mountain Lion), 64-bit Mac OS X 10.9 (Mavericks), 64-bit Linux x86-64 (RHEL 6), 64-bit
6.1.1	May 2016	Microsoft Windows 7/8/10 (x86-64), 64-bit Microsoft Windows 7/8/10, 32-bit Mac OS X 10.7 (Lion), 64-bit Mac OS X 10.8 (Mountain Lion), 64-bit Mac OS X 10.9 (Mavericks), 64-bit Linux x86-64 (RHEL 6), 64-bit

iClone

iClone is a real-time 3D animation and rendering software program that enables users to make 3D animated films. Real-time playback is enabled by using a 3D videogame engine for instant on-screen rendering.

Other functionality includes: full facial and skeletal animation of human and animal figures; lip-syncing; import of standard 3D file types including FBX; a timeline for editing and merging motions; a scripting language (Lua) for character interaction; application of standard motion-capture files; the ability to control an animated scene in the same manner as playing a videogame; and the import of models from Google 3D Warehouse, among many other features. iClone is also notable for offering users royalty-free usage of all content that they create with the software, even when using Reallusion's own assets library.

iClone is developed and marketed by Reallusion.

History

Reallusion launched iClone v1.0 in December, 2005 as a tool to create 3D animation and render animated videos. It supported real-time 3D animation and creation of avatars from photographs. Reallusion's facial mapping and lip-synch animation technology derived from the 2001 release of CrazyTalk 2D animation software. The face mapping tools and real-time 3D animation environment made iClone popular with the community of Machinima, which is a video game based filmmaking technique that transformed gamers into filmmakers by capturing live video action from within video games and virtual worlds, like Quake and Second Life. The ability of gamers to sell or broadcast their films was challenged by game makers. iClone v1.0 was adopted by many Machinima filmmakers and was showcased the 1005 Machinima Film Festival held at the Museum of the Moving Image in Queens, New York. Reallusion's Vice President John C Martin II presented the Machinima Festival attendees with a demo of iClone and news that Reallusion would provide a full commercial license for all movies produced with v1.0 and beyond as a counter-strike to game development companies' policy. Machinima Festival 2005 wiki

iClone v2.0 was released in March 2007 with an emphasis on new G2 character styles and the introduction of Clone Cloth, for creating custom clothing for actors through editing materials and applying them to pre-designed 3D avatar models; it became one of the first ways iClone users could create and sell their own content for iClone. V2.0 also brought particle effects, fog and HD video output.

iClone v3.0 was launched in August 2008, adding a revised UI featuring scene manager for organizing projects and enabling the viewport for live direct object picking and interaction. G3 characters enhanced Clone Cloth options and made character faces more refined with facial Normal Maps. The Editor Mode and Director Mode were introduced to enable a scene editing mode and a live real-time director control mode where users could pilot characters and vehicles with videogame-like keyboard controls W,A,S,D. Animation created in Director Mode built a series of live motion data on the iClone timeline and was able to be tweaked in Editor Mode. Multi cameras were added in iClone v3.0 with camera switcher for filming scenes in multiple real-time angles. Character animation was made possible with motion editing for inverse and forward kinematics. Material editing became possible from within iClone so enhancing any prop or actor was capable by exporting and editing material textures and reapplying them to iClone. The stage was enhanced with Terrain, Sky, Water and the first appearance of SpeedTree natural tree and foliage designer. Multiple shader modes in Preview, Wireframe and Pixel shading became options for users to balance the screen output with their machine performance. The Certified Content creators program opened allowing iClone users to upload and market their custom content to a Reallusion hosted portal for content sales.

iClone v4.0 – October 2009 – Drag and drop manipulation and a gizmo for transforming objects within the 3D viewport was added in iClone v4.0. Importing any image or video as a 3D object for real-time playback enabled direct compositing of real-time 3D and video in iClone. Videos were able to be imported as alpha transparent with iClone's PopVideo companion. Visual effects in iClone were further enhanced with the introduction of real-time HDR (High Dynamic Range) and IBL (Image based lighting). Characters were enhanced with G4 options for enhanced character body styles, improved body mesh and ability to import Poser and Second Life generated texture maps. Jimmy-toon G4 character was introduced as a customizable cartoon bodystyle avatar for iClone. iClone 4.2 released in May 2010 added Stereo 3D support for rendering images and video in anaglyph, side by side and top down formats.

iClone 5.0 and 5.5 released over 2011 and 2012 adding functions for motion capture, Human IK and a pipeline for importing and exporting FBX characters and
props for use in game engines and other 3D production tools. Reallusion put emphasis on cross-compatibility with Unity, UDK, Autodesk 3D Studio Max, Maya,
Z-brush, Allegorithmic, DAZ and Poser. The iClone Animation Pipeline became a
trio of products: iClone PRO, 3DXchange for import, export and rigging, and the
Mocap Device Plugin enabling real-time motion capture with the Microsoft Kinect
for Windows and OpenNI sensor supported devices. The addition of HumanIK from
Autodesk gave natural human motion to iClone and provided animation editing enhancement to generate better motions, foot & hand locking and reach targets for
prop interaction. Animation generated with 5.0 and 5.5 could be exported for use
external programs. Video game developers benefited from the iClone Animation
Pipeline as a way to prepare custom actors for games with face and body animation
ready to import into game projects. The iClone Animation Pipeline opened a portal
for artists to access the Reallusion marketplace to acquire models, characters and
motions for use in games and 3D development.

iClone 6.0 released in December 2014, offered a large amount of visual and performance improvements like improved soft cloth physics simulation, object-oriented
constraints, a new lighting system with the possibility for infinite lights instead of the
previous 8 light system, light props, support for Allegorithmic's procedurally generated
materials, and ultra realistic rendering with iClone's Indigo plug-in allowing users to
raytrace their projects in Indigo RT for photo realistic results. This new iClone iteration was designed to allow for easy, future plug-in compatibility with other programs
and applications. iClone 6.0 came updated for DirectX 11 bringing with it tessellation
effects to add real-time geometric details to models, real-time surface smoothing to
improve the appearance of objects and characters with more details and higher quality.
Later iClone 6.02 was offered in a DirectX 9 version for legacy users that could not immediately upgrade to DirectX 11.

Applications

Besides being used as a 3D moviemaking tool, iClone is also a platform for video game
development and previsualization allowing users to import and export content such
as characters, props and animation data with external 3D tools like Unity, Autodesk
Maya, 3ds Max, Blender, ZBrush, Poser and many others through popular industry file
formats like FBX, OBJ and BVH.

Other applications include using iClone as a 3D simulator for education, industry and
business since iClone's real-time capabilities allow for direct "WASD" controls through
keyboards or other input devices.

Motion capture, known as Mocap, is another iClone application allowing users to connect any infrared depth camera, or Microsoft Kinect sensor via a USB port in order to live capture body motions in real-time. These motions can then be exported by using iClone's 3DXchange Pipeline software using FBX and BVH.

Since its 6.5 update, iClone allows for quick 360-Video output, allowing users to turn animation projects into 360 panorama videos. Another update is the Alembic export capability, an interchange point cache format used by visual effects and animation professionals, that allows iClone animation detail export to other game engines, or 3D tools.

Features

- Production – Preset Layouts for Directing, In-screen Editing, Drag-n-Drop Creation, Play-to-Create Controls, Animation Path & Transition.

- Actor – Character Base & Templates, Custom 3D Head from Photo, Facial & Body Deformation, Custom Clothing Design.

- Animation – MixMoves Motion Graph System, Motion Capture with Depth Cam, Face and Body Puppeteering, Face and Body Motion Key Editing, Audio Lipsyncing, Character Embedded Performances.

- Prop – Interactive Props with iScript, Soft and Rigid Body Physics Animation, FLEX & Spring simulation, Multi-channel Material Textures, Animated UV Props, Prop Puppet.

- Stage – Modular Scene Construction, Flexible environment System (Atmosphere, HDR, IBL), Ambient Occlusion, Toon Shader, Fog.

- Camera – Camera Gizmo & Camera Studio (PIP), Animatable Lenses, Link-to & Look-at, Lighting Systems, Depth of Field, Shadow.

- Video Effects – Real-time Particle FX, Material FX, Media Compositing, Post FX.

- Render & Output – Real-time Render, Image Sequence for Post Editing, Popular Image & Video Format Output, 3D Stereo Output.

Content

Users can purchase content from the Reallusion Content Store for iClone, CrazyTalk, CrazyTalk Animator, FaceFilter and 3DXChange. The store also hosts content packs from third-party developers such as DAZ 3D, 3D Total Materials, 3D Universe, Dexsoft, Quantum Theory Ent. and others. The Reallusion Marketplace provides a trading platform for independent content developers.

Indigo Renderer

A photorealistic image rendered with Indigo.

A render demonstrating Indigo's realistic light simulation

Indigo Renderer is a 3D rendering software that uses unbiased rendering technologies to create photo-realistic images. In doing so, Indigo uses equations that simulate the behaviour of light, with no approximations or guesses taken. By accurately simulating all the interactions of light, Indigo is capable of producing effects such as:

- Depth of field, as when a camera is focused on one object and the background is blurred

- Spectral effects, as when a beam of light goes through a prism and a rainbow of colours is produced

- Refraction, as when light enters a pool of water and the objects in the pool seem to be "bent"

- Reflections, from subtle reflections on a polished concrete floor to the pure reflection of a silvered mirror

- Caustics, as in light that has been focused through a magnifying glass and has made a pattern of brightness on a surface

Indigo uses methods such as Metropolis light transport (MLT), spectral light calculus, and virtual camera model. Scene data is stored in XML or IGS format.

Indigo features Monte-Carlo path tracing, bidirectional path tracing and MLT on top of bidirectional path tracing, distributed render capabilities, and progressive rendering (image gradually becomes less noisy as rendering progresses). Indigo also supports subsurface scattering and has its own image format (.igi).

Indigo was originally released as freeware until the 2.0 release, when it became a commercial product.

CityEngine

Esri CityEngine is a three-dimensional (3D) modeling software application developed by Esri R&D Center Zurich (formerly Procedural Inc.) and is specialized in the generation of 3D urban environments. With the procedural modeling approach, CityEngine supports the creation of detailed large-scale 3D city models. CityEngine works with architectural object placement and arrangement in the same manner that VUE manages terrain, ecosystems and atmosphere mapping.

History and Releases

Current

Procedural Inc. was acquired by Esri in the summer of 2011 ()

Early

CityEngine was developed at ETH Zurich by the original author Pascal Mueller, co-founder and CEO of Procedural Inc. During his PhD research at ETH Computer Vision Lab, Mueller invented a number of techniques for procedural modeling of 3D architectural content which make up the foundation of CityEngine. In the 2001 Siggraph publication CityEngine was presented for the first time outside of the research community. Several more research papers have featured CityEngine since then.

In 2008, the first commercial version of CityEngine was released by the Swiss company Procedural Inc and is used by professionals in urban planning, architecture, visualization, game development, entertainment, GIS, archeology and cultural heritage.

Releases

Date	Version
July 21, 2008	CityEngine 2008
Nov 20, 2008	CityEngine 2008.2
Dec 17, 2008	CityEngine 2008.3
May 19, 2009	CityEngine 2009
Sept 15, 2009	CityEngine 2009.2
Dec 10, 2009	CityEngine 2009.3
June 23, 2010	CityEngine 2010
Oct 12, 2010	CityEngine 2010.2
Dec 9, 2010	CityEngine 2010.3
Oct 26, 2011	Esri CityEngine 2011.1
Feb 23, 2012	Esri CityEngine 2011.2
Oct 3, 2012	Esri CityEngine 2012.1
Nov 13, 2013	Esri CityEngine 2013.1
June 1, 2014	Esri CityEngine 2014
Sept 15, 2014	Esri CityEngine 2014.1
----,----	Esri CityEngine 2015.0
----,----	Esri CityEngine 2015.1
----,----	Esri CityEngine 2015.2

Features

GIS/CAD Data Support: Support for industry-standard formats such as Esri Shapefile, File Geodatabase and OpenStreetMap which allow to import/export any geo-spatial/vector data.

Rule-based Modeling Core: Procedural modeling based on CGA rules allows to control mass, geometry assets, proportions, or texturing of buildings or streets on a city-wide scale.

Parametric Modeling Interface: An interface to interactively control specific street or building parameters, such as the height or age (defined by the CGA rules)

Dynamic City Layouts: Interactive design, editing and modification of urban layouts consisting of (curved) streets, blocks and parcels.

Map-Controlled City Modeling: Global control of buildings and street parameters through image maps (for example the building heights or the landuse-mix).

Street Networks Patterns: Street grow tools to design and construct urban layouts.

Facade Wizard: Rule creator and visual facade authoring tool.

Industry-Standard 3D Formats: CityEngine supports Collada, Autodesk FBX, 3DS, Wavefront OBJ, RenderMan RIB, mental ray MI and e-on software's Vue.

Reporting (BIM for Cities): Rule-based reports to analyze urban design, e.g. automatically calculate quantities such as GFA, FAR, etc.

Python: Integrated Python scripting interface.

Available for All Platforms: Available for Windows (64bit only), Mac OS X (64bit), and Linux (32/64bit).

Procedural Modeling

CityEngine uses a procedural modeling approach to automatically generate models through a predefined rule set. The rules are defined through a CGA shape grammar system enabling the creation of complex parametric models. Users can change or add the shape grammar as much as needed providing room for new designs.

Modeling an urban environment within CityEngine can start out with creating a street network either with the street drawing tool or with data imported from open-streetmap.org or from Esri data formats such as Shapefiles or File Geodatabase. The next step is to subdivide all the lots as many times as specified resulting in a map of lots and streets. By selecting all or some of the lots CityEngine can be instructed to start generating the buildings. Due to the procedural modeling technology, all buildings can be made to vary from one another to achieve an urban aesthetic. At this point the city model can be re-designed and adjusted by changing parameters or the shape grammar itself.

Geodesign

Discussions on geodesign often mention the use of Esri CityEngine, although it is not an analytical tool like GIS. It fits in with the geodesign narrative of aiding quicker iterative design.

Publications

- ACM Siggraph 2001: Procedural Modeling of Cities - Yoav Parish and Pascal Mueller

- ACM Siggraph 2006: Procedural Modeling of Buildings - Pascal Mueller, Peter Wonka, Simon Haegler, Andreas Ulmer and Luc Van Gool

- ACM Siggraph 2007: Image-based Procedural Modeling of Facades - Pascal Mueller, Gang Zeng, Peter Wonka and Luc Van Gool

- ACM Siggraph 2008: Interactive Procedural Street Modeling - Guoning Chen, Gregory Esch, Peter Wonka, Pascal Mueller and Eugene Zhang

- Eurographics 2009: Interactive Geometric Simulation of 4D Cities - Basil Weber, Pascal Mueller, Peter Wonka and Markus Gross

- Eurographics Symposium VAST 2006: Procedural 3D Reconstruction of Puuc Buildings in Xkipché - Pascal Mueller, Tijl Vereenooghe, Peter Wonka, Iken Paap and Luc Van Gool

- Eurographics Symposium VAST 2007: Populating Ancient Pompeii with Crowds of Virtual Romans - Jonathan Maïm, Simon Haegler, Barbara Yersin, Pascal Mueller, Daniel Thalmann and Luc Van Gool

See Also

- Procedural modeling

- Shape grammar

Graphic Art Software

Graphic art software is a subclass of application software used for graphic design, multimedia development, stylized image development, technical illustration, general image editing, or simply to access graphic files. Art software uses either raster or vector graphic reading and editing methods to create, edit, and view art.

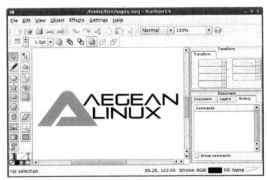

A screenshot of Karbon14 vector graphic software running on an AegeanLinux desktop.

Many artists and other creative professionals today use personal computers rather than traditional media. Using graphic art software may be more efficient than rendering using traditional media by requiring less hand–eye coordination, requiring less mental imaging skill, and utilizing the computer's quicker (sometimes more accurate) automated rendering functions to create images. However, advanced level computer styles, effects and editing methods may require a steeper learning curve of computer technical skills than what was required to learn traditional hand rendering and mental imaging skills. The potential of the software to enhance or hinder creativity may depend on the intuitiveness of the interface.

A screenshot of the GIMP 2.2.8 raster graphic software.

Specialized Software

Most art software includes common functions, creation tools, editing tools, filters, and automated rendering modes. Many, however, are designed to enhance a specialized skill or technique. Specialized software packages may be discontinued for various reasons such as lack of appreciation for the result, lack of expertise and training for the product, or simply not worth the time and money investment, but most likely due to obsolescence compared to newer methods or integration as a feature of newer more complete software packages.

Multimedia Development Software

Multimedia development professionals favor software with audio, motion and interactivity such as software for creating and editing hypermedia, electronic presentations (more specifically slide presentations), computer simulations and games.

Stylized Image Development Software

Image development professionals may use general graphic editors or may prefer more specialized software for rending or capturing images with style. Although images can be created from scratch with most art software, specialized software applications or advanced features of generalized applications are used for more accurate visual effects. These visual effects include:

Traditional Medium Effects

Vector editors are ideal for solid crisp lines seen in line art, poster, woodcut ink effects, and mosaic effects.

Some generalized image editors, such as Photoshop are used for digital painting (representing real brush and canvas textures such as watercolor or burlap canvas) or handicraft textures such as mosaic or stained glass. However, unlike Photoshop, which was originally designed for photo editing, software such as Corel Painter and Photo-Paint were originally designed for rendering with digital painting effects and continue to evolve with more emphasis on hand-rendering styles that don't appear computer generated.

Photorealistic Effects

Unlike traditional medium effects, photorealistic effects create the illusion of a photographed image. Specialized software may contain 3D modeling and ray tracing features to make images appear photographed. Some 3D software is for general 3D object modeling, whereas other 3D software is more specialized, such as Poser for characters or Bryce for scenery. Software such as Photoshop may be used to create 3D effects from 2D (flat) images instead of 3D models. AddDepth is a discontinued software for extruding 2D shapes into 3D images with the option of beveled effects. MetaCreations Detailer and Painter 3D are discontinued software applications specifically for painting texture maps on 3D Models.

Hyperrealistic Effects

Specialized software may be used to combine traditional medium effects and photorealistic effects. 3-D modeling software may be exclusively for, include features for, or include the option of 3rd party plugins for rendering 3-D models with 2-D effects (e.g. cartoons, illustrations) for hyperrealistic effects. Other 2-D image editing software may be used to trace photographs or rotoscope animations from film. This allows artists to rapidly apply unique styles to what would be purely photorealistic images from computer generated imagery from 3-D models or photographs. Some styles of hyperrealism may require motion visual effects (e.g. geometrically accurate rotation, accurate kinetics, simulated organic growth, lifelike motion constraints) to notice the realism of the imagery. Software may be used to bridge the gap between the imagination and the laws of physics.

Technical Graphic Software

Technical professionals and technical illustrators may use technical graphic software that might allow for stylized effects with more emphasis on clarity and accuracy and little or no emphasis on creative expression and aesthetics. For this reason, the results are seldom referred to as "art." For designing or technical illustration of synthetic physical objects, the software is usually referred to as CAD or CADD, Computer-Aided Design and Drafting. This software allows for more precise handling of measurements and mathematical calculations, some of which simulate physics to conduct virtual testing of the models. Aside from physical objects, technical graphic software may include software for visualizing concepts, manually representing scientific data, visualizing algorithms, visual instructions, and navigational aids in the form of information graphics. Specialized software for concept maps may be used for both technical purposes and non-technical conceptualizing, which may or may not be considered technical illustration.

Specialized Graphic Format Handling

This may include software for handling specialized graphic file formats such as Fontographer software, which is dedicated to creating and editing computer fonts. Some general image editing software has unique image file handling features as well. Vector graphic editors handle vector graphic files and are able to load PostScript files natively. Some tools enable professional photographers to use nondestructive image processing for editing digital photography without permanently changing or duplicating the original, using the Raw image format. Other special handling software includes software for capturing images such as 2D scanning software, 3D scanning software and screen-capturing, or software for specialized graphic format processing such as raster image processing and file format conversion. Some tools may reduce the file size of graphics for web performance optimization while maintaining the image quality as best as possible.

Lists of Software

- List of raster graphics editors
- List of vector graphics editors
- List of computer-aided design editors
- List of information graphics software
- List of concept- and mind-mapping software
- 3D computer graphics software (description and list)
- Presentation software (description and list)
- Desktop publishing (description and list)
- List of media players (viewing access only)
- Comparison of media players

References

- "DFG Project: Algorithmen zur Planung und Kontrolle von Hyperthermiebehandlungen". DFG Deutsche Forschungsgemeinschaft. Retrieved 28 January 2015.
- Ricky Grove (15 October 2009). "Reallusion's iClone4 Pro: Building on Quality". Renderosity reviews. Retrieved 12 May 2010.
- Chris White (22 February 2010). "Machinima made easy: iClone 4 reviewed". Icrontic. Retrieved 1 May 2010.

Applications of Computer Graphics

The applications of computer graphics discussed in the section are special effect, ambient occlusion, web design, texture mapping, molecular graphics, drug design etc. Special effects are the visual tricks used in movies or video games whereas web designing deals with the production of websites. The topics elaborated in the section will help in gaining a better perspective about the applications of computer graphics.

Special Effect

Special effects (often abbreviated as SFX, SPFX, or simply FX) are illusions or visual tricks used in the film, television, theatre, video game, and simulator industries to simulate the imagined events in a story or virtual world.

Bluescreens are commonly used in chroma key special effects.

Special effects are traditionally divided into the categories of optical effects and mechanical effects. With the emergence of digital filmmaking a distinction between special effects and visual effects has grown, with the latter referring to digital post-production while "special effects" referring to mechanical and optical effects.

Mechanical effects (also called practical or physical effects) are usually accomplished during the live-action shooting. This includes the use of mechanized props, scenery, scale models, animatronics, pyrotechnics and atmospheric effects: creating physical wind, rain, fog, snow, clouds, etc. Making a car appear to drive by itself and blowing up a building are examples of mechanical effects. Mechanical effects are often incorporated into set design and makeup. For example, a set may be built with break-away doors or walls to enhance a fight scene, or prosthetic makeup can be used to make an actor look like a non-human creature.

Optical effects (also called photographic effects) are techniques in which images or film frames are created photographically, either "in-camera" using multiple exposure, mattes, or the Schüfftan process, or in post-production using an optical printer. An optical effect might be used to place actors or sets against a different background.

A methane bubble bursting

Since the 1990s, computer generated imagery (CGI) has come to the forefront of special effects technologies. It gives filmmakers greater control, and allows many effects to be accomplished more safely and convincingly and—as technology improves—at lower costs. As a result, many optical and mechanical effects techniques have been superseded by CGI.

Developmental History

Early Development

In 1857, Oscar Rejlander created the world's first "trick photograph" by combining different sections of 30 negatives into a single image. In 1895, Alfred Clark created what is commonly accepted as the first-ever motion picture special effect. While filming a reenactment of the beheading of Mary, Queen of Scots, Clark instructed an actor to step up to the block in Mary's costume. As the executioner brought the axe above his head, Clark stopped the camera, had all of the actors freeze, and had the person playing Mary step off the set. He placed a Mary dummy in the actor's place, restarted filming, and allowed the executioner to bring the axe down, severing the dummy's head. Techniques like these would dominate the production of special effects for a century.

It wasn't only the first use of trickery in cinema, it was also the first type of photographic trickery only possible in a motion picture, i.e. the "stop trick". Georges Méliès accidentally discovered the same "stop trick." According to Méliès, his camera jammed while filming a street scene in Paris. When he screened the film, he found that the "stop trick" had caused a truck to turn into a hearse, pedestrians to change direction, and men to turn into women. Méliès, the stage manager at the Theatre Robert-Houdin, was inspired to develop a series of more than 500 short films, between 1914, in the process developing or inventing such techniques as multiple exposures, time-lapse photography, dissolves, and hand painted colour. Because of his ability to seemingly manipulate and transform reality with the cinematograph, the prolific Méliès is sometimes referred to as the "Cinemagician." His most famous film, *Le Voyage dans la lune* (1902), a whimsical parody of Jules Verne's *From the Earth to the Moon*, featured a combination of live action and animation, and also incorporated extensive miniature and matte painting work.

From 1910 to 1920, the main innovations in special effects were the improvements on the matte shot by Norman Dawn. With the original matte shot, pieces of cardboard were placed to block the exposure of the film, which would be exposed later. Dawn combined this technique with the "glass shot." Rather than using cardboard to block certain areas of the film exposure, Dawn simply painted certain areas black to prevent any light from exposing the film. From the partially exposed film, a single frame is then projected onto an easel, where the matte is then drawn. By creating the matte from an image directly from the film, it became incredibly easy to paint an image with proper respect to scale and perspective (the main flaw of the glass shot). Dawn's technique became the textbook for matte shots due to the natural images it created.

During the 1920s and 30s, special effects techniques were improved and refined by the motion picture industry. Many techniques—such as the Schüfftan process—were modifications of illusions from the theater (such as pepper's ghost) and still photography (such as double exposure and matte compositing). Rear projection was a refinement of the use of painted backgrounds in the theater, substituting moving pictures to create moving backgrounds. Lifecasting of faces was imported from traditional maskmaking. Along with makeup advances, fantastic masks could be created which fit the actor perfectly. As material science advanced, horror film maskmaking followed closely.

Several techniques soon developed, such as the "stop trick", wholly original to motion pictures. Animation, creating the illusion of motion, was accomplished with drawings (most notably by Winsor McCay in *Gertie the Dinosaur*) and with three-dimensional models (most notably by Willis O'Brien in *The Lost World* and *King Kong*). Many studios established in-house "special effects" departments, which were responsible for nearly all optical and mechanical aspects of motion-picture trickery.

Also, the challenge of simulating spectacle in motion encouraged the development of the use of miniatures. Naval battles could be depicted with models in studio. Tanks and airplanes could be flown (and crashed) without risk of life and limb. Most impressively, miniatures and matte paintings could be used to depict worlds that never existed. Fritz Lang's film *Metropolis* was an early special effects spectacular, with innovative use of miniatures, matte paintings, the Schüfftan process, and complex compositing.

An important innovation in special-effects photography was the development of the optical printer. Essentially, an optical printer is a projector aiming into a camera lens, and it was developed to make copies of films for distribution. Until Linwood G. Dunn refined the design and use of the optical printer, effects shots were accomplished as in-camera effects. Dunn demonstrating that it could be used to combine images in novel ways and create new illusions. One early showcase for Dunn was Orson Welles' *Citizen Kane*, where such locations as Xanadu (and some of Gregg Toland's famous 'deep focus' shots) were essentially created by Dunn's optical printer.

Color Era

The development of color photography required greater refinement of effects techniques. Color enabled the development of such *travelling matte* techniques as bluescreen and the sodium vapour process. Many films became landmarks in special-effects accomplishments: *Forbidden Planet* used matte paintings, animation, and miniature work to create spectacular alien environments. In *The Ten Commandments*, Paramount's John P. Fulton, A.S.C., multiplied the crowds of extras in the Exodus scenes with careful compositing, depicted the massive constructions of Rameses with models, and split the Red Sea in a still-impressive combination of travelling mattes and water tanks. Ray Harryhausen extended the art of stop-motion animation with his special techniques of compositing to create spectacular fantasy adventures such as Jason and the Argonauts (whose climax, a sword battle with seven animated skeletons, is considered a landmark in special effects).

The Science Fiction Boom

Through the 1950s and 60s numerous new special effects were developed which would dramatically increase the level of realism achievable in science fiction films.

If one film could be said to have established a new high-bench mark for special effects, it would be 1968's *2001: A Space Odyssey*, directed by Stanley Kubrick, who assembled his own effects team (Douglas Trumbull, Tom Howard, Con Pedersen and Wally Veevers) rather than use an in-house effects unit. In this film, the spaceship miniatures were highly detailed and carefully photographed for a realistic depth of field. The shots of spaceships were combined through hand-drawn rotoscoping and careful motion-control work, ensuring that the elements were precisely combined in the camera – a surprising throwback to the silent era, but with spectacular results. Backgrounds of the African vistas in the "Dawn of Man" sequence were combined with soundstage photography via the then-new front projection technique. Scenes set in zero-gravity environments were staged with hidden wires, mirror shots, and large-scale rotating sets. The finale, a voyage through hallucinogenic scenery, was created by Douglas Trumbull using a new technique termed slit-scan.

The 1970s provided two profound changes in the special effects trade. The first was economic: during the industry's recession in the late 1960s and early 1970s, many studios closed down their in-house effects houses. Many technicians became freelancers or founded their own effects companies, sometimes specializing on particular techniques (opticals, animation, etc.).

The second was precipitated by the blockbuster success of two science fiction and fantasy films in 1977. George Lucas's *Star Wars* ushered in an era of science-fiction films with expensive and impressive special-effects. Effects supervisor John Dykstra, A.S.C. and crew developed many improvements in existing effects technology. They developed a computer-controlled camera rig called the "Dykstraflex" that allowed precise repeatability of camera motion, greatly facilitating travelling-matte compositing. Degradation of film images during compositing was minimized by other innovations: the Dykstraflex used VistaVision cameras that photographed widescreen images horizontally along stock, using far more of the film per frame, and thinner-emulsion filmstocks were used in the compositing process. The effects crew assembled by Lucas and Dykstra was dubbed Industrial Light & Magic, and since 1977 has spearheaded most effects innovations.

That same year, Steven Spielberg's film *Close Encounters of the Third Kind* boasted a finale with impressive special effects by *2001* veteran Douglas Trumbull. In addition to developing his own motion-control system, Trumbull also developed techniques for creating intentional "lens flare" (the shapes created by light reflecting in camera lenses) to provide the film's undefinable shapes of flying saucers.

The success of these films, and others since, has prompted massive studio investment in effects-heavy science-fiction films. This has fueled the establishment of many independent effects houses, a tremendous degree of refinement of existing techniques, and the development of new techniques such as CGI. It has also encouraged within the industry a greater distinction between special effects and visual effects; the latter is used to characterize post-production and optical work, while *special effects* refers more often to on-set and mechanical effects.

Introduction of Computer Generated Imagery (CGI)

A recent and profound innovation in special effects has been the development of computer generated imagery, or CGI which has changed nearly every aspect of motion picture special effects. Digital compositing allows far more control and creative freedom than optical compositing, and does not degrade the image like analog (optical) processes. Digital imagery has enabled technicians to create detailed models, matte "paintings," and even fully realized characters with the malleability of computer software.

Arguably the biggest and most "spectacular" use of CGI is in the creation of photo-realistic images of science-fiction and fantasy characters, settings, and objects. Images can be created in a computer using the techniques of animated cartoons and model animation. In 1993, stop-motion animators working on the realistic dinosaurs of Steven Spielberg's *Jurassic Park* were retrained in the use of computer input devices.

By 1995, films such as *Toy Story* underscored that the distinction between live-action films and animated films was no longer clear. Other landmark examples include a character made up of broken pieces of a stained-glass window in *Young Sherlock Holmes*, a shapeshifting character in *Willow*, a tentacle of water in *The Abyss*, the T-1000 Terminator in *Terminator 2: Judgment Day*, hordes of armies of robots and fantastic creatures in the *Star Wars prequel trilogy* and *The Lord of the Rings* trilogy and the planet Pandora in *Avatar*.

Planning and Use

Although most special effects work is completed during post-production, it must be carefully planned and choreographed in pre-production and production. A visual effects supervisor is usually involved with the production from an early stage to work closely with the Director and all related personnel to achieve the desired effects.

Live Special Effects

Live special effects are effects that are used in front of a live audience, mostly during sporting events, concerts and corporate shows. Types of effects that are commonly used include: flying effects, laser lighting, Theatrical smoke and fog, CO_2 effects, pyrotechnics, confetti and other atmospheric effects such as bubbles and snow.

Spinning fiery steel wool at night

Visual Special Effects Techniques

- Bullet time
- Computer-generated imagery (often using Shaders)
- Digital compositing
- Dolly zoom
- In-camera effects

- Match moving
- Matte (filmmaking) and Matte painting
- Miniature effects
- Morphing
- Motion control photography
- Optical effects
- Optical printing
- Practical effects
- Prosthetic makeup effects
- Rotoscoping
- Stop motion
- Go motion
- Schüfftan process
- Travelling matte
- Virtual cinematography
- Wire removal

Notable Special Effects Companies

- *Adobe Systems Incorporated* (San Jose, CA)
- *Animal Logic* (Sydney, AU and Venice, CA)
- *Bird Studios* (London UK)
- *BUF Compagnie* (Paris, FR)
- *CA Scanline* (München, DE)
- *Cinesite* (London/Hollywood)
- *Creature Effects, Inc.* (LA, CA, US)
- *Digital Domain* (Venice, LA, CA, US)
- *Double Negative (VFX)* (London, UK)
- *DreamWorks* (LA, CA, US)
- *Flash Film Works* (LA, CA, US)

- *Framestore* (London, UK)
- *Giantsteps* (Venice, CA)
- *Hydraulx* (Santa Monica, LA, US)
- *Image Engine* (Vancouver, BC, CA)
- *Industrial Light & Magic*, founded by George Lucas
- *Intelligent Creatures* (Toronto, ON, CA)
- *Intrigue FX* (Canada)
- *Legacy Effects*, (Los Angeles, CA)
- *Look Effects*, (Culver City, CA, USA)
- *M5 Industries* (San Francisco i.e. Mythbusters)
- *Mac Guff* (LA, CA, US; Paris, FR)
- *Machine Shop* (London, UK)
- *Makuta VFX* (Universal City, CA) (Hyderabad, India)
- *Matte World Digital* (Novato, CA)
- *The Mill* (London, UK; NY and LA, US)
- *Modus FX* (Montreal, QC, CA)
- *Moving Picture Company* (Soho, London, UK)
- *Pixomondo* (Frankfurt, DE; Munich, DE; Stuttgart, DE; Los Angeles, CA, USA; Beijing, CH; Toronto, ON, CA; Baton Rouge, LA, USA)
- *Rhythm and Hues Studios* (LA, CA, US)
- *Rising Sun Pictures* (Adelaide, AU)
- *Snowmasters* (Lexington, AL, USA)
- *Sony Pictures Imageworks* (Culver City, CA, USA)
- *Strictly FX*, live special effects company
- *Surreal World* (Melbourne, AU)
- *Super FX*, Special Effects Company, ITALY
- *Tippett Studio* (Berkeley, CA, US)
- *Tsuburaya Productions* (Hachimanyama, Setagaya, Tokyo, Jap)
- *Vision Crew Unlimited*

- *Weta Digital*
- *Zoic Studios* (Culver City, CA, USA)
- *ZFX Inc* a flying effects company
- *Method Studios*

Ambient Occlusion

In computer graphics, ambient occlusion is a shading and rendering technique used to calculate how exposed each point in a scene is to ambient lighting. The interior of a tube is typically more occluded (and hence darker) than the exposed outer surfaces, and the deeper you go inside the tube, the more occluded (and darker) the lighting becomes. Ambient occlusion can be seen as an accessibility value that is calculated for each surface point. In scenes with open sky this is done by estimating the amount of visible sky for each point, while in indoor environments only objects within a certain radius are taken into account and the walls are assumed to be the origin of the ambient light. The result is a diffuse, non-directional shading effect that casts no clear shadows but that darkens enclosed and sheltered areas and can affect the rendered image's overall tone. It is often used as a post-processing effect.

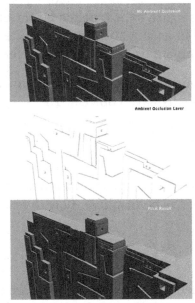

The ambient occlusion map (middle image) for this scene darkens only the innermost angles of corners.

Unlike local methods such as Phong shading, ambient occlusion is a global method, meaning that the illumination at each point is a function of other geometry in the scene.

However, it is a very crude approximation to full global illumination. The appearance achieved by ambient occlusion alone is similar to the way an object might appear on an overcast day.

Implementation

In real-time applications, such as computer games, Screen space ambient occlusion can be used as a faster approximation of true ambient occlusion, using pixel depth rather than scene geometry to form an ambient occlusion map. However, newer technologies are making true ambient occlusion feasible even in real-time.

3D animation of ambient occlusion

Ambient occlusion is related to accessibility shading, which determines appearance based on how easy it is for a surface to be touched by various elements (e.g., dirt, light, etc.). It has been popularized in production animation due to its relative simplicity and efficiency. In the industry, ambient occlusion is often referred to as "sky light".

The ambient occlusion shading model has the nice property of offering a better perception of the 3D shape of the displayed objects. This was shown in a paper where the authors report the results of perceptual experiments showing that depth discrimination under diffuse uniform sky lighting is superior to that predicted by a direct lighting model.

The occlusion $A_{\bar{p}}$ at a point $\bar{p}$ on a surface with normal $\hat{}$ can be computed by integrating the visibility function over the hemisphere Ω with respect to projected solid angle:

$$A_{\bar{p}} = \frac{1}{\pi} \int_{\Omega} V_{\bar{p},\hat{\omega}} (\hat{n} \cdot \hat{\omega}) \mathrm{d}\omega$$

where $V_{\bar{p},\hat{\omega}}$ is the visibility function at $\bar{p}$, defined to be zero if $\bar{p}$ is occluded in the direction $\hat{\omega}$ and one otherwise, and $\mathrm{d}\omega$ is the infinitesimal solid angle step of the integration variable $\hat{\omega}$. A variety of techniques are used to approximate this integral in practice: perhaps the most straightforward way is to use the Monte Carlo method by casting rays from the point $\bar{p}$ and testing for intersection with other scene geometry (i.e., ray casting). Another approach (more suited to hardware acceleration) is to render the view from $\overline{p}$ by rasterizing black geometry against a white background and taking the (cosine-weighted) average of rasterized fragments. This approach is an example of a "gathering" or "inside-out" approach, whereas other algorithms (such as depth-map ambient occlusion) employ "scattering" or "outside-in" techniques.

In addition to the ambient occlusion value, a "bent normal" vector $\hat{n}_b$ is often generated, which points in the average direction of unoccluded samples. The bent normal can be used to look up incident radiance from an environment map to approximate image-based lighting. However, there are some situations in which the direction of the bent normal is a misrepresentation of the dominant direction of illumination, e.g.,

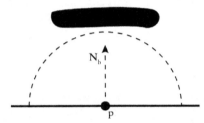

In this example the bent normal N_b has an unfortunate direction, since it is pointing at an occluded surface.

In this example, light may reach the point p only from the left or right sides, but the bent normal points to the average of those two sources, which is, unfortunately, directly toward the obstruction.

Variants

- SSAO-Screen space ambient occlusion

- SSDO-Screen space directional occlusion

- HDAO-High Definition Ambient Occlusion

- HBAO+-Horizon Based Ambient Occlusion+

- AAO-Alchemy Ambient Occlusion

- ABAO-Angle Based Ambient Occlusion

- PBAO

- VXAO-Voxel Accelerated Ambient Occlusion

Recognition

In 2010, Hayden Landis, Ken McGaugh and Hilmar Koch were awarded a Scientific and Technical Academy Award for their work on ambient occlusion rendering.

Web Design

Web design encompasses many different skills and disciplines in the production and maintenance of websites. The different areas of web design include web graphic design; interface design; authoring, including standardised code and proprietary software; user experience design; and search engine optimization. Often many individuals will work in teams covering different aspects of the design process, although some designers will cover them all. The term web design is normally used to describe the design process relating to the front-end (client side) design of a website including writing mark up. Web design partially overlaps web engineering in the broader scope of web development. Web designers are expected to have an awareness of usability and if their role involves creating mark up then they are also expected to be up to date with web accessibility guidelines.

History

Web design books in a store

1988—2001

Although web design has a fairly recent history, it can be linked to other areas such as graphic design. However web design can also be seen from a technological standpoint. It has become a large part of people's everyday lives. It is hard to imagine the Internet without animated graphics, different styles of typography, background and music.

The Start of the Web and Web Design

In 1989, whilst working at CERN Tim Berners-Lee proposed to create a global hypertext project, which later became known as the World Wide Web. During 1991 to 1993 the World Wide Web was born. Text-only pages could be viewed using a simple line-mode browser. In 1993 Marc Andreessen and Eric Bina, created the Mosaic browser. At the time there were multiple browsers, however the majority of them were Unix-based and naturally text heavy. There had been no integrated approach to graphic design elements such as images or sounds. The Mosaic browser broke this mould. The W3C was created in October 1994 to "lead the World Wide Web to its full potential by developing common protocols that promote its evolution and ensure its interoperability." This discouraged any one company from monopolizing a propriety browser and programming language, which could have altered the effect of the World Wide Web as a whole. The W3C continues to set standards, which can today be seen with JavaScript. In 1994 Andreessen formed Communications Corp. that later became known as Netscape Communications, the Netscape 0.9 browser. Netscape created its own HTML tags without regard to the traditional standards process. For example, Netscape 1.1 included tags for changing background colours and formatting text with tables on web pages. Throughout 1996 to 1999 the browser wars began, as Microsoft and Netscape fought for ultimate browser dominance. During this time there were many new technologies in the field, notably Cascading Style Sheets, JavaScript, and Dynamic HTML. On the whole, the browser competition did lead to many positive creations and helped web design evolve at a rapid pace.

Evolution of Web Design

In 1996, Microsoft released its first competitive browser, which was complete with its own features and tags. It was also the first browser to support style sheets, which at the time was seen as an obscure authoring technique. The HTML markup for tables was originally intended for displaying tabular data. However designers quickly realized the potential of using HTML tables for creating the complex, multi-column layouts that were otherwise not possible. At this time, as design and good aesthetics seemed to take precedence over good mark-up structure, and little attention was paid to semantics and web accessibility. HTML sites were limited in their design options, even more so with earlier versions of HTML. To create complex designs, many web designers had to use complicated table structures or even use blank spacer .GIF images to stop empty table cells from collapsing. CSS was introduced in December 1996 by the W3C to support presentation and layout. This allowed HTML code to be semantic rather than both semantic and presentational, and improved web accessibility, see tableless web design.

In 1996, Flash (originally known as FutureSplash) was developed. At the time, the Flash content development tool was relatively simple compared to now, using basic layout and drawing tools, a limited precursor to ActionScript, and a timeline, but it enabled web designers to go beyond the point of HTML, animated GIFs and JavaScript. However, because Flash required a plug-in, many web developers avoided using it for fear of limiting their market share due to lack of compatibility. Instead, designers reverted to gif animations (if they didn't forego using motion graphics altogether) and JavaScript for widgets. But the benefits of Flash made it popular enough among specific target markets to eventually work its way to the vast majority of browsers, and powerful enough to be used to develop entire sites.

End of the First Browser Wars

During 1998 Netscape released Netscape Communicator code under an open source licence, enabling thousands of developers to participate in improving the software. However, they decided to start from the beginning, which guided the development of the open source browser and soon expanded to a complete application platform. The Web Standards Project was formed and promoted browser compliance with HTML and CSS standards by creating Acid1, Acid2, and Acid3 tests. 2000 was a big year for Microsoft. Internet Explorer was released for Mac; this was significant as it was the first browser that fully supported HTML 4.01 and CSS 1, raising the bar in terms of standards compliance. It was also the first browser to fully support the PNG image format. During this time Netscape was sold to AOL and this was seen as Netscape's official loss to Microsoft in the browser wars.

2001—2012

Since the start of the 21st century the web has become more and more integrated into peoples lives. As this has happened the technology of the web has also moved on. There have also been significant changes in the way people use and access the web, and this has changed how sites are designed.

Since the end of the browsers wars new browsers have been released. Many of these are open source meaning that they tend to have faster development and are more supportive of new standards. The new options are considered by many to be better than Microsoft's Internet Explorer.

The W3C has released new standards for HTML (HTML5) and CSS (CSS3), as well as new JavaScript API's, each as a new but individual standard. While the term HTML5 is only used to refer to the new version of HTML and *some* of the JavaScript API's, it has become common to use it to refer to the entire suite of new standards (HTML5, CSS3 and JavaScript).

In 2016, the term "web brutalism" was applied to web design that emphasized simple presentation and fast page loading.

Tools and Technologies

Web designers use a variety of different tools depending on what part of the production process they are involved in. These tools are updated over time by newer standards and software but the principles behind them remain the same. Web designers use both vector and raster graphics editors to create web-formatted imagery or design prototypes. Technologies used to create websites include W3C standards like HTML and CSS, which can be hand-coded or generated by WYSIWYG editing software. Other tools web designers might use include mark up validators and other testing tools for usability and accessibility to ensure their web sites meet web accessibility guidelines.

Skills and Techniques

Marketing and Communication Design

Marketing and communication design on a website may identify what works for its target market. This can be an age group or particular strand of culture; thus the designer may understand the trends of its audience. Designers may also understand the type of website they are designing, meaning, for example, that (B2B) business-to-business website design considerations might differ greatly from a consumer targeted website such as a retail or entertainment website. Careful consideration might be made to ensure that the aesthetics or overall design of a site do not clash with the clarity and accuracy of the content or the ease of web navigation, especially on a B2B website. Designers may also consider the reputation of the owner or business the site is representing to make sure they are portrayed favourably.

User Experience Design and Interactive Design

User understanding of the content of a website often depends on user understanding of how the website works. This is part of the user experience design. User experience is related to layout, clear instructions and labeling on a website. How well a user understands how they can interact on a site may also depend on the interactive design of the site. If a user perceives the usefulness of the website, they are more likely to continue using it. Users who are skilled and well versed with website use may find a more distinctive, yet less intuitive or less user-friendly website interface useful nonetheless. However, users with less experience are less likely to see the advantages or usefulness of a less intuitive website interface. This drives the trend for a more universal user experience and ease of access to accommodate as many users as possible regardless of user skill. Much of the user experience design and interactive design are considered in the user interface design.

Advanced interactive functions may require plug-ins if not advanced coding language skills. Choosing whether or not to use interactivity that requires plug-ins is a critical decision in user experience design. If the plug-in doesn't come pre-installed with most browsers, there's a risk that the user will have neither the know how or the patience to install a plug-in just to access the content. If the function requires advanced coding language skills, it may be too costly in either time or money to code compared to the amount of enhancement the function will add to the user experience. There's also a risk that advanced interactivity may be incompatible with older browsers or hardware configurations. Publishing a function that doesn't work reliably is potentially worse for the user experience than making no attempt. It depends on the target audience if it's likely to be needed or worth any risks.

Page Layout

Part of the user interface design is affected by the quality of the page layout. For example, a designer may consider whether the site's page layout should remain consistent on different pages when designing the layout. Page pixel width may also be considered vital for aligning objects in the layout design. The most popular fixed-width websites generally have the same set width to match the current most popular browser window, at the current most popular screen resolution, on the current most popular monitor size. Most pages are also center-aligned for concerns of aesthetics on larger screens.

Fluid layouts increased in popularity around 2000 as an alternative to HTML-table-based layouts and grid-based design in both page layout design principle and in coding technique, but were very slow to be adopted. This was due to considerations of screen reading devices and varying windows sizes which designers have no control over. Accordingly, a design may be broken down into units (sidebars, content blocks, embedded advertising areas, navigation areas) that are sent to the browser and which will be fitted into the display window by the browser, as best it can. As the browser does recognize the details of the reader's screen (window size, font size relative to window etc.) the browser can make user-specific layout adjustments to fluid layouts, but not fixed-width layouts. Although such a display may often change the relative position of major content units, sidebars may be displaced below body text rather than to the side of it. This is a more flexible display than a hard-coded grid-based layout that doesn't fit the device window. In particular, the relative position of content blocks may change while leaving the content within the block unaffected. This also minimizes the user's need to horizontally scroll the page.

Responsive Web Design is a newer approach, based on CSS3, and a deeper level of per-device specification within the page's stylesheet through an enhanced use of the CSS @media rule.

Typography

Web designers may choose to limit the variety of website typefaces to only a few which are of a similar style, instead of using a wide range of typefaces or type styles. Most browsers recognize a specific number of safe fonts, which designers mainly use in order to avoid complications.

Font downloading was later included in the CSS3 fonts module and has since been implemented in Safari 3.1, Opera 10 and Mozilla Firefox 3.5. This has subsequently increased interest in web typography, as well as the usage of font downloading.

Most site layouts incorporate negative space to break the text up into paragraphs and also avoid center-aligned text.

Motion Graphics

The page layout and user interface may also be affected by the use of motion graphics. The choice of whether or not to use motion graphics may depend on the target market for the website. Motion graphics may be expected or at least better received with an entertainment-oriented website. However, a website target audience with a more serious or formal interest (such as business, community, or government) might find animations unnecessary and distracting if only for entertainment or decoration purposes. This doesn't mean that more serious content couldn't be enhanced with animated or video presentations that is relevant to the content. In either case, motion graphic design may make the difference between more effective visuals or distracting visuals.

Motion graphics that are not initiated by the site visitor can produce accessibility issues. The World Wide Web consortium accessibility standards require that site visitors be able to disable the animations.

Quality of Code

Website designers may consider it to be good practice to conform to standards. This is usually done via a description specifying what the element is doing. Failure to conform to standards may not make a website unusable or error prone, but standards can relate to the correct layout of pages for readability as well making sure coded elements are closed appropriately. This includes errors in code, more organized layout for code, and making sure IDs and classes are identified properly. Poorly-coded pages are sometimes colloquially called tag soup. Validating via W3C can only be done when a correct DOC-TYPE declaration is made, which is used to highlight errors in code. The system identifies the errors and areas that do not conform to web design standards. This information can then be corrected by the user.

Homepage Design

Usability experts, including Jakob Nielsen and Kyle Soucy, have often emphasised homepage design for website success and asserted that the homepage is the most important page on a website. However practitioners into the 2000s were starting to find that a growing number of website traffic was bypassing the homepage, going directly to internal content pages through search engines, e-newsletters and RSS feeds. Leading many practitioners to argue that homepages are less important than most people think. Jared Spool argued in 2007 that a site's homepage was actually the least important page on a website.

In 2012 and 2013, carousels (also called 'sliders' and 'rotating banners') have become an extremely popular design element on homepages, often used to showcase featured or recent content in a confined space. Many practitioners argue that carousels are an ineffective design element and hurt a website's search engine optimisation and usability.

Occupations

There are two primary jobs involved in creating a website: the web designer and web developer, who often work closely together on a website. The web designers are responsible for the visual aspect, which includes the layout, coloring and typography of a web page. Web designers will also have a working knowledge of markup languages such as HTML and CSS, although the extent of their knowledge will differ from one web designer to another. Particularly in smaller organizations one person will need the necessary skills for designing and programming the full web page, while larger organizations may have a web designer responsible for the visual aspect alone.

Further jobs which may become involved in the creation of a website include:

- Graphic designers to create visuals for the site such as logos, layouts and buttons

- Internet marketing specialists to help maintain web presence through strategic solutions on targeting viewers to the site, by using marketing and promotional techniques on the internet

- SEO writers to research and recommend the correct words to be incorporated into a particular website and make the website more accessible and found on numerous search engines

- Internet copywriter to create the written content of the page to appeal to the targeted viewers of the site

- User experience (UX) designer incorporates aspects of user focused design considerations which include information architecture, user centered design, user testing, interaction design, and occasionally visual design.

Computer-generated Imagery

Computer-generated imagery (CGI) is the application of computer graphics to create or contribute to images in art, printed media, video games, films, television programs, shorts, commercials, videos, and simulators. The visual scenes may be dynamic or static, and may be two-dimensional (2D), though the term "CGI" is most commonly used to refer to 3D computer graphics used for creating scenes or special effects in films and television. Additionally, the use of 2D CGI is often mistakenly referred to as "traditional animation", most often in the case when dedicated animation software such as Adobe Flash or Toon Boom is not used or the CGI is hand drawn using a tablet and mouse.

The term 'CGI animation' refers to dynamic CGI rendered as a movie. The term virtual world refers to agent-based, interactive environments. Computer graphics software is used to make computer-generated imagery for films, etc. Availability of CGI software and increased computer speeds have allowed individual artists and small companies to produce professional-grade films, games, and fine art from their home computers. This has brought about an Internet subculture with its own set of global celebrities, clichés, and technical vocabulary. The evolution of CGI led to the emergence of virtual cinematography in the 1990s where runs of the simulated camera are not constrained by the laws of physics.

Static Images and Landscapes

Not only do animated images form part of computer-generated imagery, natural look-ing landscapes (such as fractal landscapes) are also generated via computer algorithms. A simple way to generate fractal surfaces is to use an extension of the triangular mesh method, relying on the construction of some special case of a de Rham curve, e.g. mid-point displacement. For instance, the algorithm may start with a large triangle, then re-cursively zoom in by dividing it into four smaller Sierpinski triangles, then interpolate the height of each point from its nearest neighbors. The creation of a Brownian surface may be achieved not only by adding noise as new nodes are created, but by adding additional noise at multiple levels of the mesh. Thus a topographical map with varying levels of height can be created using relatively straightforward fractal algorithms. Some typical, easy-to-program fractals used in CGI are the *plasma fractal* and the more dra-matic *fault fractal*.

Fractal landscape

The large number of specific techniques have been researched and developed to pro-duce highly focused computer-generated effects — e.g. the use of specific models to represent the chemical weathering of stones to model erosion and produce an "aged appearance" for a given stone-based surface.

Architectural Scenes

Modern architects use services from computer graphic firms to create 3-dimension-al models for both customers and builders. These computer generated models can be more accurate than traditional drawings. Architectural animation (which provides an-imated movies of buildings, rather than interactive images) can also be used to see the possible relationship a building will have in relation to the environment and its surrounding buildings. The rendering of architectural spaces without the use of paper and pencil tools is now a widely accepted practice with a number of computer-assisted architectural design systems.

Architectural modelling tools allow an architect to visualize a space and perform "walk-throughs" in an interactive manner, thus providing "interactive environments" both at the urban and building levels. Specific applications in architecture not only include the specification of building structures (such as walls and windows) and walk-throughs, but the effects of light and how sunlight will affect a specific design at different times of the day.

A computer generated image featuring a house, made in Blender.

Architectural modelling tools have now become increasingly internet-based. However, the quality of internet-based systems still lags behind those of sophisticated inhouse modelling systems.

In some applications, computer-generated images are used to "reverse engineer" historical buildings. For instance, a computer-generated reconstruction of the monastery at Georgenthal in Germany was derived from the ruins of the monastery, yet provides the viewer with a "look and feel" of what the building would have looked like in its day.

Anatomical Models

Computer generated models used in skeletal animation are not always anatomically correct. However, organizations such as the Scientific Computing and Imaging Institute have developed anatomically correct computer-based models. Computer generated anatomical models can be used both for instructional and operational purposes. To date, a large body of artist produced medical images continue to be used by medical students, such as images by Frank Netter, e.g. Cardiac images. However, a number of online anatomical models are becoming available.

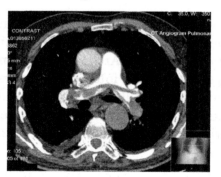

A CT pulmonary angiogram image generated by a computer from a collection of x-rays.

A single patient X-ray is not a computer generated image, even if digitized. However, in applications which involve CT scans a three dimensional model is automatically produced from a large number of single slice x-rays, producing "computer generated image". Applications involving magnetic resonance imaging also bring together a number of "snapshots" (in this case via magnetic pulses) to produce a composite, internal image.

In modern medical applications, patient specific models are constructed in 'computer assisted surgery'. For instance, in total knee replacement, the construction of a detailed patient specific model can be used to carefully plan the surgery. These three dimensional models are usually extracted from multiple CT scans of the appropriate parts of the patient's own anatomy. Such models can also be used for planning aortic valve implantations, one of the common procedures for treating heart disease. Given that the shape, diameter and position of the coronary openings can vary greatly from patient to patient, the extraction (from CT scans) of a model that closely resembles a patient's valve anatomy can be highly beneficial in planning the procedure.

Generating Cloth and Skin Images

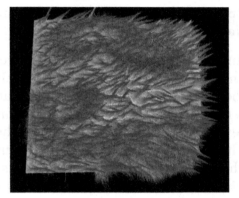

Computer-generated wet fur

Models of cloth generally fall into three groups:

- The geometric-mechanical structure at yarn crossing

- The mechanics of continuous elastic sheets

- The geometric macroscopic features of cloth.

To date, making the clothing of a digital character automatically fold in a natural way remains a challenge for many animators.

In addition to their use in film, advertising and other modes of public display, computer generated images of clothing are now routinely used by top fashion design firms.

The challenge in rendering human skin images involves three levels of realism:

- Photo realism in resembling real skin at the static level

- Physical realism in resembling its movements

- Function realism in resembling its response to actions.

The finest visible features such as fine wrinkles and skin pores are size of about 100 μm or 0.1 millimetres. Skin can be modelled as a 7-dimensional bidirectional texture function (BTF) or a collection of bidirectional scattering distribution function (BSDF) over the target's surfaces.

Interactive Simulation and Visualization

Interactive visualization is a general term that applies to the rendering of data that may vary dynamically and allowing a user to view the data from multiple perspectives. The applications areas may vary significantly, ranging from the visualization of the flow patterns in fluid dynamics to specific computer aided design applications. The data rendered may correspond to specific visual scenes that change as the user interacts with the system — e.g. simulators, such as flight simulators, make extensive use of CGI techniques for representing the world.

At the abstract level an interactive visualization process involves a "data pipeline" in which the raw data is managed and filtered to a form that makes it suitable for rendering. This is often called the "visualization data". The visualization data is then mapped to a "visualization representation" that can be fed to a rendering system. This is usually called a "renderable representation". This representation is then rendered as a displayable image. As the user interacts with the system (e.g. by using joystick controls to change their position within the virtual world) the raw data is fed through the pipeline to create a new rendered image, often making real-time computational efficiency a key consideration in such applications.

Computer Animation

While computer generated images of landscapes may be static, the term computer animation only applies to dynamic images that resemble a movie. However, in general the term computer animation refers to dynamic images that do not allow user interaction, and the term virtual world is used for the interactive animated environments.

Computer animation is essentially a digital successor to the art of stop motion animation of 3D models and frame-by-frame animation of 2D illustrations. Computer generated animations are more controllable than other more physically based processes, such as constructing miniatures for effects shots or hiring extras for crowd scenes, and because it allows the creation of images that would not be feasible using any other technology. It can also allow a single graphic artist to produce such content without the use of actors, expensive set pieces, or props.

To create the illusion of movement, an image is displayed on the computer screen and repeatedly replaced by a new image which is similar to the previous image, but advanced slightly in the time domain (usually at a rate of 24 or 30 frames/second). This technique is identical to how the illusion of movement is achieved with television and motion pictures.

Virtual Worlds

A yellow submarine in Second Life

A virtual world is a simulated environment, which allows user to interact with animated characters, or interact with other users through the use of animated characters known as avatars. Virtual worlds are intended for its users to inhabit and interact, and the term today has become largely synonymous with interactive 3D virtual environments, where the users take the form of avatars visible to others graphically. These avatars are usually depicted as textual, two-dimensional, or three-dimensional graphical representations, although other forms are possible (auditory and touch sensations for example). Some, but not all, virtual worlds allow for multiple users.

Metallic balls

In Courtrooms

Computer-generated imagery has been used in courtrooms, primarily since the early 2000s. However, some experts have argued that it is prejudicial. They are used to help judges or the jury to better visualize the sequence of events, evidence or hypothesis. However, a 1997 study showed that people are poor intuitive physicists and easily influenced by computer generated images. Thus it is important that jurors and other legal decision-makers be made aware that such exhibits are merely a representation of one potential sequence of events.

Texture Mapping

Texture mapping is a method for defining high frequency detail, surface texture, or color information on a computer-generated graphic or 3D model. Its application to 3D graphics was pioneered by Edwin Catmull in 1974.

1 = 3D model without textures2 = 3D model with textures

Texture mapping originally referred to a method (now more accurately called diffuse mapping) that simply wrapped and mapped pixels from a texture to a 3D surface. In recent decades the advent of multi-pass rendering and complex mapping such as height mapping, bump mapping, normal mapping, displacement mapping, reflection mapping, specular mapping, mipmaps, occlusion mapping, and many other variations on the technique (controlled by a materials system) have made it possible to simulate near-photorealism in real time by vastly reducing the number of polygons and lighting calculations needed to construct a realistic and functional 3D scene.

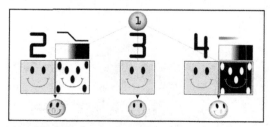

Examples of multitexturing (click for larger image); 1: Untextured sphere, 2: Texture and bump maps, 3: Texture map only, 4: Opacity and texture maps.

Texture Maps

A texture map is an image applied (mapped) to the surface of a shape or polygon. This may be a bitmap image or a procedural texture. They may be stored in common image file formats, referenced by 3d model formats or material definitions, and assembled into resource bundles.

They may have 1-3 dimensions, although 2 dimensions are most common for visible surfaces. For use with modern hardware, texture map data may be stored in swizzled or tiled orderings to improve cache coherency. Rendering APIs typically manage texture map resources (which may be located in device memory) as buffers or surfaces, and may allow 'render to texture' for additional effects such as post processing, environment mapping.

They usually contain RGB color data (either stored as direct color, compressed formats, or indexed color), and sometimes an additional channel for alpha blending (RGBA) especially for billboards and *decal* overlay textures. It is possible to use the alpha channel (which may be convenient to store in formats parsed by hardware) for other uses such as specularity.

Multiple texture maps (or channels) may be combined for control over specularity, normals, displacement, or subsurface scattering for skin rendering.

Multiple texture images may be combined in texture atlases or array textures to reduce state changes for modern hardware. (They may be considered a modern evolution of tile map graphics). Modern hardware often supports cube map textures with multiple faces for environment mapping.

Authoring

They may be acquired by scanning/digital photography, authored in image manipulation software such as Photoshop, or painted onto 3D surfaces directly in a 3D paint tool such as Mudbox or zbrush.

Texture Application

This process is akin to applying patterned paper to a plain white box. Every vertex in a polygon is assigned a texture coordinate (which in the 2d case is also known as a UV coordinates). This may be done through explicit assignment of vertex attributes, manually edited in a 3D modelling package through UV unwrapping tools. It is also possible to associate a procedural transformation from 3d space to texture space with the material. This might be accomplished via planar projection or, alternatively, cylindrical or spherical mapping. More complex mappings may consider the distance along a surface to minimize distortion. These coordinates are interpolated across the faces of polygons to sample the texture map during rendering.

Textures may be repeated or mirrored to extend a finite rectangular bitmap over a larger area, or they may have a one to one unique "injective" mapping from every piece of a surface (which is important for render mapping and light mapping, also known as baking)

Texture Space

Texture mapping maps from the model surface (or screen space during rasterization) into texture space; in this space, the texture map is visible in its undistorted form. UV unwrapping tools typically provide a view in texture space for manual editing of texture coordinates. Some rendering techniques such as subsurface scattering may be performed approximately by texture-space operations.

Multitexturing

Multitexturing is the use of more than one texture at a time on a polygon. For instance, a light map texture may be used to light a surface as an alternative to recalculating that lighting every time the surface is rendered. Microtextures or detail textures are used to add higher frequency details, and dirt maps may add weathering and variation; this can greatly reduce the apparent periodicity of repeating textures. Modern graphics may use in excess of 10 layers for greater fidelity which are combined using shaders. Another multitexture technique is bump mapping, which allows a texture to directly control the facing direction of a surface for the purposes of its lighting calculations; it can give a very good appearance of a complex surface (such as tree bark or rough concrete) that takes on lighting detail in addition to the usual detailed coloring. Bump mapping has become popular in recent video games, as graphics hardware has become powerful enough to accommodate it in real-time.

Texture Filtering

The way that samples (e.g. when viewed as pixels on the screen) are calculated from the texels (texture pixels) is governed by texture filtering. The cheapest method is to use the nearest-neighbour interpolation, but bilinear interpolation or trilinear interpolation between mipmaps are two commonly used alternatives which reduce aliasing or jaggies. In the event of a texture coordinate being outside the texture, it is either clamped or wrapped. Anisotropic filtering better eliminates directional artefacts when viewing textures from oblique viewing angles.

Baking

As an optimization, it is possible to render detail from a high resolution model or expensive process (such as global illumination) into a surface texture (possibly on a low resolution model). This is also known as render mapping. This technique is most commonly used for lightmapping but may also be used to generate normal maps and displacement maps. Some video games (e.g. Messiah) have used this technique. The original Quake software engine used on-the-fly baking to combine light maps and colour texture-maps ("surface caching").

Baking can be used as a form of level of detail generation, where a complex scene with many different elements and materials may be approximated by a single element with a single texture which is then algorithmically reduced for lower rendering cost and fewer drawcalls. It is also used to take high detail models from 3D sculpting software and point cloud scanning and approximate them with meshes more suitable for realtime rendering.

Rasterisation Algorithms

Various techniques have evolved in software and hardware implementations. Each offers different trade-offs in precision, versatility and performance :-

Because affine texture mapping does not take into account the depth information about a polygon's vertices, where the polygon is not perpendicular to the viewer it produces a noticeable defect.

Forward Texture Mapping

Some hardware systems e.g. Sega Saturn and the NV1 traverse texture coordinates directly, interpolating the projected position in screen space through texture space and splatting the texels into a frame buffer. (in the case of the NV1, quadratic interpolation was used allowing curved rendering). Sega provided tools for baking suitable per-quad texture tiles from UV mapped models.

This has the advantage that texture maps are read in a simple linear fashion.

Forward texture mapping may also sometimes produce more natural looking results than affine texture mapping if the primitives are aligned with prominent texture directions (e.g. road markings or layers of bricks). However, perspective distortion is still visible as primitives near the camera. (e.g. the saturn port of Sega Rally exhibited texture-squashing artefacts as nearby polygons were near clipped without UV coordinates.).

This technique is not used in modern hardware because UV coordinates have proved more versatile for modelling and more consistent for clipping.

Inverse Texture Mapping

Most approaches use inverse texture mapping, which traverses the rendering primitives in screen space whilst interpolating texture coordinates for sampling. This interpolation may be affine or perspective correct. One advantage is that each output pixel is guaranteed to only be traversed once; generally the source texture map data is stored in some lower bit-depth or compressed form whilst the frame buffer uses a higher bit-depth. Another is greater versatility for UV mapping. A texture cache becomes important for buffering reads, since the memory access pattern in texture space is more complex.

Affine Texture Mapping

It is cheapest to linearly interpolate texture coordinates across a surface. Some software and hardware systems (such as the original PlayStation), project 3D vertices onto the screen during rendering and linearly interpolate the texture coordinates in screen space between them (inverse-texture mapping). This may be done by incrementing fixed point UV coordinates or by an incremental error algorithm akin to Bresenham's line algorithm.

This leads to noticeable distortion with perspective transformations (see figure – textures (the checker boxes) appear bent), especially as primitives near the camera. Such distortion may be reduced with subdivision.

Perspective Correctness

Perspective correct texturing accounts for the vertices' positions in 3D space rather than simply interpolating coordinates in 2D screen space. This achieves the correct visual effect but it is more expensive to calculate. Instead of interpolating the texture coordinates directly, the coordinates are divided by their depth (relative to the viewer) and the reciprocal of the depth value is also interpolated and used to recover the perspective-correct coordinate. This correction makes it so that in parts of the polygon that are closer to the viewer the difference from pixel to pixel between texture coordinates is smaller (stretching the texture wider) and in parts that are farther away this difference is larger (compressing the texture).

Affine texture mapping directly interpolates a texture coordinate u_α between two endpoints u_0 and u_1 :

$$u_\alpha = (1-\alpha)u_0 + \alpha u_1 \quad 0 \le \alpha \le 1$$

Perspective correct mapping interpolates after dividing by depth z , then uses its interpolated reciprocal to recover the correct coordinate:

$$u_\alpha = \frac{(1-\alpha)\dfrac{u_0}{z_0} + \alpha \dfrac{u_1}{z_1}}{(1-\alpha)\dfrac{1}{z_0} + \alpha \dfrac{1}{z_1}}$$

All modern 3D graphics hardware implements perspective correct texturing.

Various techniques have evolved for rendering texture mapped geometry into images with different quality/precision tradeoffs, which can be applied to both software and hardware.

Doom renders vertical spans (walls) with perspective-correct texture mapping.

Classic software texture mappers generally did only simple mapping with at most one lighting effect (typically applied through a lookup table), and the perspective correctness was about 16 times more expensive.

Restricted Camera Rotation

The *Doom engine* restricted the world to vertical walls and horizontal floors/ceilings, with a camera that could only rotate about the vertical axis. This meant the walls would be a constant depth coordinate along a vertical line and the floors/ceilings would have a constant depth along a horizontal line. A fast affine mapping could be used along those lines because it would be correct. Some later renderers of this era simulated a small amount of camera pitch with shearing which allowed the appearance of greater freedom whilst using the same rendering technique.

Some engines with were able to render texture mapped Heightmaps (e.g. Nova Logic's Voxel Space, and the engine for outcast) via Bresenham-like incremental algorithms, producing the appearance of a texture mapped landscape without the use of traditional geometric primitives.

Subdivision for Perspective Correction

Every triangle can be further subdivided into groups of about 16 pixels in order to achieve two goals. First, keeping the arithmetic mill busy at all times. Second, producing faster arithmetic results.

World Space Subdivision

For perspective texture mapping without hardware support, a triangle is broken down into smaller triangles for rendering and affine mapping is used on them. The reason this technique works is that the distortion of affine mapping becomes much less noticeable on smaller polygons. The Sony Playstation made extensive use of this because it only supported affine mapping in hardware but had a relatively high triangle through-put compared to its peers.

Screen Space Subdivision

Software renderers generally preferred screen subdivision because it has less overhead. Additionally, they try to do linear interpolation along a line of pixels to simplify the set-up (compared to 2d affine interpolation) and thus again the overhead (also affine tex-ture-mapping does not fit into the low number of registers of the x86 CPU; the 68000 or any RISC is much more suited).

A different approach was taken for *Quake*, which would calculate perspective correct coordinates only once every 16 pixels of a scanline and linearly interpolate between them, effectively running at the speed of linear interpolation because the perspective correct calculation runs in parallel on the co-processor. The polygons are rendered in-dependently, hence it may be possible to switch between spans and columns or diag-onal directions depending on the orientation of the polygon normal to achieve a more constant z but the effort seems not to be worth it.

Screen space sub division techniques. Top left: Quake-like, top right:
bilinear, bottom left: const-z

Other Techniques

Another technique was approximating the perspective with a faster calculation, such as a polynomial. Still another technique uses 1/z value of the last two drawn pixels to linearly extrapolate the next value. The division is then done starting from those values so that only a small remainder has to be divided but the amount of bookkeeping makes this method too slow on most systems.

Finally, the Build engine extended the constant distance trick used for Doom by finding the line of constant distance for arbitrary polygons and rendering along it.

Hardware Implementations

Texture mapping hardware was originally developed for simulation (e.g. as implement-ed in the Evans and Sutherland ESIG image generators), and professional graphics workstations such as Silicon Graphics, broadcast digital video effects machines such as the Ampex ADO and later appeared in arcade machines, consumer video game con-soles, and PC graphics cards in the mid 1990s. In flight simulation, texture mapping provided important motion cues.

Modern Graphics processing units provide specialised fixed function units called texture samplers or texture mapping units to perform texture mapping, usually with trilinear filtering or better multi-tap anisotropic filtering and hardware for decoding specific formats such as DXTn. As of 2016, texture mapping hardware is ubiquitous as most SOCs contain a suitable GPU.

Some hardware combines texture mapping with hidden surface determination in tile based deferred rendering or scanline rendering; such systems only fetch the visible texels at the expense of using greater workspace for transformed vertices. Most systems have settled on the Z-buffer approach, which can still reduce the texture mapping workload with front to back sorting.

Applications

Beyond 3d rendering, the availability of texture mapping hardware has inspired its use for accelerating other tasks:

Tomography

It is possible to use texture mapping hardware to accelerate both the reconstruction of voxel data sets from tomographic scans, and to visualise the results

User Interfaces

Many user interfaces use texture mapping to accelerate animated transitions of screen elements, e.g. Expose in Mac OSX.

Morphing

Morphing is a special effect in motion pictures and animations that changes (or morphs) one image or shape into another through a seamless transition. Most often it is used to depict one person turning into another through technological means or as part of a fantasy or surreal sequence. Traditionally such a depiction would be achieved through cross-fading techniques on film. Since the early 1990s, this has been replaced by computer software to create more realistic transitions.

Three frames form a morph from George W. Bush to Arnold Schwarzenegger showing the midpoint between the two extremes

Early Examples

Though the 1986 movie *The Golden Child* implemented very crude morphing effects from animal to human and back, the first movie to employ detailed morphing was *Willow*, in 1988. A similar process was used a year later in *Indiana Jones and the Last Crusade* to create Walter Donovan's gruesome demise. Both effects were created by Industrial Light & Magic using grid warping techniques developed by Tom Brigham and Doug Smythe (AMPAS).

In 1985, Godley & Creme created a "morph" effect using analogue cross-fades in the video for "Cry". The cover for Queen's 1989 album *The Miracle* featured the technique to morph the four band members' faces into one gestalt image. In 1991, morphing appeared notably in the Michael Jackson music video "Black or White" and in the movies *Terminator 2: Judgment Day* and *Star Trek VI: The Undiscovered Country*. The first application for personal computers to offer morphing was Gryphon Software Morph on the Macintosh. Other early morphing systems included ImageMaster, MorphPlus and CineMorph, all of which premiered for the Commodore Amiga in 1992. Other programs became widely available within a year, and for a time the effect became common to the point of cliché. For high-end use, Elastic Reality (based on MorphPlus) saw its first feature film use in *In The Line of Fire* (1993) and was used in Quantum Leap (work performed by the Post Group). At VisionArt Ted Fay used Elastic Reality to morph Odo for *Star Trek: Deep Space Nine*. Elastic Reality was later purchased by Avid, having already become the de facto system of choice, used in many hundreds of films. The technology behind Elastic Reality earned two Academy Awards in 1996 for Scientific and Technical Achievement going to Garth Dickie and Perry Kivolowitz. The effect is technically called a "spatially warped cross-dissolve". The first social network designed for user-generated morph examples to be posted online was Galleries by Morpheus (morphing software).

In Taiwan, Aderans, a hair loss solutions provider, did a TV commercial featuring a morphing sequence in which people with lush, thick hair morph into one another, reminiscent of the end sequence of the "Black or White" video.

Modern Techniques

An animated example of an ape morphing into a bird.

In the early 1990s computer techniques that often produced more convincing results began to be widely used. These involved distorting one image at the same time that it faded into another through marking corresponding points and vectors on the "before" and "after" images used in the morph. For example, one would morph one face into another by marking key points on the first face, such as the contour of the nose or location of an eye, and mark where these same points existed on the second face. The computer would then distort the first face to have the shape of the second face at the same time that it faded the two faces. To compute the transformation of image coordinates required for the distortion, the algorithm of Beier and Neely can be used.

Later, more sophisticated cross-fading techniques were employed that vignetted different parts of one image to the other gradually instead of transitioning the entire image at once. This style of morphing was perhaps most famously employed in the video that former 10cc members Kevin Godley and Lol Creme (performing as Godley & Creme) produced in 1985 for their song *Cry*. It comprised a series of black and white close-up shots of faces of many different people that gradually faded from one to the next. In a strict sense, this had little to do with modern-day computer generated morphing effects, since it was merely a dissolve using fully analog equipment.

Present Use

Morphing algorithms continue to advance and programs can automatically morph images that correspond closely enough with relatively little instruction from the user. This has led to the use of morphing techniques to create convincing slow-motion effects where none existed in the original film or video footage by morphing between each individual frame using optical flow technology. Morphing has also appeared as a transition technique between one scene and another in television shows, even if the contents of the two images are entirely unrelated. The algorithm in this case attempts to find corresponding points between the images and distort one into the other as they crossfade.

While perhaps less obvious than in the past, morphing is used heavily today. Whereas the effect was initially a novelty, today, morphing effects are most often designed to be seamless and invisible to the eye.

A particular use for morphing effects is modern digital font design. Using morphing technology, called interpolation or multiple master technology, a designer can create an intermediate between two styles, for example generating a semibold font by compromising between a bold and regular style, or extend a trend to create an ultra-light or ultra-bold. The technique is commonly used by font design studios.

Software

- Morpheus
- Nuke

- After Effects

- FantaMorph

- Gryphon Software Morph

- MorphThing

- SilhouetteFX (new algorithms by the above cited Perry Kivolowitz)

- Angelmorph

Molecular Graphics

Molecular graphics (MG) is the discipline and philosophy of studying molecules and their properties through graphical representation. IUPAC limits the definition to representations on a "graphical display device". Ever since Dalton's atoms and Kekulé's benzene, there has been a rich history of hand-drawn atoms and molecules, and these representations have had an important influence on modern molecular graphics. This article concentrates on the use of computers to create molecular graphics. Note, however, that many molecular graphics programs and systems have close coupling between the graphics and editing commands or calculations such as in molecular modelling.

Relation to Molecular Models

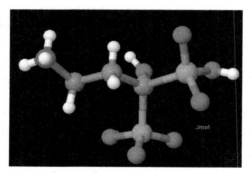

Fig. Key: Hydrogen = white, carbon = grey, nitrogen = blue, oxygen = red,}
and phosphorus = orange.

There has been a long tradition of creating molecular models from physical materials. Perhaps the best known is Crick and Watson's model of DNA built from rods and planar sheets, but the most widely used approach is to represent all atoms and bonds explicitly using the "ball and stick" approach. This can demonstrate a wide range of properties, such as shape, relative size, and flexibility. Many chemistry courses expect that students will have access to ball and stick models. One goal of mainstream molecular graphics has been to represent the "ball and stick" model as realistically as possible and to couple this with calculations of molecular properties.

Figure shows a small molecule ($NH_3CH_2CH_2C(OH)(PO_3H)(PO_3H)-$), as drawn by the Jmol program. It is important to realize that the colors and shapes are purely a convention, as individual atoms are not colored, nor do they have hard surfaces. Bonds between atoms are also not rod-shaped.

Comparison of Physical Models with Molecular Graphics

Physical models and computer models have partially complementary strengths and weaknesses. Physical models can be used by those without access to a computer and now can be made cheaply out of plastic materials. Their tactile and visual aspects cannot be easily reproduced by computers (although haptic devices have occasionally been built). On a computer screen, the flexibility of molecules is also difficult to appreciate; illustrating the pseudorotation of cyclohexane is a good example of the value of mechanical models.

However, it is difficult to build large physical molecules, and all-atom physical models of even simple proteins could take weeks or months to build. Moreover, physical models are not robust and they decay over time. Molecular graphics is particularly valuable for representing global and local properties of molecules, such as electrostatic potential. Graphics can also be animated to represent molecular processes and chemical reactions, a feat that is not easy to reproduce physically.

History

Initially the rendering was on early Cathode ray tube screens or through plotters drawing on paper. Molecular structures have always been an attractive choice for developing new computer graphics tools, since the input data are easy to create and the results are usually highly appealing. The first example of MG was a display of a protein molecule (Project MAC, 1966) by Cyrus Levinthal and Robert Langridge. Among the milestones in high-performance MG was the work of Nelson Max in "realistic" rendering of macromolecules using reflecting spheres.

By about 1980 many laboratories both in academia and industry had recognized the power of the computer to analyse and predict the properties of molecules, especially in materials science and the pharmaceutical industry. The discipline was often called "molecular graphics" and in 1982 a group of academics and industrialists in the UK set up the Molecular Graphics Society (MGS). Initially much of the technology concentrated either on high-performance 3D graphics, including interactive rotation or 3D rendering of atoms as spheres (sometimes with radiosity). During the 1980s a number of programs for calculating molecular properties (such as molecular dynamics and quantum mechanics) became available and the term "molecular graphics" often included these. As a result, the MGS has now changed its name to the Molecular Graphics and Modelling Society (MGMS).

The requirements of macromolecular crystallography also drove MG because the traditional techniques of physical model-building could not scale. The first two protein structures solved by molecular graphics without the aid of the Richards' Box were built with Stan Swanson's program FIT on the Vector General graphics display in the laboratory of Edgar Meyer at Texas A&M University: First Marge Legg in Al Cotton's lab at A&M solved the structure of staph. nuclease (1975) and then Jim Hogle solved the structure of monoclinic lysozyme in 1976. A full year passed before other graphics systems were used to replace the Richards' Box for modelling into density in 3-D. Alwyn Jones' FRODO program (and later "O") were developed to overlay the molecular electron density determined from X-ray crystallography and the hypothetical molecular structure.

In 2009 BALLView became the first software to use Raytracing for molecular graphics.

Art, Science and Technology in Molecular Graphics

Both computer technology and graphic arts have contributed to molecular graphics. The development of structural biology in the 1950s led to a requirement to display molecules with thousands of atoms. The existing computer technology was limited in power, and in any case a naive depiction of all atoms left viewers overwhelmed. Most systems therefore used conventions where information was implicit or stylistic. Two vectors meeting at a point implied an atom or (in macromolecules) a complete residue (10-20 atoms).

Fig. Image of hemagglutinin with alpha helices depicted as cylinders and the rest of the chain as silver coils. The individual protein molecules (several thousand) have been hidden. All of the non-hydrogen atoms in the two ligands (presumably sialic acid) have been shown near the top of the diagram. Key: Carbon = grey, oxygen = red, nitrogen = blue.

The macromolecular approach was popularized by Dickerson and Geis' presentation of proteins and the graphic work of Jane Richardson through high-quality hand-drawn diagrams such as the "ribbon" representation. In this they strove to capture the intrinsic 'meaning' of the molecule. This search for the "messages in the molecule" has always accompanied the increasing power of computer graphics processing. Typically the depiction would concentrate on specific areas of the molecule (such as the active site) and this might have different colors or more detail in the number of explicit atoms or the type of depiction (e.g., spheres for atoms).

In some cases the limitations of technology have led to serendipitous methods for rendering. Most early graphics devices used vector graphics, which meant that rendering spheres and surfaces was impossible. Michael Connolly's program "MS" calculated points on the surface-accessible surface of a molecule, and the points were rendered as dots with good visibility using the new vector graphics technology, such as the Evans and Sutherland PS300 series. Thin sections ("slabs") through the structural display showed very clearly the complementarity of the surfaces for molecules binding to active sites, and the "Connolly surface" became a universal metaphor.

The relationship between the art and science of molecular graphics is shown in the exhibitions sponsored by the Molecular Graphics Society. Some exhibits are created with molecular graphics programs alone, while others are collages, or involve physical materials. An example from Mike Hann (1994), inspired by Magritte's painting *Ceci n'est pas une pipe*, uses an image of a salmeterol molecule. "*Ceci n'est pas une molecule*," writes Mike Hann, "serves to remind us that all of the graphics images presented here are not molecules, not even pictures of molecules, but pictures of icons which we believe represent some aspects of the molecule's properties."

Colour molecular graphics is often use on chemistry journal covers in an artistic manner.

Space-filling Models

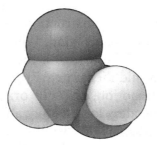

Fig. Space-filling model of formic acid. Key: Hydrogen = white, carbon = black, oxygen = red.

Fig. is a "space-filling" representation of formic acid, where atoms are drawn as solid spheres to suggest the space they occupy. This and all space-filling models are necessarily icons or abstractions: atoms are nuclei with electron "clouds" of varying density surrounding them, and as such have no actual surfaces. For many years the size of atoms has been approximated by physical models (CPK) in which the volumes of plastic balls describe where much of the electron density is to be found (often sized to van der Waals radii). That is, the surface of these models is meant to represent a specific *level of density* of the electron cloud, not any putative physical surface of the atom.

Since the atomic radii (e.g. in Fig.) are only slightly less than the distance between bonded atoms, the iconic spheres intersect, and in the CPK models, this was achieved by planar truncations along the bonding directions, the section being circular. When raster graphics became affordable, one of the common approaches was to replicate CPK models *in silico*. It is relatively straightforward to calculate the circles of intersection, but more complex to represent a model with hidden surface removal. A useful side product is that a conventional value for the molecular volume can be calculated.

The use of spheres is often for convenience, being limited both by graphics libraries and the additional effort required to compute complete electronic density or other space-filling quantities. It is now relatively common to see images of surfaces that have been colored to show quantities such as electrostatic potential. Common surfaces in molecular visualization include solvent-accessible ("Lee-Richards") surfaces, solvent-excluded ("Connolly") surfaces, and isosurfaces. The isosurface in Fig. appears to show the electrostatic potential, with blue colors being negative and red/yellow (near the metal) positive (there is no absolute convention of coloring, and red/positive, blue/negative are often reversed). Opaque isosurfaces do not allow the atoms to be seen and identified and it is not easy to deduce them. Because of this, isosurfaces are often drawn with a degree of transparency.

Technology

Early interactive molecular computer graphics systems were vector graphics machines, which used stroke-writing vector monitors, sometimes even oscilloscopes. The electron beam does not sweep left-and-right as in a raster display. The display hardware followed a sequential list of digital drawing instructions (the display list), directly drawing at an angle one stroke for each molecular bond. When the list was complete, drawing would begin again from the top of the list, so if the list was long (a large number of molecular bonds), the display would flicker heavily. Later vector displays could rotate complex structures with smooth motion, since the orientation of all of the coordinates in the display list could be changed by loading just a few numbers into rotation registers in the display unit, and the display unit would multiply all coordinates in the display list by the contents of these registers as the picture was drawn.

The early black-and white vector displays could somewhat distinguish for example a molecular structure from its surrounding electron density map for crystallographic structure solution work by drawing the molecule brighter than the map. Color display makes them easier to tell apart. During the 1970s two-color stroke-writing Penetron tubes were available, but not used in molecular computer graphics systems. In about 1980 Evans & Sutherland made the first practical full-color vector displays for molecular graphics, typically attached to an E&S PS-300 display. This early color tube was expensive, because it was originally engineered to withstand the shaking of a flight-simulator motion base.

Color raster graphics display of molecular models began around 1978 as seen in this paper by Porter on spherical shading of atomic models. Early raster molecular graphics systems displayed static images that could take around a minute to generate. Dynamically rotating color raster molecular display phased in during 1982-1985 with the introduction of the Ikonas programmable raster display.

Molecular graphics has always pushed the limits of display technology, and has seen a number of cycles of integration and separation of compute-host and display. Early systems like Project MAC were bespoke and unique, but in the 1970s the MMS-X and similar systems used (relatively) low-cost terminals, such as the Tektronix 4014 series, often over dial-up lines to multi-user hosts. The devices could only display static pictures but were able to evangelize MG. In the late 1970s, it was possible for departments (such as crystallography) to afford their own hosts (e.g., PDP-11) and to attach a display (such as Evans & Sutherland's MPS) directly to the bus. The display list was kept on the host, and interactivity was good since updates were rapidly reflected in the display—at the cost of reducing most machines to a single-user system.

In the early 1980s, Evans & Sutherland (E&S) decoupled their PS300 display, which contained its own display information transformable through a dataflow architecture. Complex graphical objects could be downloaded over a serial line (e.g. 9600 baud) and then manipulated without impact on the host. The architecture was excellent for high performance display but very inconvenient for domain-specific calculations, such as electron-density fitting and energy calculations. Many crystallographers and modellers spent arduous months trying to fit such activities into this architecture.

The benefits for MG were considerable, but by the later 1980s, UNIX workstations such as Sun-3 with raster graphics (initially at a resolution of 256 by 256) had started to appear. Computer-assisted drug design in particular required raster graphics for the display of computed properties such as atomic charge and electrostatic potential. Although E&S had a high-end range of raster graphics (primarily aimed at the aerospace industry) they failed to respond to the low-end market challenge where single users, rather than engineering departments, bought workstations. As a result, the market for MG displays passed to Silicon Graphics, coupled with the development of minisupercomputers (e.g., CONVEX and Alliant) which were affordable for well-supported MG laboratories. Silicon Graphics provided a graphics language, IrisGL, which was easier to use and more productive than the PS300 architecture. Commercial companies (e.g., Biosym, Polygen/MSI) ported their code to Silicon Graphics, and by the early 1990s, this was the "industry standard". Dial boxes were often used as control devices.

Stereoscopic displays were developed based on liquid crystal polarized spectacles, and while this had been very expensive on the PS300, it now became a commodity item. A common alternative was to add a polarizable screen to the front of the display and to provide viewers with extremely cheap spectacles with orthogonal polarization for separate eyes. With projectors such as Barco, it was possible to project stereoscopic display onto special silvered screens and supply an audience of hundreds with spectacles. In this way molecular graphics became universally known within large sectors of chemical and biochemical science, especially in the pharmaceutical industry. Because the backgrounds of many displays were black by default, it was common for modelling sessions and lectures to be held with almost all lighting turned off.

In the last decade almost all of this technology has become commoditized. IrisGL evolved to OpenGL so that molecular graphics can be run on any machine. In 1992, Roger Sayle released his RasMol program into the public domain. RasMol contained a very high-performance molecular renderer that ran on Unix/X Window, and Sayle later ported this to the Windows and Macintosh platforms. The Richardsons developed kinemages and the Mage software, which was also multi-platform. By specifying the chemical MIME type, molecular models could be served over the Internet, so that for the first time MG could be distributed at zero cost regardless of platform. In 1995, Birkbeck College's crystallography department used this to run "Principles of Protein Structure", the first multimedia course on the Internet, which reached 100 to 200 scientists.

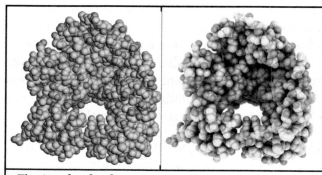

Fig. A molecule of Porin (protein) shown without ambient occlusion (left) and with (right). Advanced rendering effects can improve the comprehension of the 3D shape of a molecule.

MG continues to see innovation that balances technology and art, and currently zero-cost or open source programs such as PyMOL and Jmol have very wide use and acceptance.

Recently the widespread diffusion of advanced graphics hardware has improved the rendering capabilities of the visualization tools. The capabilities of current shading languages allow the inclusion of advanced graphic effects (like ambient occlusion, cast shadows and non-photorealistic rendering techniques) in the interactive visualization of molecules. These graphic effects, beside being eye candy, can improve the comprehension of the three-dimensional shapes of the molecules. An example of the effects that can be achieved exploiting recent graphics hardware can be seen in the simple open source visualization system QuteMol.

Algorithms

Reference Frames

Drawing molecules requires a transformation between molecular coordinates (usually, but not always, in Angstrom units) and the screen. Because many molecules are chiral it is essential that the handedness of the system (almost always right-handed) is preserved. In molecular graphics the origin (0, 0) is usually at the lower left, while in many computer systems the origin is at top left. If the z-coordinate is out of the screen (towards the viewer) the molecule will be referred to right-handed axes, while the screen display will be left-handed.

Molecular transformations normally require:

- scaling of the display (but not the molecule).

- translations of the molecule and objects on the screen.

- rotations about points and lines.

Conformational changes (e.g. rotations about bonds) require rotation of one part of the molecule relative to another. The programmer must decide whether a transformation on the screen reflects a change of view or a change in the molecule or its reference frame.

Simple

In early displays only vectors could be drawn e.g. (Fig. 7) which are easy to draw because no rendering or hidden surface removal is required.

Fig. Stick model of caffeine drawn in Jmol.

On vector machines the lines would be smooth but on raster devices Bresenham's algorithm is used (note the "jaggies" on some of the bonds, which can be largely removed with antialiasing software.)

Atoms can be drawn as circles, but these should be sorted so that those with the largest z-coordinates (nearest the screen) are drawn last. Although imperfect, this often gives a reasonably attractive display. Other simple tricks which do not include hidden surface algorithms are:

- coloring each end of a bond with the same color as the atom to which it is at-tached (Fig.).

- drawing less than the whole length of the bond (e.g. 10%-90%) to simulate the bond sticking out of a circle.

- adding a small offset white circle within the circle for an atom to simulate reflection.

Typical pseudocode for creating Fig. (to fit the molecule exactly to the screen): //

assume:

// atoms with x, y, z coordinates (Angstrom) and elementSymbol

// bonds with pointers/references to atoms at ends

// table of colors for elementTypes

// find limits of molecule in molecule coordinates as xMin, yMin, xMax, yMax

scale = min(xScreenMax/(xMax-xMin), yScreenMax/(yMax-yMin))

xOffset = -xMin * scale; yOffset = -yMin * scale

for (bond in $bonds) {

  atom0 = bond.getAtom(0)

  atom1 = bond.getAtom(1)

  x0 = xOffset+atom0.getX()*scale; y0 = yOffset+atom0.getY()*scale // (1)

  x1 = xOffset+atom1.getX()*scale; y1 = yOffset+atom1.getY()*scale // (2)

  x1 = atom1.getX(); y1 = atom1.getY()

  xMid = (x0 + x1) /2; yMid = (y0 + y1) /2;

  color0 = ColorTable.getColor(atom0.getSymbol())

  drawLine (color0, x0, y0, xMid, yMid)

  color1 = ColorTable.getColor(atom1.getSymbol())

  drawLine (color1, x1, y1, xMid, yMid)

Note that this assumes the origin is in the bottom left corner of the screen, with Y up the screen. Many graphics systems have the origin at the top left, with Y down the screen. In this case the lines (1) and (2) should have the y coordinate generation as:

y0 = yScreenMax -(yOffset+atom0.getY()*scale) // (1)

y1 = yScreenMax -(yOffset+atom1.getY()*scale) // (2)

Changes of this sort change the handedness of the axes so it is easy to reverse the chirality of the displayed molecule unless care is taken.

Advanced

For greater realism and better comprehension of the 3D structure of a molecule many computer graphics algorithms can be used. For many years molecular graphics has stressed the capabilities of graphics hardware and has required hardware-specific approaches. With the increasing power of machines on the desktop, portability is more important and programs such as Jmol have advanced algorithms that do not rely on hardware. On the other hand, recent graphics hardware is able to interactively render very complex molecule shapes with a quality that would not be possible with standard software techniques.

Chronology

Developer(s)	Approximate date	Technology	Comments
Crystallographers < 1960		Hand-drawn	Crystal structures, with hidden atom and bond removal. Often clinographic projections.
Johnson, Motherwell	ca 1970	Pen plotter	ORTEP, PLUTO. Very widely deployed for publishing crystal structures.
Cyrus Levinthal, Bob Langridge, Ward, Stots	1966	Project MAC display system, two-degree of freedom, spring-return velocity joystick for rotating the image.	First protein display on screen. System for interactively building protein structures.
Barry	1969	LINC 300 computer with a dual trace oscilloscope display.	Interactive molecular structure viewing system. Early examples of dynamic rotation, intensity depth-cueing, and side-by-side stereo. Early use of the small angle approximations (a = sin a, 1 = cos a) to speed up graphical rotation calculations.

Developer(s)	Approximate date	Technology	Comments
Ortony	1971	Designed a stereo viewer (British patent appl. 13844/70) for molecular computer graphics.	Horizontal two-way (half-silvered) mirror combines images drawn on the upper and lower halves of a CRT. Crossed polarizers isolate the images to each eye.
Ortony	1971	Light pen, knob.	Interactive molecular structure viewing system. Select bond by turning another knob until desired bond lights up in sequence, a technique later used on the MMS-4 system below, or by picking with the light pen. Points in space are specified with a 3-D "bug" under dynamic control.
Barry, Graesser, Marshall	1971	CHEMAST: LINC 300 computer driving an oscilloscope. Two-axis joystick, similar to one used later by GRIP-75 (below).	Interactive molecular structure viewing system. Structures dynamically rotated using the joystick.
Tountas and Katz	1971	Adage AGT/50 display	Interactive molecular structure viewing system. Mathematics of nested rotation and for laboratory-space rotation.
Perkins, Piper, Tattam, White	1971	Honeywell DDP 516 computer, EAL TR48 analog computer, Lanelec oscilloscope, 7 linear potentiometers. Stereo.	Interactive molecular structure viewing system.
Wright	1972	GRIP-71 at UNC-CH: IBM System/360 Model 40 time-shared computer, IBM 2250 display, buttons, light pen, keyboard.	Discrete manipulation and energy relaxation of protein structures. Program code became the foundation of the GRIP-75 system below.
Barry and North	1972	Oxford Univ.: Ferranti Argus 500 computer, Ferranti model 30 display, keyboard, track ball, one knob. Stereo.	Prototype large-molecule crystallographic structure solution system. Track ball rotates a bond, knob brightens the molecule vs. electron density map.
North, Ford, Watson	Early 1970s	Leeds Univ.: DEC PDP-11/40 computer, Hewlett-Packard display. 16 knobs, keyboard, spring-return joystick. Stereo.	Prototype large-molecule crystallographic structure solution system. Six knobs rotate and translate a small molecule.

Developer(s)	Approxi-mate date	Technology	Comments
Barry, Boss-hard, Ellis, Marshall, Fritch, Jacobi	1974	MMS-4: Washington Univ. at St. Louis, LINC 300 computer and an LDS-1 / LINC 300 display, custom display modules. Rotation joystick, knobs. Stereo.	Prototype large-molecule crystallographic structure solution system. Select bond to rotate by turning another knob until desired bond lights up in sequence.
Cohen and Feldmann	1974	DEC PDP-10 computer, Adage display, push buttons, keyboard, knobs	Prototype large-molecule crystallographic structure solution system.
Stellman	1975	Princeton: PDP-10 computer, LDS-1 display, knobs	Prototype large-molecule crystallographic structure solution system. Electron density map not shown; instead an "H Factor" figure of merit is updated as the molecular structure is manipulated.
Collins, Cotton, Hazen, Meyer, Morimoto	1975	CRYSNET, Texas A&M Univ. DEC PDP-11/40 computer, Vector General Series 3 display, knobs, keyboard. Stereo.	Prototype large-molecule crystallographic structure solution system. Variety of viewing modes: rocking, spinning, and several stereo display modes.
Cornelius and Kraut	1976 (approx.)	Univ, of Calif. at San Diego: DEC PDP-11/40 emulator (CalData 135), Evans and Sutherland Picture System display, keyboard, 6 knobs. Stereo.	Prototype large-molecule crystallographic structure solution system.
(Yale Univ.)	1976 (approx.)	PIGS: DEC PDP-11/70 computer, Evans and Sutherland Picture System 2 display, data tablet, knobs.	Prototype large-molecule crystallographic structure solution system. The tablet was used for most interactions.
Feldmann and Porter	1976	NIH: DEC PDP—11/70 computer. Evans and Sutherland Picture System 2 display, knobs. Stereo.	Interactive molecular structure viewing system. Intended to display interactively molecular data from the AMSOM – Atlas of Macromolecular Structure on Microfiche.
Rosenberger et al.	1976	MMS-X: Washington Univ. at St. Louis, TI 980B computer, Hewlett-Packard 1321A display, Beehive video terminal, custom display modules, pair of 3-D spring-return joysticks, knobs.	Prototype (and later successful) large-molecule crystallographic structure solution system. Successor to the MMS-4 system above. The 3-D spring-return joysticks either translate and rotate the molecular structure for viewing or a molecular substructure for fitting, mode controlled by a toggle switch.

Developer(s)	Approxi-mate date	Technology	Comments
Britton, Lip-scomb, Pique, Wright, Brooks	1977	GRIP-75 at UNC-CH: Time-shared IBM System/360 Model 75 computer, DEC PDP 11/45 computer, Vector General Series 3 display, 3-D movement box from A.M. Noll and 3-D spring return joystick for substructure manipulation, Measurement Systems nested joystick, knobs, sliders, but-tons, keyboard, light pen.	First large-molecule crystallo-graphic structure solution.
Jones	1978	FRODO and RING Max Planck Inst., Germany, RING: DEC PDP-11/40 and Siemens 4004 computers, Vector General 3404 display, 6 knobs.	Large-molecule crystallographic structure solution. FRODO may have run on a DEC VAX-780 as a follow-on to RING.
Diamond	1978	Bilder Cambridge, England, DEC PDP-11/50 computer, Evans and Sutherland Picture System display, tablet.	Large-molecule crystallographic structure solution. All input is by data tablet. Molecular structures built on-line with ideal geometry. Later passes stretch bonds with idealization.
Langridge, White, Marshall	Late 1970s	Departmental systems (PDP-11, Tektronix displays or DEC-VT11, e.g. MMS-X)	Mixture of commodity computing with early displays.
Davies, Hub-bard	Mid-1980s	CHEM-X, HYDRA	Laboratory systems with multi-color, raster and vector devices (Sigmex, PS300).
Biosym, Tripos, Polygen	Mid-1980s	PS300 and lower cost dumb terminals (VT200, SIGMEX)	Commercial integrated modelling and display packages.
Silicon Graph-ics, Sun	Late 1980s	IRIS GL (UNIX) workstations	Commodity-priced single-user workstations with stereoscopic display.
EMBL - WHAT IF	1989, 2000	Machine independent	Nearly free, multifunctional, still fully supported, many free servers based on it
Sayle, Richard-son	1992, 1993	RasMol, Kinemage	Platform-independent MG.
MDL (van Vliet, Maffett, Adler, Holt)	1995–1998	Chime	proprietary C++ ; free browser plugin for Mac (OS9) and PCs

Developer(s)	Approximate date	Technology	Comments
MolSoft	1997-	ICM-Browser	proprietary; free download for Windows, Mac, and Linux.
1998-	Marvin-Sketch & MarvinView. MarvinSpace (2005)	proprietary Java applet or stand-alone application.	
Community efforts	2000-	DINO, Jmol, PyMol, Avogadro, PDB, OpenStructure	Open-source Java applet or stand-alone application.
NOCH	2002-	NOC	Open source code molecular structure explorer
LION Bioscience / EMBL	2004-	SRS 3D	Free, open-source system based on Java3D. Integrates 3D structures with sequence and feature data (domains, SNPs, etc.).
San Diego Supercomputer Center	2006-	Sirius	Free for academic/non-profit institutions
Community efforts	2011-	HTML5/JavaScript viewers (GLMol, jolecule, pv, Molmil, iCn3D, 3DMol, NGL, Speck, xtal.js, UglyMol, LiteMol, JSmol)	All Open-source. Require WebGL support in the browser (except for JSmol).

Electronic Richards Box Systems

Before computer graphics could be employed, mechanical methods were used to fit large molecules to their electron density maps. Using techniques of X-ray crystallography crystal of a substance were bombarded with X-rays, and the diffracted beams that came off were assembled by computer using a Fourier transform into a usually blurry 3-D image of the molecule, made visible by drawing contour circles around high electron density to produce a contoured electron density map.

In the earliest days, contoured electron density maps were hand drawn on large plastic sheets. Sometimes, bingo chips were placed on the plastic sheets where atoms were interpreted to be.

This was superseded by the Richards Box in which an adjustable brass Kendrew molecular model was placed front of a 2-way mirror, behind which were plastic sheets of the electron density map. This optically superimposed the molecular model and the electron density map. The model was moved to within the contour lines of the superimposed map. Then, atomic coordinates were recorded using a plumb bob and a meter stick. Computer graphics held out the hope of vastly speeding up this process, as well as giving a clearer view in many ways.

A noteworthy attempt to overcome the low speed of graphics displays of the time took place at Washington University in St. Louis, USA. Dave Barry's group attempted to leapfrog the state of the art in graphics displays by making custom display hardware to display images complex enough for large-molecule crystallographic structure solution, fitting molecules to their electron-density maps. The MMS-4 (table above) display modules were slow and expensive, so a second generation of modules was produced for the MMS-X (table above) system.

The first large molecule whose atomic structure was *partly* determined on a molecular computer graphics system was Transfer RNA by Sung-Hou Kim's team in 1976. after initial fitting on a mechanical Richards Box. The first large molecule whose atomic structure was *entirely* determined on a molecular computer graphics system is said to be neurotoxin A from venom of the Philippines sea snake, by Tsernoglou, Petsko, and Tu, with a statement of being first in 1977. The Richardson group published partial atomic structure results of the protein superoxide dismutase the same year, in 1977. All of these were done using the GRIP-75 system.

Other structure fitting systems, FRODO, RING, Builder, MMS-X, etc. (table above) succeeded as well within three years and became dominant.

The reason that most of these systems succeeded in just those years, not earlier or later, and within a short timespan had to do with the arrival of commercial hardware that was powerful enough. Two things were needed and arrived at about the same time. First, electron density maps are large and require either a computer with at least a 24-bit address space or a combination of a computer with a lesser 16-bit address space plus several years to overcome the difficulties of an address space that is smaller than the data. The second arrival was that of interactive computer graphics displays that were fast enough to display electron-density maps, whose contour circles require the display of numerous short vectors. The first such displays were the Vector General Series 3 and the Evans and Sutherland Picture System 2, MultiPicture System, and PS-300.

Nowadays, fitting of the molecular structure to the electron density map is largely automated by algorithms with computer graphics a guide to the process. An example is the XtalView XFit program.

Scientific Visualization

Scientific visualization (also spelled scientific visualisation) is an interdisciplinary branch of science. According to Friendly (2008), it is "primarily concerned with the visualization of three-dimensional phenomena (architectural, meteorological, medical, biological, etc.), where the emphasis is on realistic renderings of volumes, surfaces, illumination sources, and so forth, perhaps with a dynamic (time) component". It is also considered a subset of computer graphics, a branch of computer science. The purpose of scientific visualization is to graphically illustrate scientific data to enable scientists to understand, illustrate, and glean insight from their data.

A scientific visualization of a simulation of a Rayleigh–Taylor instability caused by two mixing fluids.

Surface rendering of *Arabidopsis thaliana* pollen grains with confocal microscope.

History

One of the earliest examples of three-dimensional scientific visualisation was Maxwell's thermodynamic surface, sculpted in clay in 1874 by James Clerk Maxwell. This prefigured modern scientific visualization techniques that use computer graphics.

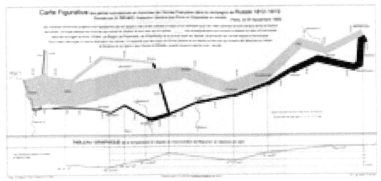

Charles Minard's flow map of Napoleon's March.

Notable early two-dimensional examples include the flow map of Napoleon's March on Moscow produced by Charles Joseph Minard in 1869; the "coxcombs" used by Florence Nightingale in 1857 as part of a campaign to improve sanitary conditions in the British army; and the dot map used by John Snow in 1855 to visualise the Broad Street cholera outbreak.

Methods for Visualizing Two-dimensional Data Sets

Scientific visualization using computer graphics gained in popularity as graphics matured. Primary applications were scalar fields and vector fields from computer simulations and also measured data. The primary methods for visualizing two-dimensional (2D) scalar fields are color mapping and drawing contour lines. 2D vector fields are visualized using glyphs and streamlines or line integral convolution methods. 2D tensor fields are often resolved to a vector field by using one of the two eigenvectors to represent the tensor each point in the field and then visualized using vector field visualization methods.

Methods for Visualizing Three-dimensional Data Sets

For 3D scalar fields the primary methods are volume rendering and isosurfaces. Methods for visualizing vector fields include glyphs (graphical icons) such as arrows, streamlines and streaklines, particle tracing, line integral convolution (LIC) and topological methods. Later, visualization techniques such as hyperstreamlines were developed to visualize 2D and 3D tensor fields.

Scientific Visualization Topics

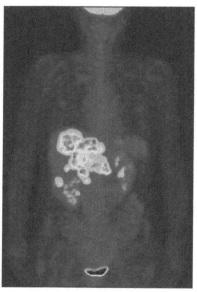

Maximum intensity projection (MIP) of a whole body PET scan.

Scientific visualization of Fluid Flow: Surface waves in water

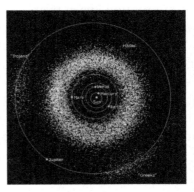

Solar system image of the main asteroid belt and the Trojan asteroids.

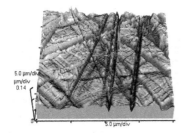

Topographic scan of a glass surface by an Atomic force microscope.

Chemical imaging of a simultaneous release of SF_6 and NH_3.

Computer Animation

Computer animation is the art, technique, and science of creating moving images via the use of computers. It is becoming more common to be created by means of 3D computer graphics, though 2D computer graphics are still widely used for stylistic, low bandwidth, and faster real-time rendering needs. Sometimes the target of the animation is the computer itself, but sometimes the target is another medium, such as film. It is also referred to as CGI (Computer-generated imagery or computer-generated imaging), especially when used in films.

Computer Simulation

Computer simulation is a computer program, or network of computers, that attempts to simulate an abstract model of a particular system. Computer simulations have become a useful part of mathematical modelling of many natural systems in physics, and computational physics, chemistry and biology; human systems in economics, psychology, and social science; and in the process of engineering and new technology, to gain insight into the operation of those systems, or to observe their behavior. The simultaneous visualization and simulation of a system is called visulation.

Computer simulations vary from computer programs that run a few minutes, to network-based groups of computers running for hours, to ongoing simulations that run for months. The scale of events being simulated by computer simulations has far exceeded anything possible (or perhaps even imaginable) using the traditional paper-and-pencil mathematical modeling: over 10 years ago, a desert-battle simulation, of one force invading another, involved the modeling of 66,239 tanks, trucks and other vehicles on simulated terrain around Kuwait, using multiple supercomputers in the DoD High Performance Computer Modernization Program.

Information Visualization

Information visualization is the study of "the visual representation of large-scale collections of non-numerical information, such as files and lines of code in software systems, library and bibliographic databases, networks of relations on the internet, and so forth".

Information visualization focused on the creation of approaches for conveying abstract information in intuitive ways. Visual representations and interaction techniques take advantage of the human eye's broad bandwidth pathway into the mind to allow users to see, explore, and understand large amounts of information at once. The key difference between scientific visualization and information visualization is that information visualization is often applied to data that is not generated by scientific inquiry. Some examples are graphical representations of data for business, government, news and social media.

Interface Technology and Perception

Interface technology and perception shows how new interfaces and a better understanding of underlying perceptual issues create new opportunities for the scientific visualization community.

Surface Rendering

Rendering is the process of generating an image from a model, by means of computer programs. The model is a description of three-dimensional objects in a strictly defined language or data structure. It would contain geometry, viewpoint, texture, lighting, and shading information. The image is a digital image or raster graphics image. The term may be by analogy with an "artist's rendering" of a scene. 'Rendering' is also used to describe the process of calculating effects in a video editing file to produce final video output. Important rendering techniques are:

Scanline rendering and rasterisation

A high-level representation of an image necessarily contains elements in a different domain from pixels. These elements are referred to as primitives.

In a schematic drawing, for instance, line segments and curves might be primitives. In a graphical user interface, windows and buttons might be the primitives. In 3D rendering, triangles and polygons in space might be primitives.

Ray casting

Ray casting is primarily used for realtime simulations, such as those used in 3D computer games and cartoon animations, where detail is not important, or where it is more efficient to manually fake the details in order to obtain better performance in the computational stage. This is usually the case when a large number of frames need to be animated. The resulting surfaces have a characteristic 'flat' appearance when no additional tricks are used, as if objects in the scene were all painted with matte finish.

Radiosity

Radiosity, also known as Global Illumination, is a method that attempts to simulate the way in which directly illuminated surfaces act as indirect light sources that illuminate other surfaces. This produces more realistic shading and seems to better capture the 'ambience' of an indoor scene. A classic example is the way that shadows 'hug' the corners of rooms.

Ray tracing

Ray tracing is an extension of the same technique developed in scanline rendering and ray casting. Like those, it handles complicated objects well, and the objects may be described mathematically. Unlike scanline and casting, ray tracing is almost always a Monte Carlo technique, that is one based on averaging a number of randomly generated samples from a model.

Volume Rendering

Volume rendering is a technique used to display a 2D projection of a 3D discretely sampled data set. A typical 3D data set is a group of 2D slice images acquired by a CT or MRI scanner. Usually these are acquired in a regular pattern (e.g., one slice every millimeter) and usually have a regular number of image pixels in a regular pattern. This is an example of a regular volumetric grid, with each volume element, or voxel represented by a single value that is obtained by sampling the immediate area surrounding the voxel.

Volume Visualization

According to Rosenblum (1994) "volume visualization examines a set of techniques that allows viewing an object without mathematically representing the other surface. Initially used in medical imaging, volume visualization has become an essential technique for many sciences, portraying phenomena become an essential technique such as clouds, water flows, and molecular and biological structure. Many volume visualization algorithms are computationally expensive and demand large data storage. Advances in hardware and software are generalizing volume visualization as well as real time performances".

Scientific Visualization Applications

This section will give a series of examples how scientific visualization can be applied today.

In The Natural Sciences

Star formation: The featured plot is a Volume plot of the logarithm of gas/dust density in an Enzo star and galaxy simulation. Regions of high density are white while less dense regions are more blue and also more transparent.

Gravitational waves

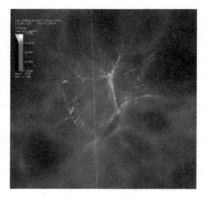

Star formation

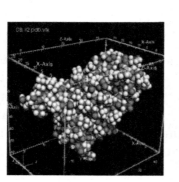

Molecular rendering

Massive Star Supernovae Explosions

Gravitational waves: Researchers used the Globus Toolkit to harness the power of multiple supercomputers to simulate the gravitational effects of black-hole collisions.

Massive Star Supernovae Explosions: In the image, three-Dimensional Radiation Hydrodynamics Calculations of Massive Star Supernovae Explosions The DJEHUTY stellar evolution code was used to calculate the explosion of SN 1987A model in three dimensions.

Molecular rendering: VisIt's general plotting capabilities were used to create the molecular rendering shown in the featured visualization. The original data was taken from the Protein Data Bank and turned into a VTK file before rendering.

In Geography and Ecology

Terrain visualization: VisIt can read several file formats common in the field of Geographic Information Systems (GIS), allowing one to plot raster data such as terrain data in visualizations. The featured image shows a plot of a DEM dataset containing mountainous areas near Dunsmuir, CA. Elevation lines are added to the plot to help delineate changes in elevation.

Terrain rendering

Tornado Simulation: This image was created from data generated by a tornado simulation calculated on NCSA's IBM p690 computing cluster. High-definition television animations of the storm produced at NCSA were included in an episode of the PBS television series NOVA called "Hunt for the Supertwister." The tornado is shown by spheres that are colored according to pressure; orange and blue tubes represent the rising and falling airflow around the tornado.

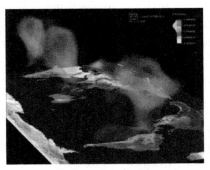

Climate visualization

Climate visualization: This visualization depicts the carbon dioxide from various sources that are advected individually as tracers in the atmosphere model. Carbon dioxide from the ocean is shown as plumes during February 1900.

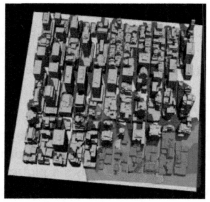

Atmospheric Anomaly in Times Square

Atmospheric Anomaly in Times Square In the image the results from the SAMRAI simulation framework of an atmospheric anomaly in and around Times Square are visualized.

View of a 4D cube projected into 3D: orthogonal projection (left) and perspective projection (right).

In Mathematics

Scientific visualization of mathematical structures has been undertaken for purposes of building intuition and for aiding the forming of mental models.

Higher-dimensional objects can be visualized in form of projections (views) in lower dimensions. In particular, 4-dimensional objects are visualized by means of projection in three dimensions. The lower-dimensional projections of higher-dimensional objects can be used for purposes of virtual object manipulation, allowing 3D objects to be manipulated by operations performed in 2D, and 4D objects by interactions performed in 3D.

In the Formal Sciences

Computer mapping of topographical surfaces: Through computer mapping of topographical surfaces, mathematicians can test theories of how materials will change when stressed. The imaging is part of the work on the NSF-funded Electronic Visualization Laboratory at the University of Illinois at Chicago.

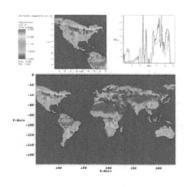

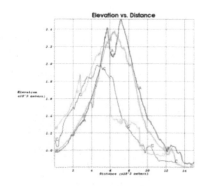

Image annotations   Curve plots

Curve plots: VisIt can plot curves from data read from files and it can be used to extract and plot curve data from higher-dimensional datasets using lineout operators or queries. The curves in the featured image correspond to elevation data along lines drawn on DEM data and were created with the feature lineout capability. Lineout allows you to interactively draw a line, which specifies a path for data extraction. The resulting data was then plotted as curves.

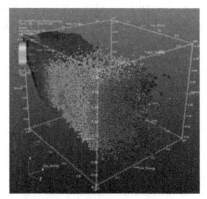

Scatter plot

Image annotations: The featured plot shows Leaf Area Index (LAI), a measure of global vegetative matter, from a NetCDF dataset. The primary plot is the large plot at the bottom, which shows the LAI for the whole world. The plots on top are actually annotations that contain images generated earlier. Image annotations can be used to include material that enhances a visualization such as auxiliary plots, images of experimental data, project logos, etc.

Scatter plot: VisIt's Scatter plot allows to visualize multivariate data of up to four dimensions. The Scatter plot takes multiple scalar variables and uses them for different axes in phase space. The different variables are combined to form coordinates in the phase space and they are displayed using glyphs and colored using another scalar variable.

In The Applied Sciences

Porsche 911 model (NASTRAN model): The featured plot contains a Mesh plot of a Porsche 911 model imported from a NASTRAN bulk data file. VisIt can read a limited subset of NASTRAN bulk data files, in general enough to import model geometry for visualization.

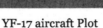

YF-17 aircraft Plot   Porsche 911 model

YF-17 aircraft Plot: The featured image displays plots of a CGNS dataset representing a YF-17 jet aircraft. The dataset consists of an unstructured grid with solution. The image was created by using a pseudocolor plot of the dataset's Mach variable, a Mesh plot of the grid, and Vector plot of a slice through the Velocity field.

City rendering

City rendering: An ESRI shapefile containing a polygonal description of the building footprints was read in and then the polygons were resampled onto a rectilinear grid, which was extruded into the featured cityscape.

Inbound traffic measured: This image is a visualization study of inbound traffic measured in billions of bytes on the NSFNET T1 backbone for the month of September 1991. The traffic volume range is depicted from purple (zero bytes) to white (100 billion bytes). It represents data collected by Merit Network, Inc.

Scientific Visualization Organizations

Important laboratory in the field are:

- Electronic Visualization Laboratory

- NASA Goddard Scientific Visualization Studio.

Conferences in this field, ranked by significance in scientific visualization research, are:

- IEEE Visualization

- EuroVis

- SIGGRAPH

- Eurographics

- Graphicon

Drug Design

Drug design, often referred to as rational drug design or simply rational design, is the inventive process of finding new medications based on the knowledge of a biological target. The drug is most commonly an organic small molecule that activates or inhibits the function of a biomolecule such as a protein, which in turn results in a therapeutic benefit to the patient. In the most basic sense, drug design involves the design of molecules that are complementary in shape and charge to the biomolecular target with which they interact and therefore will bind to it. Drug design frequently but not necessarily relies on computer modeling techniques. This type of modeling is sometimes referred to as computer-aided drug design. Finally, drug design that relies on the knowledge of the three-dimensional structure of the biomolecular target is known as structure-based drug design. In addition to small molecules, biopharmaceuticals and especially therapeutic antibodies are an increasingly important class of drugs and computational methods for improving the affinity, selectivity, and stability of these protein-based therapeutics have also been developed.

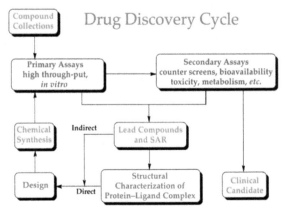

The phrase "drug design" is to some extent a misnomer. A more accurate term is ligand design (i.e., design of a molecule that will bind tightly to its target). Although design techniques for prediction of binding affinity are reasonably successful, there are many other properties, such as bioavailability, metabolic half-life, side effects, etc., that first must be optimized before a ligand can become a safe and efficacious drug. These other characteristics are often difficult to predict with rational design techniques. Nevertheless, due to high attrition rates, especially during clinical phases of drug development, more attention is being focused early in the drug design process on selecting candidate drugs whose physicochemical properties are predicted to result in fewer complications during development and hence more likely to lead to an approved, marketed drug. Furthermore, in vitro experiments complemented with computation methods are increasingly used in early drug discovery to select compounds with more favorable ADME (absorption, distribution, metabolism, and excretion) and toxicological profiles.

Drug Targets

A biomolecular target (most commonly a protein or nucleic acid) is a key molecule involved in a particular metabolic or signaling pathway that is associated with a specific disease condition or pathology or to the infectivity or survival of a microbial pathogen. Potential drug targets are not necessarily disease causing but must by definition be disease modifying. In some cases, small molecules will be designed to enhance or inhibit the target function in the specific disease modifying pathway. Small molecules (for example receptor agonists, antagonists, inverse agonists, or modulators; enzyme activators or inhibitors; or ion channel openers or blockers) will be designed that are complementary to the binding site of target. Small molecules (drugs) can be designed so as not to affect any other important "off-target" molecules (often referred to as anti-targets) since drug interactions with off-target molecules may lead to undesirable side effects. Due to similarities in binding sites, closely related targets identified through sequence homology have the highest chance of cross reactivity and hence highest side effect potential.

Most commonly, drugs are organic small molecules produced through chemical synthesis, but biopolymer-based drugs (also known as biopharmaceuticals) produced through biological processes are becoming increasingly more common. In addition, mRNA-based gene silencing technologies may have therapeutic applications.

Rational Drug Discovery

In contrast to traditional methods of drug discovery (known as forward pharmacology), which rely on trial-and-error testing of chemical substances on cultured cells or animals, and matching the apparent effects to treatments, rational drug design (also called reverse pharmacology) begins with a hypothesis that modulation of a specific biological target may have therapeutic value. In order for a biomolecule to be selected as a drug target, two essential pieces of information are required. The first is evidence that modulation of the target will be disease modifying. This knowledge may come from, for example, disease linkage studies that show an association between mutations in the biological target and certain disease states. The second is that the target is "druggable". This means that it is capable of binding to a small molecule and that its activity can be modulated by the small molecule.

Once a suitable target has been identified, the target is normally cloned and produced and purified. The purified protein is then used to establish a screening assay. In addition, the three-dimensional structure of the target may be determined.

The search for small molecules that bind to the target is begun by screening libraries of potential drug compounds. This may be done by using the screening assay (a "wet screen"). In addition, if the structure of the target is available, a virtual screen may be performed of candidate drugs. Ideally the candidate drug compounds should be "drug-like", that is they should possess properties that are predicted to lead to oral bioavailability, adequate chemical and metabolic stability, and minimal toxic effects. Several methods are available to estimate druglikeness such as Lipinski's Rule of Five and a range of scoring methods such as lipophilic efficiency. Several methods for predicting drug metabolism have also been proposed in the scientific literature.

Due to the large number of drug properties that must be simultaneously optimized during the design process, multi-objective optimization techniques are sometimes employed. Finally because of the limitations in the current methods for prediction of activity, drug design is still very much reliant on serendipity and bounded rationality.

Computer-aided Drug Design

The most fundamental goal in drug design is to predict whether a given molecule will bind to a target and if so how strongly. Molecular mechanics or molecular dynamics is most often used to estimate the strength of the intermolecular interaction between the small molecule and its biological target. These methods are also used to predict the conformation of the small molecule and to model conformational changes in the target that may occur when the small molecule binds to it. Semi-empirical, ab initio quantum chemistry methods, or density functional theory are often used to provide optimized parameters for the molecular mechanics calculations and also provide an estimate of the electronic properties (electrostatic potential, polarizability, etc.) of the drug candidate that will influence binding affinity.

Molecular mechanics methods may also be used to provide semi-quantitative prediction of the binding affinity. Also, knowledge-based scoring function may be used to provide binding affinity estimates. These methods use linear regression, machine learning, neural nets or other statistical techniques to derive predictive binding affinity equations by fitting experimental affinities to computationally derived interaction energies between the small molecule and the target.

Ideally, the computational method will be able to predict affinity before a compound is synthesized and hence in theory only one compound needs to be synthesized, saving enormous time and cost. The reality is that present computational methods are imperfect and provide, at best, only qualitatively accurate estimates of affinity. In practice it still takes several iterations of design, synthesis, and testing before an optimal drug is discovered. Computational methods have accelerated discovery by reducing the number of iterations required and have often provided novel structures.

Drug design with the help of computers may be used at any of the following stages of drug discovery:

1. hit identification using virtual screening (structure- or ligand-based design)

2. hit-to-lead optimization of affinity and selectivity (structure-based design, QSAR, etc.)

3. lead optimization of other pharmaceutical properties while maintaining affinity

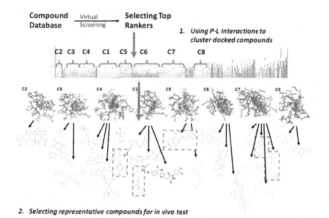

Flowchart of a Usual Clustering Analysis for Structure-Based Drug Design

In order to overcome the insufficient prediction of binding affinity calculated by recent scoring functions, the protein-ligand interaction and compound 3D structure information are used for analysis. For structure-based drug design, several post-screening analyses focusing on protein-ligand interaction have been developed for improving enrichment and effectively mining potential candidates:

- Consensus scoring

  ○ Selecting candidates by voting of multiple scoring functions

  ○ May lose the relationship between protein-ligand structural information and scoring criterion

- Cluster analysis

o   Represent and cluster candidates according to protein-ligand 3D information

o   Needs meaningful representation of protein-ligand interactions.

Types

There are two major types of drug design. The first is referred to as ligand-based drug design and the second, structure-based drug design.

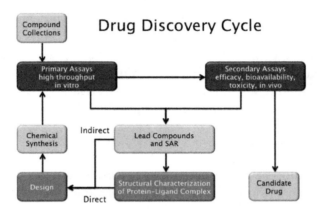

Drug discovery cycle highlighting both ligand-based (indirect) and structure-based (direct) drug design strategies.

Ligand-based

Ligand-based drug design (or indirect drug design) relies on knowledge of other molecules that bind to the biological target of interest. These other molecules may be used to derive a pharmacophore model that defines the minimum necessary structural characteristics a molecule must possess in order to bind to the target. In other words, a model of the biological target may be built based on the knowledge of what binds to it, and this model in turn may be used to design new molecular entities that interact with the target. Alternatively, a quantitative structure-activity relationship (QSAR), in which a correlation between calculated properties of molecules and their experimentally determined biological activity, may be derived. These QSAR relationships in turn may be used to predict the activity of new analogs.

Structure-based

Structure-based drug design (or direct drug design) relies on knowledge of the three dimensional structure of the biological target obtained through methods such as x-ray crystallography or NMR spectroscopy. If an experimental structure of a target is not available, it may be possible to create a homology model of the target based on the experimental structure of a related protein. Using the structure of the biological target, candidate drugs that are predicted to bind with high affinity and selectivity to the target may be designed using interactive graphics and the intuition of a medicinal chemist. Alternatively various automated computational procedures may be used to suggest new drug candidates.

Current methods for structure-based drug design can be divided roughly into three main categories. The first method is identification of new ligands for a given receptor by searching large databases of 3D structures of small molecules to find those fitting the binding pocket of the receptor using fast approximate docking programs. This method is known as virtual screening. A second category is de novo design of new ligands. In this method, ligand molecules are built up within the constraints of the binding pocket by assembling small pieces in a stepwise manner. These pieces can be either individual atoms or molecular fragments. The key advantage of such a method is that novel structures, not contained in any database, can be suggested. A third method is the optimization of known ligands by evaluating proposed analogs within the binding cavity.

Binding Site Identification

Binding site identification is the first step in structure based design. If the structure of the target or a sufficiently similar homolog is determined in the presence of a bound ligand, then the ligand should be observable in the structure in which case location of the binding site is trivial. However, there may be unoccupied allosteric binding sites that may be of interest. Furthermore, it may be that only apoprotein (protein without ligand) structures are available and the reliable identification of unoccupied sites that have the potential to bind ligands with high affinity is non-trivial. In brief, binding site identification usually relies on identification of concave surfaces on the protein that can accommodate drug sized molecules that also possess appropriate "hot spots" (hydrophobic surfaces, hydrogen bonding sites, etc.) that drive ligand binding.

Scoring Functions

Structure-based drug design attempts to use the structure of proteins as a basis for designing new ligands by applying the principles of molecular recognition. Selective high affinity binding to the target is generally desirable since it leads to more efficacious drugs with fewer side effects. Thus, one of the most important principles for designing or obtaining potential new ligands is to predict the binding affinity of a certain ligand to its target (and known antitargets) and use the predicted affinity as a criterion for selection.

One early general-purposed empirical scoring function to describe the binding energy of ligands to receptors was developed by Böhm. This empirical scoring function took the form:

$$\Delta G_{bind} = \Delta G_0 + \Delta G_{hb}\Sigma_{h-bonds} + \Delta G_{ionic}\Sigma_{ionic-int} + \Delta G_{lipophilic}\left|A\right| + \Delta G_{rot}NROT$$

where:

- ΔG_o – empirically derived offset that in part corresponds to the overall loss of translational and rotational entropy of the ligand upon binding.

- ΔG_{hb} – contribution from hydrogen bonding

- ΔG_{ionic} – contribution from ionic interactions

- ΔG_{lip} – contribution from lipophilic interactions where $|A_{lipo}|$ is surface area of lipophilic contact between the ligand and receptor

- ΔG_{rot} – entropy penalty due to freezing a rotatable in the ligand bond upon binding

A more general thermodynamic "master" equation is as follows:

$$\Delta G_{bind} = -RT \ln K_d$$
$$K_d = \frac{[\text{Ligand}][\text{Receptor}]}{[\text{Complex}]}$$

$$\Delta G_{bind} = \Delta G_{desolvation} + \Delta G_{motion} + \Delta G_{configuration} + \Delta G_{interaction}$$

where:

- desolvation – enthalpic penalty for removing the ligand from solvent

- motion – entropic penalty for reducing the degrees of freedom when a ligand binds to its receptor

- configuration – conformational strain energy required to put the ligand in its "active" conformation

- interaction – enthalpic gain for "resolvating" the ligand with its receptor

The basic idea is that the overall binding free energy can be decomposed into independent components that are known to be important for the binding process. Each component reflects a certain kind of free energy alteration during the binding process between a ligand and its target receptor. The Master Equation is the linear combination of these components. According to Gibbs free energy equation, the relation between dissociation equilibrium constant, K_d, and the components of free energy was built.

Various computational methods are used to estimate each of the components of the master equation. For example, the change in polar surface area upon ligand binding can be used to estimate the desolvation energy. The number of rotatable bonds frozen upon ligand binding is proportional to the motion term. The configurational or strain energy can be estimated using molecular mechanics calculations. Finally the interaction energy can be estimated using methods such as the change in non polar surface, statistically derived potentials of mean force, the number of hydrogen bonds formed, etc. In practice, the components of the master equation are fit to experimental data using multiple linear regression. This can be done with a diverse training set including many types of ligands and receptors to produce a less accurate but more general "global" model or a more restricted set of ligands and receptors to produce a more accurate but less general "local" model.

Examples

A particular example of rational drug design involves the use of three-dimensional information about biomolecules obtained from such techniques as X-ray crystallography and NMR spectroscopy. Computer-aided drug design in particular becomes much more tractable when there is a high-resolution structure of a target protein bound to a potent ligand. This approach to drug discovery is sometimes referred to as structure-based drug design. The first unequivocal example of the application of structure-based drug design leading to an approved drug is the carbonic anhydrase inhibitor dorzolamide, which was approved in 1995.

Another important case study in rational drug design is imatinib, a tyrosine kinase inhibitor designed specifically for the *bcr-abl* fusion protein that is characteristic for Philadelphia chromosome-positive leukemias (chronic myelogenous leukemia and occasionally acute lymphocytic leukemia). Imatinib is substantially different from previous drugs for cancer, as most agents of chemotherapy simply target rapidly dividing cells, not differentiating between cancer cells and other tissues.

Additional examples include:

- Many of the atypical antipsychotics
- Cimetidine, the prototypical H_2-receptor antagonist from which the later members of the class were developed
- Selective COX-2 inhibitor NSAIDs
- Enfuvirtide, a peptide HIV entry inhibitor
- Nonbenzodiazepines like zolpidem and zopiclone
- Raltegravir, an HIV integrase inhibitor
- SSRIs (selective serotonin reuptake inhibitors), a class of antidepressants
- Zanamivir, an antiviral drug

Case Studies

- 5-HT3 antagonists

- Acetylcholine receptor agonists

- Angiotensin receptor antagonists

- Bcr-Abl tyrosine-kinase inhibitors

- Cannabinoid receptor antagonists

- CCR5 receptor antagonists

- Cyclooxygenase 2 inhibitors

- Dipeptidyl peptidase-4 inhibitors

- HIV protease inhibitors

- NK1 receptor antagonists

- Non-nucleoside reverse transcriptase inhibitors

- Nucleoside and nucleotide reverse transcriptase inhibitors

- PDE5 inhibitors

- Proton pump inibitors

- Renin inhibitors

- Triptans

- TRPV1 antagonists

- c-Met inhibitors

Criticism

It has been argued that the highly rigid and focused nature of rational drug design suppresses serendipity in drug discovery. Because many of the most significant medical discoveries have been inadvertent, the recent focus on rational drug design may limit the progress of drug discovery. Furthermore, the rational design of a drug may be limited by a crude or incomplete understanding of the underlying molecular processes of the disease it is intended to treat.

Pixel Art

Pixel art is a form of digital art, created through the use of raster graphics software, where images are edited on the pixel level. Graphics in most old (or relatively limited) computer, console, graphing calculator and mobile games are mostly pixel art.

An example of pixel art.

History

The term *pixel art* was first published by Adele Goldberg and Robert Flegal of Xerox Palo Alto Research Center in 1982. The concept, however, goes back about 11 years before that, for example in Richard Shoup's SuperPaint system in 1972, also at Xerox PARC.

Some traditional art forms, such as counted-thread embroidery (including cross-stitch) and some kinds of mosaic and beadwork, are very similar to pixel art. These art forms construct pictures out of small colored units similar to the pixels of modern digital computing. A similar concept on a much bigger scale can be seen in the North Korean Arirang Festival.

There are some similarities of technique and style between pixel art and older artistic movements like Impressionism, Abstract Art, and especially Cubism.

Definition

Image filters (such as blurring or alpha-blending) or tools with automatic anti-aliasing are considered by most advanced pixel artists as invalid tools for pixel art, as such tools calculate new pixel values automatically, contrasting with the precise manual arrangement of pixels associated with pixel art.

Types

Drawings usually start with what is called the line art, which is the basic line that defines the character, building or anything else the artist is intending to draw. Linearts are usually traced over scanned drawings and are often shared among other pixel artists. Other techniques, some resembling painting, also exist.

The limited palette often implemented in pixel art usually promotes dithering to achieve different shades and colors, but due to the nature of this form of art this is done completely by hand. *Hand-made* anti-aliasing is also used.

Here are a few parts of the above image of "The Gunk" in detail, depicting a few of the techniques involved:

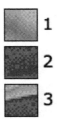

1. The basic form of dithering, using two colors in a 2×2 checkerboard pattern. Changing the density of each color will lead to different subtones.

2. Stylized dithering with 2×2 pixel squares randomly scattered can produce interesting textures. Small circles are also frequent.

3. Anti-aliasing can be done, by hand, to smooth curves and transitions. Some artists only do this internally, to keep crisp outlines that can go over any background. The PNG alpha channel can be used to create external anti-aliasing for any background.

Saving and Compression

Pixel art is preferably stored in a file format utilizing lossless data compression, such as run-length encoding or an indexed color palette. GIF and PNG are two file formats commonly used for storing pixel art. The JPEG format is avoided because its lossy compression algorithm is designed for smooth continuous-tone images and introduces visible artifacts in the presence of dithering.

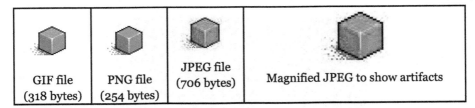

| GIF file (318 bytes) | PNG file (254 bytes) | JPEG file (706 bytes) | Magnified JPEG to show artifacts |

Categories

Pixel art is commonly divided in two subcategories: isometric and non-isometric. The isometric kind is drawn in a near-isometric dimetric projection. This is commonly seen in games to provide a three-dimensional view without using any real three-dimensional processing. Technically, an isometric angle would be of 30 degrees from the horizontal, but this is avoided since the pixels created by a line drawing algorithm would not follow a neat pattern. To fix this, lines with a 1:2 pixel ratio are picked, leading to an angle of about 26.57 degrees (arctan 0.5). One subcategory is planometric, which is done at a 1:1 angle, giving a more top-down look. Another subcategory is "rpg perspective", in which the x and z (vertical) axes are combined into a side/top view. This view is facing an edge, instead of a vertex.

- Examples of near-isometric pixel art

PixelPlaza *City*

Non-isometric pixel art is any pixel art that does not fall in the isometric category, such as views from the top, side, front, bottom or perspective views.

Scaling

When pixel art is displayed at a higher resolution than the source image, it is often scaled using the nearest neighbor interpolation algorithm. This avoids blurring caused by other algorithms, such as bilinear and bicubic interpolation—which interpolate between adjacent pixels and work best on continuous tones, but not sharp edges or lines. Nearest-neighbor interpolation preserves these sharp edges, but it makes diagonal lines and curves look blocky, an effect called pixelation. Thus, hybrid algorithms have been devised to interpolate between continuous tones while preserving the sharpness of lines in the piece; such attempts include the 2xSaI, Super Eagle, and the high-quality hqx algorithms.

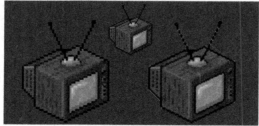

2x zoom interpolated using nearest-neighbor interpolation (left) and the 2xSaI algorithm (right)

Uses

Pixel art was very often used in older computer and console video games. With the increasing use of 3D graphics in games, pixel art lost some of its use. Despite that, this is still a very active professional/amateur area, since mobile phones and other portable devices still have low resolution and therefore require skillful use of space and memory. Sometimes pixel art is used for advertising too. One such company that uses pixel art to advertise is Bell. The group eboy specializes in isometric pixel graphics for advertising and has been featured in magazines such as *Wired*, *Popular Science*, and *Fortune 500*.

Icons for operating systems with limited graphics abilities are also pixel art. The limited number of colors and resolution presents a challenge when attempting to convey complicated concepts and ideas in an efficient way. On the Microsoft Windows desktop icons are raster images of various sizes, the smaller of which are not necessarily scaled from the larger ones and could be considered pixel art. On the GNOME and KDE desktops, icons are represented primarily by SVG images, but also with hand-optimized, pixel art PNGs for smaller sizes such as 16x16 and 24x24. Another use of pixel art on modern desktop computers is favicons.

An example of pixel art in a modern video game, *Broforce*

Modern pixel art has been seen as a reaction to the 3D graphics industry by amateur game/graphic hobbyists. Many retro enthusiasts often choose to mimic the style of the past. Some view the pixel art revival as restoring the golden age of second and third generation consoles, where it is argued graphics were more aesthetically pleasing. Pixel art still remains popular and has been used in social networking virtual worlds such as Citypixel and Habbo, as well as among hand-held devices such as the Nintendo DS, Nintendo 3DS, PSP, PS Vita and Cellphones, and in modern indie games such as Hotline Miami and FTL: Faster Than Light. Pixel art is also used in textures for Minecraft.

Software

- GraphicsGale, for Windows, has both freeware and shareware versions, and has features designed for animation and cursor creation.

- Deluxe Paint, a graphics editor for the Amiga frequently used by demoscene pixel artists.

- GrafX2, a Free Software bitmap editor.

- Cosmigo Pro Motion, a professional graphics editor used for creating images and animations with pixel precision, it has a similar design to Deluxe Paint.

- Microsoft Paint, the raster graphic editor bundled with Microsoft Windows.

- Pixen, a graphics and animation editor for Mac OS X tailored toward pixel art

- Piskel, a free online program

- Pixel Art Studio, Windows 10 universal app for making sprites, pixel art and animations

References

- Zwicky, E.D, Cooper, S and Chapman, D,B. (2000). Building Internet Firewalls. United States: O'Reily & Associates. p. 804. ISBN 1-56592-871-7.

- Niederst, Jennifer (2006). Web Design In a Nutshell. United States of America: O'Reilly Media. pp. 12–14. ISBN 0-596-00987-9.

- Oleksy, Walter (2001). Careers in Web Design. New York: The Rosen Publishing Group,Inc. pp. 9–11. ISBN 9780823931910.

- Chaos and fractals: new frontiers of science by Heinz-Otto Peitgen, Hartmut Jürgens, Dietmar Saupe 2004 ISBN 0-387-20229-3.

- Digital modeling of material appearance by Julie Dorsey, Holly E. Rushmeier, François X. Sillion 2007 ISBN 0-12-221181-2.

- Interactive environments with open-source software: 3D walkthroughs by Wolfgang Höhl, Wolfgang Höhl 2008 ISBN 3-211-79169-8.

- Interactive storytelling: First Joint International Conference by Ulrike Spierling, Nicolas Szilas 2008 ISBN 3-540-89424-1.

- Mathematical optimization in computer graphics and vision by Luiz Velho, Paulo Cezar Pinto Carvalho 2008 ISBN 0-12-715951-7.

- Trends in interactive visualization by Elena van Zudilova-Seinstra, Tony Adriaansen, Robert Liere 2008 ISBN 1-84800-268-8.

- Abrash, Michael. Michael Abrash's Graphics Programming Black Book Special Edition. The Coriolis Group, Scottsdale Arizona, 1997. ISBN 1-57610-174-6.

- James Clerk Maxwell and P. M. Harman (2002), The Scientific Letters and Papers of James Clerk Maxwell, Volume 3; 1874–1879, Cambridge University Press, ISBN 0-521-25627-5.

- Madsen U, Krogsgaard-Larsen P, Liljefors T (2002). Textbook of Drug Design and Discovery. Washington, DC: Taylor & Francis. ISBN 0-415-28288-8.

- Reynolds CH, Merz KM, Ringe D, eds. (2010). Drug Design: Structure- and Ligand-Based Approaches (1 ed.). Cambridge, UK: Cambridge University Press. ISBN 978-0521887236.

- Wu-Pong S, Rojanasakul Y (2008). Biopharmaceutical drug design and development (2nd ed.). Totowa, NJ Humana Press: Humana Press. ISBN 978-1-59745-532-9.

- Hopkins AL (2011). "Chapter 25: Pharmacological space". In Wermuth CG. The Practice of Medicinal Chemistry (3 ed.). Academic Press. pp. 521–527. ISBN 978-0-12-374194-3.

- Kirchmair J (2014). Drug Metabolism Prediction. Wiley's Methods and Principles in Medicinal Chemistry. 63. Wiley-VCH. ISBN 978-3-527-67301-8.

- Guner OF (2000). Pharmacophore Perception, Development, and use in Drug Design. La Jolla, Calif: International University Line. ISBN 0-9636817-6-1.

Evolution of Computer Graphics

The history of computer graphics is an important part of the subject of computer graphics. The initial use of this technology was for scientific reasons and research purposes but as this subject grew, the focus shifted to art and media. This chapter helps the readers in understanding the growth and evolution of computer graphics over a period of decades.

History of Computer Animation

As early as the 1940s and '50s, experiments in computer graphics were beginning, most notably by John Whitney—but it was only by the early 1960s when digital computers had become widely established, that new avenues for innovative computer graphics blossomed. Initially, uses were mainly for scientific, engineering and other research purposes, but artistic experimentation began to make its appearance by the mid-1960s. By the mid-'70s, many such efforts were beginning to enter into public media. Much computer graphics at this time involved 2-dimensional imagery, though increasingly, as computer power improved, efforts to achieve 3-dimensional realism become the emphasis. By the late 1980s, photo-realistic 3D was beginning to appear in cinema movies, and by mid-'90s had developed to the point where 3D animation could be used for entire feature film production.

The Earliest Pioneers: 1940s to Mid-1960s

John Whitney

John Whitney, Sr was an American animator, composer and inventor, widely considered to be one of the fathers of computer animation. In the '40s and '50s, he and his brother James created a series of experimental films made with a custom-built device based on old anti-aircraft analog computers (Kerrison Predictors) connected by servos to control the motion of lights and lit objects — the first example of motion control photography. One of Whitney's best known works from this early period was the animated title sequence from Alfred Hitchcock's 1958 film *Vertigo*, which he collaborated on with graphic designer Saul Bass. In 1960, Whitney established his company Motion Graphics Inc, which largely focused on producing titles for film and television, while continuing further experimental works. In 1968, his pioneering motion control model photography was used on Stanley Kubrick's movie *2001: A Space Odyssey*, and also for the slit-scan photography technique used in the film's "Star Gate" finale. All of John

Whitney's sons (Michael, Mark and John Jr.) are also film-makers. John Whitney died in 1995.

The First Digital Image

One of the first programmable digital computers was SEAC (the Standards Eastern Automatic Computer), which entered service in 1950 at the National Bureau of Standards (NBS) in Maryland, USA. In 1957, computer pioneer Russell Kirsch and his team unveiled a drum scanner for SEAC, to "trace variations of intensity over the surfaces of photographs", and so doing made the first digital image by scanning a photograph. The image, picturing Kirsch's three-month-old son, consisted of just 176×176 pixels. They used the computer to extract line drawings, count objects, recognize types of characters and display digital images on an oscilloscope screen. This breakthrough can be seen as the forerunner of all subsequent computer imaging, and recognising the importance of this first digital photograph, Life magazine in 2003 credited this image as one of the "100 Photographs That Changed the World".

> From the late 1950s and early '60s, mainframe digital computers were becoming commonplace within large organisations and universities, and increasingly these would be equipped with graphic plotting and graphics screen devices. Consequently, a new field of experimentation began to open up.

Boeing-Wichita

In 1960, William Fetter was a graphic designer for Boeing at Wichita, and was credited with coining the phrase "Computer Graphics" to describe what he was doing at Boeing at the time (though Fetter himself credited this to colleague Verne Hudson). Fetter's work included the development of ergonomic descriptions of the human body that are both accurate and adaptable to different environments, and this resulted in the first 3D animated "wire-frame" figures. Such human figures became one of the most iconic images of the early history of computer graphics, and often were referred to as the "Boeing Man". Fetter died in 2002.

Bell Labs

Bell Labs in Murray Hill, New Jersey, was a leading research contributor in computer graphics, computer animation and electronic music from its beginnings in the early 1960s. Initially, researchers were interested in what the computer could be made to do, but the results of the visual work produced by the computer during this period established people like Edward Zajac, Michael Noll and Ken Knowlton as pioneering computer artists.

Edward Zajac produced one of the first computer generated films at Bell Labs in 1963, titled *A Two Gyro Gravity Gradient Attitude Control System*, which demonstrated that a satellite could be stabilized to always have a side facing the Earth as it orbited.

Ken Knowlton developed the Beflix (Bell Flicks) animation system in 1963, which was used to produce dozens of artistic films by artists Stan VanDerBeek, Knowlton and Lillian Schwartz. Instead of raw programming, Beflix worked using simple "graphic primitives", like draw a line, copy a region, fill an area, zoom an area, and the like.

In 1965, Michael Noll created computer-generated stereographic 3D movies, including a ballet of stick figures moving on a stage. Some movies also showed four-dimensional hyper-objects projected to three dimensions. Around 1967, Noll used the 4D animation technique to produce computer animated title sequences for the commercial film short *Incredible Machine* (produced by Bell Labs) and the TV special *The Unexplained* (produced by Walt DeFaria). Many projects in other fields were also undertaken at this time.

Ivan Sutherland

Ivan Sutherland is considered by many to be the creator of Interactive Computer Graphics, and an internet pioneer. He worked at the Lincoln Laboratory at MIT (Massachusetts Institute of Technology) in 1962, where he developed a program called *Sketchpad I*, which allowed the user to interact directly with the image on the screen. This was the first Graphical User Interface, and is considered one of the most influential computer programs ever written by an individual.

Mid-1960s to Mid-1970s

The University of Utah

Utah was a major center for computer animation in this period. The computer science faculty was founded by David Evans in 1965, and many of the basic techniques of 3D computer graphics were developed here in the early 70s with ARPA funding (*Advanced Research Projects Agency*). Research results included Gouraud, Phong, and Blinn shading, texture mapping, hidden surface algorithms, curved surface subdivision, real-time line-drawing and raster image display hardware, and early virtual reality work. In the words of Robert Rivlin in his 1986 book *The Algorithmic Image: Graphic Visions of the Computer Age*, "almost every influential person in the modern computer-graphics community either passed through the University of Utah or came into contact with it in some way".

Evans & Sutherland

In 1968, Ivan Sutherland teamed up with David Evans to found the company Evans & Sutherland—both were professors in the Computer Science Department at the University of Utah, and the company was formed to produce new hardware designed to run the systems being developed in the University. Many such algorithms have later resulted in the generation of significant hardware implementation, including the Geometry Engine, the Head-mounted display, the Frame buffer, and Flight simulators. Most of the employees were active or former students, and included Jim Clark, who started Silicon Graphics in 1981, Ed Catmull, co-founder of Pixar in 1979, and John Warnock of Adobe Systems in 1982.

First Computer Animated Character, Nikolai Konstantinov

In 1968 a group of soviet physicists and mathematicians with N.Konstantinov as its head created a mathematical model for the motion of a cat. On a BESM-4 computer they devised a programme for solving the ordinary differential equations for this model. The Computer printed hundreds of frames on paper using alphabet symbols that were latter filmed in sequence thus creating the first computer animation of a character, a walking cat.

Ohio State

Charles Csuri, an artist at The Ohio State University (OSU), started experimenting with the application of computer graphics to art in 1963. His efforts resulted in a prominent CG research laboratory that received funding from the National Science Foundation and other government and private agencies. The work at OSU revolved around animation languages, complex modeling environments, user-centric interfaces, human and creature motion descriptions, and other areas of interest to the discipline.

Cybernetic Serendipity

In July 1968, the arts journal *Studio International* published a special issue titled *Cybernetic Serendipity - the computer and the arts*, which catalogued a comprehensive collection of items and examples of work being done in the field of computer art in organisations all over the world, and shown in exhibitions in London, UK, San Francisco, CA. and Washington, DC. This marked a milestone in the development of the medium, and was considered by many to be of widespread influence and inspiration. Apart from all the examples mentioned above, two other particularly well known iconic images from this include *Chaos to Order* by Charles Csuri (often referred to as the *Hummingbird*), created at Ohio State University in 1967, and *Running Cola is Africa* by Masao Komura and Koji Fujino created at the Computer Technique Group, Japan, also in 1967.

Scanimate

The first machine to achieve widespread public attention in the media was Scanimate, an analog computer animation system designed and built by Lee Harrison of the Computer Image Corporation in Denver. From around 1969 onward, Scanimate systems were used to produce much of the video-based animation seen on television in commercials, show titles, and other graphics. It could create animations in real time, a great advantage over digital systems at the time.

National Film Board of Canada

The National Film Board of Canada, already a world center for animation art, also began experimentation with computer techniques in 1969. Most well-known of the early pioneers with this was artist Peter Foldes, who completed *Metadata* in 1971. This film comprised drawings animated by gradually changing from one image to the next, a technique known as "interpolating" (also known as "inbetweening" or "morphing"), which also featured in a number of earlier art examples during the 1960s. In 1974, Foldes completed *Hunger / La Faim*, which was one of the first films to show solid filled (raster scanned) rendering, and was awarded the Jury Prize in the short film category at 1974 Cannes Film Festival, as well as an Academy Award nomination.

Atlas Computer Laboratory & Antics

The Atlas Computer Laboratory near Oxford was for many years a major facility for computer animation in Britain. The first entertainment cartoon made was *The Flexipede*, by Tony Pritchett, which was first shown publicly at the Cybernetic Serendipity exhibition in 1968. Artist Colin Emmett and animator Alan Kitching first developed solid filled colour rendering in 1972, notably for the title animation for the BBC's *The Burke Special* TV program.

In 1973, Kitching went on to develop a software called *Antics*, which allowed users to create animation without needing any programming. The package was broadly based on conventional "cel" (celluloid) techniques, but with a wide range of tools including camera and graphics effects, interpolation ("inbetweening"/"morphing"), use of skeleton figures and grid overlays. Any number of drawings or cels could be animated at once by "choreographing" them in limitless ways using various types of "movements". At the time, only black & white plotter output was available, but Antics was able to produce full-color output by using the Technicolor Three-strip Process. Hence the name Antics was coined as an acronym for *AN*imated *T*echnicolor-*I*mage *C*omputer *S*ystem. Antics was used for many animation works, including the first complete documentary movie *Finite Elements*, made for the Atlas Lab itself in 1975.

> From around the early 70s, much of the emphasis in computer animation development was towards ever increasing realism in 3D imagery, and on effects designed for use in feature movies.

First Digital Animation in a Feature Film

The first feature film to use digital image processing was the 1973 movie *Westworld*, a science-fiction film written and directed by novelist Michael Crichton, in which humanoid robots live amongst the humans. John Whitney, Jr, and Gary Demos at Information International, Inc. digitally processed motion picture photography to appear pixelized in order to portray the Gunslinger android's point of view. The cinegraphic block portraiture was accomplished using the Technicolor Three-strip Process to color-separate each frame of the source images, then scanning them to convert into rectangular blocks according to its tone values, and finally outputting the result back to film. The process was covered in the *American Cinematographer* article "Behind the scenes of Westworld".

SIGGRAPH

Sam Matsa whose background in graphics started with the APT project at MIT with Doug Ross and Andy Van Dam petitioned ACM to form a SICGRAPH (Special Interest Committee on Computer Graphics), the forerunner of SIGGRAPH in 1968. In 1974, the first SIGGRAPH conference on computer graphics opened. This annual conference soon became the dominant venue for presenting innovations in the field.

Towards 3D: Mid-1970s into the 1980s

Early 3D Animation in the Cinema

The first use of 3D wireframe imagery in mainstream cinema was in the sequel to *Westworld*, *Futureworld* (1976), directed by Richard T. Heffron. This featured a computer-generated hand and face created by then University of Utah graduate students Edwin Catmull and Fred Parke which had initially appeared in their 1971 experimental short *A Computer Animated Hand*. The third movie to use this technology was *Star Wars* (1977), written and directed by George Lucas, with wireframe imagery in the scenes with the Death Star plans, the targeting computers in the X-wing fighters, and the *Millennium Falcon* spacecraft. in The Oscar-winning 1975 short animated film *Great*, about the life of the Victorian engineer Isambard Kingdom Brunel, contains a brief sequence of a rotating wireframe model of Brunel's final project, the iron steam ship SS Great Eastern.

The Walt Disney film *The Black Hole* (1979, directed by Gary Nelson) used wireframe rendering to depict the titular black hole, using equipment from Disney's engineers. In the same year, the science-fiction horror film *Alien*, directed by Ridley Scott, also used wireframe model graphics, in this case to render the navigation monitors in the spaceship. The footage was produced by Colin Emmett at the Atlas Computer Laboratory.

Nelson Max

Although Lawrence Livermore Labs in California is mainly known as a centre for high-level research in science, it continued producing significant advances in computer animation throughout this period. Notably, Nelson Max, who joined the Lab in 1971, and whose 1977 film *Turning a sphere inside out* is regarded as one of the classic early films in the medium (International Film Bureau, Chicago, 1977). He also produced a series of "realistic-looking" molecular model animations that served to demonstrate the future role of CGI in scientific visualization ("CGI" = Computer-generated imagery). His research interests focused on realism in nature images, molecular graphics, computer animation, and 3D scientific visualization. He later served as computer graphics director for the Fujitsu pavilions at Expo 85 and 90 in Japan.

NYIT

In 1974, Alex Schure, a wealthy New York entrepreneur, established the Computer Graphics Laboratory (CGL) at the New York Institute of Technology (NYIT). He put together the most sophisticated studio of the time, with state of the art computers, film and graphic equipment, and hired top technology experts and artists to run it -- Ed Catmull, Malcolm Blanchard, Fred Parke and others all from Utah, plus others from around the country including Ralph Guggenheim, Alvy Ray Smith and Ed Emshwiller. During the late 70s, the staff made numerous innovative contributions to image rendering techniques, and produced many influential software, including the animation program *Tween*, the paint program *Paint*, and the animation program *SoftCel*. Several videos from NYIT become quite famous: *Sunstone*, by Ed Emshwiller, *Inside a Quark*, by Ned Greene, and *The Works*. The latter, written by Lance Williams, was begun in 1978, and was intended to be the first full-length CGI film, but it was never completed, though a trailer for it was shown at SIGGRAPH 1982. In these years, many people regarded NYIT CG Lab as the top computer animation research and development group in the world.

The quality of NYIT's work attracted the attention of George Lucas, who was interested in developing a CGI special effects facility at his company Lucasfilm. In 1979, he recruited the top talent from NYIT, including Catmull, Smith and Guggenheim to start his division, which later spun off as Pixar, founded in 1986 with funding by Apple Inc. co-founder Steve Jobs.

Framebuffer

The framebuffer or framestore is a graphics screen configured with a memory buffer that contains data for a complete screen image. Typically, it is a rectangular array (raster) of pixels, and the number of pixels in the width and the height is its "resolution". Color values stored in the pixels can be from 1-bit (monochrome), to 24-bit (true color, 8-bits each for RGB—Red, Green, & Blue), or also 32-bit, with an extra 8-bits used as a transparency mask (alpha channel). Before the framebuffer, graphics displays were all vector-based, tracing straight lines from one co-ordinate to another. The first known example of a framebuffer was built in 1969 at Bell Labs, where Joan Miller implemented a simple paint program to allow users to "paint" direct on the framebuffer. This device had just 3-bits (giving just 8 colors).

In 1972–73, Richard Shoup developed the SuperPaint system at Xerox PARC, which used a framebuffer displaying 640×480 pixels (standard NTSC video resolution) with eight-bit depth (256 colors). The SuperPaint software contained all the essential elements of later paint packages, allowing the user to paint and modify pixels, using a palette of tools and effects, and thereby making it the first complete computer hardware and software solution for painting and editing images. Shoup also experimented with modifying the output signal using color tables, to allow the system to produce a wider variety of colors than the limited 8-bit range it contained. This scheme would later become commonplace in computer framebuffers. The SuperPaint framebuffer could also be used to capture input images from video.

The first commercial framebuffer was produced in 1974 by Evans & Sutherland. It cost about $15,000, with a resolution of 512 by 512 pixels in 8-bit grayscale color, and sold well to graphics researchers without the resources to build their own framebuffer. A little later, NYIT created the first full-color 24-bit RGB framebuffer by using three of the Evans & Sutherland framebuffers linked together as one device by a minicomputer. Many of the "firsts" that happened at NYIT were based on the development of this first raster graphics system.

In 1975, the UK company Quantel, founded in 1973 by Peter Michael, produced the first commercial full-color broadcast framebuffer, the Quantel DFS 3000. It was first used in TV coverage of the 1976 Montreal Olympics to generate a picture-in-picture inset of the Olympic flaming torch while the rest of the picture featured the runner entering the stadium. Framebuffer technology provided the cornerstone for the future development of digital television products.

By the late 70s, it became possible for personal computers (such as the Apple II) to contain low-color framebuffers. However, it was not until the 1980s that a real revolution in the field was seen, and framebuffers capable of holding a standard video image were incorporated into standalone workstations. By the 90s, framebuffers eventually became the standard for all personal computers.

Fractals

At this time, a major step forward to the goal of increased realism in 3D animation came with the development of "fractals". The term was coined in 1975 by mathematician Benoit Mandelbrot, who used it to extend the theoretical concept of fractional dimensions to geometric patterns in nature, and published in English translation of his book *Fractals: Form, Chance and Dimension* in 1977.

In 1979–80, the first film using fractals to generate the graphics was made by Loren Carpenter of Boeing. Titled *Vol Libre*, it showed a flight over a fractal landscape, and was presented at SIGGRAPH 1980. Carpenter was subsequently hired by Pixar to create the fractal planet in the *Genesis Effect* sequence of *Star Trek II: The Wrath of Khan* in June 1982.

JPL and Jim Blinn

Bob Holzman of NASA's Jet Propulsion Laboratory in California established JPL's Computer Graphics Lab in 1977 as a group with technology expertise in visualizing data being returned from NASA missions. On the advice of Ivan Sutherland, Holzman hired a graduate student from Utah named Jim Blinn. Blinn had worked with imaging techniques at Utah, and developed them into a system for NASA's visualization tasks. He produced a series of widely seen "fly-by" simulations, including the Voyager, Pioneer and Galileo spacecraft fly-bys of Jupiter, Saturn and their moons. He also worked with Carl Sagan, creating animations for his *Cosmos: A Personal Voyage* TV series. Blinn developed many influential new modelling techniques, and wrote papers on them for the IEEE (Institute of Electrical and Electronics Engineers), in their journal *Computer Graphics and Applications*. Some of these included environment mapping, improved highlight modelling, "blobby" modelling, simulation of wrinkled surfaces, and simulation of butts and dusty surfaces.

Later in the 80s, Blinn developed CG animations for an Annenberg/CPB TV series, *The Mechanical Universe*, which consisted of over 500 scenes for 52 half-hour programs describing physics and mathematics concepts for college students. This he followed with production of another series devoted to mathematical concepts, called *Project Mathematics!*.

Motion Control Photography

Motion control photography is a technique that uses a computer to record (or specify) the exact motion of a film camera during a shot, so that the motion can be precisely duplicated again, or alternatively on another computer, and combined with the movement of other sources, such as CGI elements. Early forms of motion control go back to John Whitney's 1968 work on *2001: A Space Odyssey*, and the effects on the 1977 movie *Star Wars Episode IV: A New Hope*, by George Lucas' newly created company Industrial Light & Magic in California (ILM). ILM created a digitally controlled camera known as the Dykstraflex, which performed complex and repeatable motions around stationary spaceship models, enabling separately filmed elements (spaceships, backgrounds, etc.) to be coordinated more accurately with one another. However, neither of these was actually computer-based—Dykstraflex was essentially a custom-built hardwired collection of knobs and switches. The first commercial computer-based motion control and CGI system was developed in 1981 in the UK by Moving Picture Company designer Bill Mather.

The 1980s

The '80s saw a great expansion of radical new developments in commercial hardware, especially the incorporation of framebuffer technologies into graphic workstations, allied with continuing advances in computer power and affordability.

Silicon Graphics, Inc (SGI)

Silicon Graphics, Inc (SGI) was a manufacturer of high-performance computer hardware and software, founded in 1981 by Jim Clark. His idea, called the Geometry Engine, was to create a series of components in a VLSI processor that would accomplish the main operations required in image synthesis—the matrix transforms, clipping, and the scaling operations that provided the transformation to view space. Clark attempted to shop his design around to computer companies, and finding no takers, he and colleagues at Stanford University, California, started their own company, Silicon Graphics.

SGI's first product (1984) was the IRIS (Integrated Raster Imaging System). It used the 8 MHz M68000 processor with up to 2 MB memory, a custom 1024×1024 frame buffer, and the Geometry Engine to give the workstation its impressive image generation power. Its initial market was 3D graphics display terminals, but SGI's products, strategies and market positions evolved significantly over time, and for many years were a favoured choice for CGI companies in film, TV, and other fields.

Quantel

In 1981, Quantel released the "Paintbox", the first broadcast-quality turnkey system designed for creation and composition of television video and graphics. Its design emphasized the studio workflow efficiency required for live news production. Essentially, it was a framebuffer packaged with innovative user software, and it rapidly found applications in news, weather, station promos, commercials, and the like. Although it was essentially a design tool for still images, it was also sometimes used for frame-by-frame animations. Following its initial launch, it revolutionised the production of television graphics, and some Paintboxes are still in use today due to their image quality, and versatility.

This was followed in 1982 by the Quantel Mirage, or DVM8000/1 "Digital Video Manipulator", a digital real-time video effects processor. This was based on Quantel's own hardware, plus a Hewlett-Packard computer for custom program effects. It was capable of warping a live video stream by texture mapping it onto an arbitrary three-dimensional shape, around which the viewer could freely rotate or zoom in real-time. It could also interpolate, or morph, between two different shapes. It was considered the first real-time 3D video effects processor, and the progenitor of subsequent DVE (Digital video effect) machines. In 1985, Quantel went on to produce "Harry", the first all-digital non-linear editing and effects compositing system.

Osaka University

In 1982, Japan's Osaka University developed the LINKS-1 Computer Graphics System, a supercomputer that used up to 257 Zilog Z8001 microprocessors, used for rendering realistic 3D computer graphics. According to the Information Processing Society of Japan: "The core of 3D image rendering is calculating the luminance of each pixel making up a rendered surface from the given viewpoint, light source, and object position. The LINKS-1 system was developed to realize an image rendering methodology in which each pixel could be parallel processed independently using ray tracing. By developing a new software methodology specifically for high-speed image rendering, LINKS-1 was able to rapidly render highly realistic images." It was "used to create the world's first 3D planetarium-like video of the entire heavens that was made completely with computer graphics. The video was presented at the Fujitsu pavilion at the 1985 International Exposition in Tsukuba." The LINKS-1 was the world's most powerful computer, as of 1984.

3D Fictional Animated Films at the University of Montreal

In the '80s, University of Montreal was at the front run of Computer Animation with three successful short 3D animated films with 3D characters:

In 1983, Philippe Bergeron, Nadia Magnenat Thalmann, and Daniel Thalmann directed Dream Flight, considered as the first 3D generated film telling a story. The film was completely programmed using the MIRA graphical language, an extension of the Pascal programming language based on abstract graphical data types. The film got several awards and was shown at the SIGGRAPH '83 Film Show.

In 1985, Pierre Lachapelle, Philippe Bergeron, Pierre Robidoux and Daniel Langlois directed Tony de Peltrie, which shows the first animated human character to express emotion through facial expressions and body movements, which touched the feelings of the audience. *Tony de Peltrie* premiered as the closing film of SIGGRAPH '85.

In 1987, the Engineering Institute of Canada celebrated its 100th anniversary. A major event, sponsored by Bell Canada and Northern Telecom (now Nortel), was planned for the Place des Arts in Montreal. For this event, Nadia Magnenat Thalmann and Daniel Thalmann simulated Marilyn Monroe and Humphrey Bogart meeting in a cafe in the old town section of Montreal. The short movie, called Rendez-vous in Montreal was shown in numerous festivals and TV channels all over the world.

Sun Microsystems, Inc

The Sun Microsystems company was founded in 1982 by Andy Bechtolsheim with other fellow graduate students at Stanford University. Bechtolsheim originally designed the SUN computer as a personal CAD workstation for the Stanford University Network (hence the acronym "SUN"). It was designed around the Motorola 68000 processor with the Unix operating system and virtual memory, and, like SGI, had an embedded frame buffer. Later developments included computer servers and workstations built on its own RISC-based processor architecture and a suite of software products such as the Solaris operating system, and the Java platform. By the '90s, Sun workstations were popular for rendering in 3D CGI filmmaking—for example, Disney-Pixar's 1995 movie *Toy Story* used a render farm of 117 Sun workstations. Sun was a proponent of open systems in general and Unix in particular, and a major contributor to open source software.

National Film Board of Canada

The NFB's French-language animation studio founded its Centre d'animatique in 1980, at a cost of $1 million CAD, with a team of six computer graphics specialists. The unit was initially tasked with creating stereoscopic CGI sequences for the NFB's 3-D IMAX film *Transitions* for Expo 86. Staff at the Centre d'animatique included Daniel Langlois, who left in 1986 to form Softimage.

First Turnkey Broadcast Animation System

Also in 1982, the first complete turnkey system designed specifically for creating broadcast-standard animation was produced by the Japanese company Nippon Univac Kaisha ("NUK", later merged with Burroughs), and incorporated the Antics 2-D computer animation software developed by Alan Kitching from his earlier versions. The configuration was based on the VAX 11/780 computer, linked to a Bosch 1-inch VTR, via NUK's own framebuffer. This framebuffer also showed realtime instant replays of animated vector sequences ("line test"), though finished full-color recording would take many seconds per frame. The full system was successfully sold to broadcasters and animation production companies across Japan. Later in the '80s, Kitching developed versions of Antics for SGI and Apple Mac platforms, and these achieved a wider global distribution.

First Solid 3D CGI in the Movies

The first cinema feature movie to make extensive use of solid 3D CGI was Walt Disney's *Tron*, directed by Steven Lisberger, in 1982. The film is celebrated as a milestone in the industry, though less than twenty minutes of this animation were actually used—mainly the scenes that show digital "terrain", or include vehicles such as *Light Cycles*, tanks and ships. To create the CGI scenes, Disney turned to the four leading computer graphics firms of the day: Information International Inc, Robert Abel and Associates (both in California), MAGI, and Digital Effects (both in New York). Each worked on a separate aspect of the movie, without any particular collaboration. *Tron* was a box office success, grossing $33 million on a budget of $17 million.

In 1984, *Tron* was followed by *The Last Starfighter*, a Universal Pictures / Lorimar production, directed by Nick Castle, and was one of cinema's earliest films to use extensive CGI to depict its many starships, environments and battle scenes. This was a great step forward compared with other films of the day, such as *Return of the Jedi*, which still used conventional physical models. The computer graphics for the film were designed by artist Ron Cobb, and rendered by Digital Productions on a Cray X-MP supercomputer. A total of 27 minutes of finished CGI footage was produced—considered an enormous quantity at the time. The company estimated that using computer animation required only half the time, and one half to one third the cost of traditional special effects. The movie was a financial success, earning over $28 million on an estimated budget of $15 million.

Inbetweening and Morphing

The terms inbetweening and morphing are often used interchangeably, and signify the creating of a sequence of images where one image transforms gradually into another image smoothly by small steps. Graphically, an early example would be Charles Philipon's famous 1831 caricature of French King Louis Philippe turning into a pear (metamorphosis). "Inbetweening" (AKA "tweening") is a term specifically coined for traditional animation technique, an early example being in E.G.Lutz's 1920 book *Animated Cartoons*. In computer animation, inbetweening was used from the beginning (e.g., John Whitney in the '50s, Charles Csuri and Masao Komura in the '60s). These pioneering examples were vector-based, comprising only outline drawings (as was also usual in conventional animation technique), and would often be described mathematically as "interpolation". Inbetweening with solid-filled colors appeared in the early '70s, (e.g., Alan Kitching's *Antics* at Atlas Lab, 1973, and Peter Foldes' *La Faim* at NFBC, 1974), but these were still entirely vector-based.

The term "morphing" did not become current until the late '80s, when it specifically applied to computer inbetweening with photographic images—for example, to make one face transform smoothly into another. The technique uses grids (or "meshes") overlaid on the images, to delineate the shape of key features (eyes, nose, mouth, etc.). Morphing then inbetweens one mesh to the next, and uses the resulting mesh to distort the image and simultaneously dissolve one to another, thereby preserving a coherent internal structure throughout. Thus, several different digital techniques come together in morphing. Computer distortion of photographic images was first done by NASA, in the mid-1960s, to align Landsat and Skylab satellite images with each other. Texture mapping, which applies a photographic image to a 3D surface in another image, was first defined by Jim Blinn and Martin Newell in 1976. A 1980 paper by Ed Catmull and Alvy Ray Smith on geometric transformations, introduced a mesh-warping algorithm. The earliest full demonstration of morphing was at the 1982 SIGGRAPH conference, where Tom Brigham of NYIT presented a short film sequence in which a woman transformed, or "morphed", into a lynx.

The first cinema movie to use morphing was Ron Howard's 1988 fantasy film *Willow*, where the main character, Willow, uses a magic wand to transform animal to animal to animal and finally, to a sorceress.

3D Inbetweening

With 3D CGI, the inbetweening of photo-realistic computer models can also produce results similar to morphing, though technically, it is an entirely different process (but is nevertheless often also referred to as "morphing"). An early example is Nelson Max's 1977 film *Turning a sphere inside out*. The first cinema feature film to use this technique was the 1986 *Star Trek IV: The Voyage Home*, directed by Leonard Nimoy, with visual effects by George Lucas's company Industrial Light & Magic (ILM). The movie includes a dream sequence where the crew travel back in time, and images of their faces transform into one another. To create it, ILM employed a new 3D scanning technology developed by Cyberware to digitize the cast members' heads, and used the resulting data for the computer models. Because each head model had the same number of key points, transforming one character into another was a relatively simple inbetweening.

The Abyss

In 1989 James Cameron's underwater action movie *The Abyss* was released. This was the first cinema movie to include photo-realistic CGI integrated seamlessly into live-action scenes. A five-minute sequence featuring an animated tentacle or "pseudopod" was created by ILM, who designed a program to produce surface waves of differing sizes and kinetic properties for the pseudopod, including reflection, refraction and a morphing sequence. Although short, this successful blend of CGI and live action is widely considered a milestone in setting the direction for further future development in the field.

Walt Disney & CAPS

The late 80s saw another milestone in computer animation, this time in 2D: the development of Disney's "Computer Animation Production System", known as "CAPS". This was a custom collection of software, scanners and networked workstations developed by The Walt Disney Company in collaboration with Pixar. Its purpose was to computerize the ink-and-paint and post-production processes of traditionally animated films, to allow more efficient and sophisticated post-production by making the practice of hand-painting cels obsolete. The animators' drawings and background paintings are scanned into the computer, and animation drawings are inked and painted by digital artists. The drawings and backgrounds are then combined, using software that allows for camera movements, multiplane effects, and other techniques—including compositing with 3D image material. The system's first feature film use was in *The Little Mermaid* (1989), for the "farewell rainbow" scene near the end, but the first full-scale use was for *The Rescuers Down Under* (1990), which therefore became the first traditionally animated film to be entirely produced on computer—or indeed, the first 100% digital feature film of any kind ever produced.

3D Animation Software in the 1980s

The '80s saw the appearance of many notable new commercial software products:

- 1982: Autodesk Inc was founded in California by John Walker, with a focus on design software for the PC, with their flagship CAD package *AutoCAD*. In 1986, Autodesk's first animation package was *AutoFlix*, for use with AutoCAD. Their first full 3D animation software was *3D Studio* for DOS in 1990, which was developed under license by The Yost Group.

- 1983: Alias Research was founded in Toronto, Canada, by Stephen Bingham and others, with a focus on industrial and entertainment software for SGI workstations. Their first product was *Alias-1* and shipped in 1985. In 1989, Alias was chosen to animate the pseudopod in James Cameron's *The Abyss*, which gave the software high-profile recognition in movie animation. In 1990 this developed into *PowerAnimator*, often known just as *Alias*.

- 1984: Wavefront was founded by Bill Kovacs and others, in California, to produce computer graphics for movies and television, and also to develop and market their own software based on SGI hardware. Wavefront developed their first product, *Preview*, during the first year of business. The company's production department helped tune the software by using it on commercial projects, creating opening graphics for television programs. In 1988, the company introduced the *Personal Visualiser*.

- 1984: TDI (Thomson Digital Image) was created in France as a subsidiary of aircraft simulator company Thomson-CSF, to develop and commercialise on their own 3D system *Explore*, first released in 1986.

- 1984: Sogitec Audiovisuel, was a division of Sogitec avionics in France, founded by Xavier Nicolas for the production of computer animation films, using their own 3D software developed from 1981 by Claude Mechoulam and others at Sogitec.

- 1986: Softimage was founded by National Film Board of Canada filmmaker Daniel Langlois in Montreal. Its first product was called the *Softimage Creative Environment*, and was launched at SIGGRAPH '88. For the first time, all 3D processes (modelling, animation, and rendering) were integrated. Creative Environment (eventually to be known as *Softimage 3D* in 1988), became a standard animation solution in the industry.

- 1987: Side Effects Software was established by Kim Davidson and Greg Hermanovic in Toronto, Canada, as a production/software company based on a 3D animation package called *PRISMS*, which they had acquired from their former employer *Omnibus*. Side Effects Software developed this procedural modelling and motion product into a high-end, tightly integrated 2D/3D animation software which incorporated a number of technological breakthroughs.

- 1989: the companies TDI and Sogitec were merged to create the new company ExMachina.

CGI in the 1990s

Computer Animation Expands in Film and TV

The 90s began with much of CGI technology now sufficiently developed to allow a major expansion into film and TV production. 1991 is widely considered the "breakout year", with two major box-office successes, both making heavy use of CGI.

First of these was James Cameron's movie *Terminator 2: Judgment Day*, and was the one that first brought CGI to widespread public attention. The technique was used to animate the two "Terminator" robots. The "T-1000" robot was given a "mimetic po-ly-alloy" (liquid metal) structure, which enabled this shapeshifting character to morph into almost anything it touched. Most of the key Terminator effects were provided by Industrial Light & Magic, and this film was the most ambitious CGI project since the 1982 film *Tron*.

The other was Disney's *Beauty and the Beast*, the second traditional 2D animated film to be entirely made using CAPS. The system also allowed easier combination of hand-drawn art with 3D CGI material, notably in the "waltz sequence", where Belle and Beast dance through a computer-generated ballroom as the camera "dollies" around them in simulated 3D space. Notably, *Beauty and the Beast* was the first animated film ever to be nominated for a Best Picture Academy Award.

Another significant step came in 1993, with Steven Spielberg's *Jurassic Park*, where 3D CGI dinosaurs were integrated with life-sized animatronic counterparts. The CGI animals were created by ILM, and in a test scene to make a direct comparison of both techniques, Spielberg chose the CGI. Also watching was George Lucas who remarked "a major gap had been crossed, and things were never going to be the same."

Flocking

Flocking is the behavior exhibited when a group of birds (or other animals) move to-gether in a flock. A mathematical model of flocking behavior was first simulated on a computer in 1986 by Craig Reynolds, and soon found its use in animation. *Jurassic Park* notably featured flocking, and brought it to widespread attention by mentioning it in the actual script. Other early uses were the flocking bats in Tim Burton's *Batman Returns* (1992), and the wildebeest stampede in Disney's *The Lion King* (1994).

> With improving hardware, lower costs, and an ever-increasing range of soft-ware tools, CGI techniques were soon rapidly taken up in both film and televi-sion production.

In 1993, J. Michael Straczynski's *Babylon 5* became the first major television series to use CGI as the primary method for their visual effects (rather than using hand-built models), followed later the same year by Rockne S. O'Bannon's *SeaQuest DSV*.

Also the same year, the French company Studio Fantome produced the first full-length completely computer animated TV series, *Insektors* (26×13'), though they also pro-duced an even earlier all 3D short series, *Geometric Fables* (50 x 5') in 1991. A little later, in 1994, the Canadian TV CGI series *ReBoot* (48×23') was aired, produced by Mainframe Entertainment.

In 1995, there came the first fully computer-animation feature film, Disney-Pixar's *Toy Story*, which was a huge commercial success. This film was directed by John Lasseter, a co-founder of Pixar, and former Disney animator, who started at Pixar with short movies such as *Luxo Jr.* (1986), *Red's Dream* (1987), and *Tin Toy* (1988), which was also the first computer-generated animated short film to win an Academy Award. Then, after some long negotiations between Disney and Pixar, a partnership deal was agreed in 1991 with the aim of producing a full feature movie, and *Toy Story* was the result.

The following years saw a greatly increased uptake of digital animation techniques, with many new studios going into production, and existing companies making a transition from traditional techniques to CGI. Between 1995 and 2005 in the USA, the average effects budget for a wide-release feature film leapt from $5 million to $40 million. According to Hutch Parker, President of Production at 20th Century Fox, as of 2005, "50 percent of feature films have significant effects. They're a character in the movie." However, CGI has made up for the expenditures by grossing over 20% more than their real-life counterparts, and by the early 2000s, computer-generated imagery had become the dominant form of special effects.

Motion Capture

Motion capture, or "Mocap", records the movement of external objects or people, and has applications for medicine, sports, robotics, and the military, as well as for animation in film, TV and games. The earliest example would be in 1878, with the pioneering photographic work of Eadweard Muybridge on human and animal locomotion, which is still a source for animators today. Before computer graphics, capturing movements to use in animation would be done using Rotoscoping, where the motion of an actor was filmed, then the film used as a guide for the frame-by-frame motion of a hand-drawn animated character. The first example of this was Max Fleischer's *Out of the Inkwell* series in 1915, and a more recent notable example is the 1978 Ralph Bakshi 2D animated movie *The Lord of the Rings*.

Computer-based motion capture started as a photogrammetric analysis tool in biomechanics research in the 70s and 80s. A performer wears markers near each joint to identify the motion by the positions or angles between the markers. Many different types of markers can be used—lights, reflective markers, LEDs, infra-red, inertial, mechanical, or wireless RF—and may be worn as a form of suit, or attached direct to a performer's body. Some systems include details of face and fingers to capture subtle expressions, and such is often referred to as "performance capture". The computer records the data from the markers, and uses it to animate digital character models in 2D or 3D computer animation, and in some cases this can include camera movement as well. In the 90s, these techniques became widely used for visual effects. Video games also began to use motion capture to animate in-game characters in 1995, the earliest examples of this being the Atari Jaguar CD-based game *Highlander: The Last of the MacLeods*, and the arcade fighting game *Soul Edge*, which was the first video game to use passive optical motion-capture technology.

Another breakthrough where a cinema film used motion capture was creating hundreds of digital characters for the film *Titanic* in 1997. The technique was used extensively in 1999 to create Jar-Jar Binks and other digital characters in *Star Wars: Episode I – The Phantom Menace*.

Match Moving

Match moving (also known as motion tracking or camera tracking), although related to motion capture, is a completely different technique. Instead of using special cameras and sensors to record the motion of subjects, match moving works with pre-existing live-action footage, and uses computer software alone to track specific points in the scene through multiple frames, and thereby allow the insertion of CGI elements into the shot with correct position, scale, orientation, and motion relative to the existing material. The terms are used loosely to describe several different methods of extracting subject or camera motion information from a motion picture. The technique can be 2D or 3D, and can also include matching for camera movements. The earliest commercial software examples being *3D-Equalizer* from Science.D.Visions and *rastrack* from Hammerhead Productions, both starting mid-90s.

The first step is identifying suitable features that the software tracking algorithm can lock onto and follow. Typically, features are chosen because they are bright or dark spots, edges or corners, or a facial feature—depending on the particular tracking algorithm being used. When a feature is tracked it becomes a series of 2D coordinates that represent the position of the feature across the series of frames. Such tracks can be used immediately for 2D motion tracking, or then be used to calculate 3D information. In 3D tracking, a process known as "calibration" derives the motion of the camera from the inverse-projection of the 2D paths, and from this a "reconstruction" process is used to recreate the photographed subject from the tracked data, and also any camera movement. This then allows an identical virtual camera to be moved in a 3D animation program, so that new animated elements can be composited back into the original live-action shot in perfectly matched perspective.

In the 90s, the technology progressed to the point that it became possible to include virtual stunt doubles. Camera tracking software was refined to allow increasingly complex visual effects developments that were previously impossible. Computer-generated extras also became used extensively in crowd scenes with advanced flocking and crowd simulation software. Being mainly software-based, match moving has become increasingly affordable as computers become cheaper and more powerful. It has become an essential visual effects tool and is even used providing effects in live television broadcasts.

Virtual Studio

In television, a virtual studio, or virtual set, is a studio that allows the real-time combination of people or other real objects and computer generated environments and objects in a seamless manner. It requires that the 3D CGI environment is automatically locked to follow any movements of the live camera and lens precisely. The essence of such system is that it uses some form of camera tracking to create a live stream of data describing the exact camera movement, plus some realtime CGI rendering software that uses the camera tracking data and generates a synthetic image of the virtual set exactly linked to the camera motion. Both streams are then combined with a video mixer, typically using chroma key. Such virtual sets became common in TV programs in the 90s, with the first practical system of this kind being the *Synthevision virtual studio* developed by the Japanese broadcasting corporation NHK (Nippon Hoso Kyokai) in 1991, and first used in their science special, *Nano-space*. Virtual studio techniques are also used in filmmaking, but this medium does not have the same requirement to operate entirely in realtime. Motion control or camera tracking can be used separately to generate the CGI elements later, and then combine with the live-action as a post-production process. However, by the 2000s, computer power had improved sufficiently to allow many virtual film sets to be generated in realtime, as in TV, so it was unnecessary to composite anything in post-production.

Machinima

Machinima uses realtime 3D computer graphics rendering engines to create a cinematic production. Most often, video games machines are used for this. The Academy of Machinima Arts & Sciences (AMAS), a non-profit organization formed 2002, and dedicated to promoting machinima, defines machinima as "animated filmmaking within a real-time virtual 3-D environment". AMAS recognizes exemplary productions through awards given at its annual The practice of using graphics engines from video games arose from the animated software introductions of the '80s "demoscene", Disney Interactive Studios' 1992 video game Stunt Island, and '90s recordings of gameplay in first-person shooter video games, such as id Software's Doom and Quake. Machinima Film Festival. Machinima-based artists are sometimes called machinimists or machinimators.

3D Animation Software in the 1990s

There were many developments, mergers and deals in the 3D software industry in the '90s and later.

- Wavefront followed the success of *Personal Visualiser* with the release of *Dynamation* in 1992, a powerful tool for interactively creating and modifying realistic, natural images of dynamic events. In 1993, Wavefront acquired Thomson Digital Images (TDI), with their innovative product *Explore*, a tool suite that included *3Design* for modelling, *Anim* for animation, and *Interactive Photore-alistic Renderer* (IPR) for rendering. In 1995, Wavefront was bought by Silicon Graphics, and merged with Alias.

- Alias Research continued the success of *PowerAnimator* with movies like *Terminator 2: Judgment Day*, *Batman Returns* and *Jurassic Park*, and in 1993 started the development of a new entertainment software, which was later to be named *Maya*. Alias found customers in animated film, TV series, visual effects, and video games, and included many prominent studios, such as Industrial Light & Magic, Pixar, Sony Pictures Imageworks, Walt Disney, and Warner Brothers. Other Alias products were developed for applications in architecture and engineering. In 1995, SGI purchased both Alias Research and Wavefront in a 3-way deal, and the merged company Alias Wavefront was launched.

- Alias Wavefront's new mission was to focus on developing the world's most advanced tools for the creation of digital content. *PowerAnimator* continued to be used for visual effects and movies (such as *Toy Story* and *Batman Forever*), and also for video games. Further development of the *Maya* software went ahead, adding new features such as motion capture, facial animation, motion blur, and "time warp" technology. CAD industrial design products like *AliasStudio* and *Alias Designer* became standardized on Alias|Wavefront software. In 1998, Alias|Wavefront launched *Maya* as its new 3D flagship product, and this soon became the industry's most important animation tool. *Maya* was the merger of three packages—Wavefront's *Advanced Visualizer*, Alias's *Power Animator*, and TDI's *Explore*. In 2003 the company was renamed simply "Alias". In 2004, SGI sold the business to a private investment firm, and it was later renamed to Alias Systems Corporation. In 2006, the company was bought by Autodesk.

- Softimage developed further features for *Creative Environment*, including the *Actor Module* (1991) and *Eddie* (1992), including tools such as inverse kinematics, enveloping, metaclay, flock animation, and many others. Softimage customers include many prominent production companies, and Softimage has been used to create animation for hundreds of major feature films and games. In 1994, Microsoft acquired Softimage, and renamed the package *Softimage 3D*, releasing a Windows NT port two years later. In 1998, after helping to port the products to Windows and financing the development of *Softimage* and *Softimage|DS*, Microsoft sold the Softimage unit to Avid Technology, who was looking to expand its visual effect capabilities. Then, in 2008, Autodesk acquired the brand and the animation assets of Softimage from Avid, thereby ending Softimage Co. as a distinct entity. The video-related assets of Softimage, including *Softimage|DS* (now *Avid|DS*) continue to be owned by Avid.

- Autodesk Inc's PC DOS-based *3D Studio* was eventually superseded in 1996 when The Yost Group developed 3D Studio Max for Windows NT. Priced much lower than most competitors, *3D Studio Max* was quickly seen as an affordable solution for many professionals. Of all animation software, *3D Studio Max* serves the widest range of users. It is used in film and broadcast, game development, corporate and industrial design, education, medical, and web design. In 2006, Autodesk acquired Alias, bringing the *StudioTools* and *Maya* software products under the Autodesk banner, with *3D Studio Max* rebranded as *Autodesk 3ds Max*, and *Maya* as *Autodesk Maya*. Now one of the largest software companies in the world, Autodesk serves more than 4 million customers in over 150 countries.

- Side Effects Software's *PRISMS* was used extensively to create visual effects for broadcast and feature films into the '90s, with projects like *Twister, Independence Day*, and *Titanic*. In 1996, Side Effects Software introduced *Houdini*, a next-generation 3D package that proved to be more sophisticated and artist-friendly than its predecessor. *Houdini* is used around the world to develop cutting edge 3D animation in the film, broadcast and gaming industries, and Side Effects Software has consistently proved itself to be an industry innovator.

CGI in the 2000s

2000 breakthrough capture of the reflectance field over the human face

In 2000, a team led by Paul Debevec managed to adequately capture (and simulate) the reflectance field over the human face using the simples of light stages. which was the last missing piece of the puzzle to make digital look-alikes of known actors.

Motion Capture, Photorealism, and Uncanny Valley

The first mainstream cinema film fully made with motion capture was the 2001 Japanese-American *Final Fantasy: The Spirits Within* directed by Hironobu Sakaguchi, which was also the first to use photorealistic CGI characters. The film was not a box-office success. Some commentators have suggested this may be partly because the lead CGI characters had facial features which fell into the "uncanny valley". In 2002, Peter Jackson's *The Lord of the Rings: The Two Towers* was the first feature film to use a real-time motion capture system, which allowed the actions of actor Andy Serkis to be fed direct into the 3D CGI model of Gollum as it was being performed.

Motion capture is seen by many as replacing the skills of the animator, and lacking the animator's ability to create exaggerated movements that are impossible to perform live. The end credits of Pixar's film *Ratatouille* (2007) carry a stamp certifying it as "100% Pure Animation — No Motion Capture!" However, proponents point out that the technique usually includes a good deal of adjustment work by animators as well. Nevertheless, in 2010, the US Film Academy (AMPAS) announced that motion-capture films will no longer be considered eligible for "Best Animated Feature Film" Oscars, stating "Motion capture by itself is not an animation technique."

Virtual Cinematography

The early 2000s saw the advent of fully virtual cinematography with its audience debut considered to be in the 2003 movies Matrix Reloaded and Matrix Revolutions with its digital look-alikes so convincing that it is often impossible to know if some image is a human imaged with a camera or a digital look-alike shot with a simulation of a camera. The scenes built and imaged within virtual cinematography are the *"Burly brawl"* and the end showdown between Neo and Agent Smith. With conventional cinematographic methods the burly brawl would have been prohibitively time consuming to make with years of compositing required for a scene of few minutes. Also a human actor could not have been used for the end showdown in Matrix Revolutions: Agent Smith's cheekbone gets punched in by Neo leaving the digital look-alike naturally unhurt.

3D animation Software in the 2000s

- Blender (software) is a free open source virtual cinematography package, used by professionals and enthusiasts alike.

- Poser is another DIY 3D graphics program especially aimed at user-friendly animation of soft objects

- Pointstream Software is a professional optical flow program that uses a pixel as its basic primitive form usually tracked over a multi-camera setup from the esteemed Arius3D, makers of the XYZRGB scanner, used in the production process of the Matrix sequels

CGI in the 2010s

In SIGGRAPH 2013 Activision and USC presented a real-time digital face look-alike of "Ira" utilizing the USC light stage X by Ghosh et al. for both reflectance field and motion capture. The end result, both precomputed and real-time rendered with the state-of-the-art Graphics processing unit: *Digital Ira*, looks fairly realistic. Techniques previously confined to high-end virtual cinematography systems are rapidly moving into the video games and leisure applications.

References

- The algorithmic image: graphic visions of the computer age, Harper & Row Publishers, Inc. New York, NY, USA 1986. ISBN 0914845802

- Dealers of Lightning: Xerox PARC and the Dawn of the Computer Age, 1999, Michael A. Hiltzik, HarperBusiness, ISBN 0-88730-891-0

- Mandelbrot, Benoît B, 1983. "The Fractal Geometry of Nature", Macmillan, ISBN 978-0-7167-1186-5 (retrieved 1 February 2012).

- Albers; Alexanderson, 2008. "Benoit Mandelbrot: In his own words". Mathematical people: profiles and interviews. Wellesley, Mass: AK Peters. p. 214, ISBN 978-1-56881-340-0.

- Shone, Tom. Blockbuster: How Hollywood learned to stop worrying and love the summer Pg 218. Simon and Schuster, 2004 ISBN 0-7432-3568-1, ISBN 978-0-7432-3568-6

- Paik, Karen (2007). To Infinity and Beyond!: The Story of Pixar Animation Studios. San Francisco: Chronicle Books. p. 103. ISBN 0-8118-5012-9. Retrieved March 13, 2009.

- "Pixar founder's Utah-made Hand added to National Film Registry". The Salt Lake Tribune. December 28, 2011. Retrieved January 8, 2012.

- "The Quantel Paintbox -- a pioneering computer graphics workstation", Quantel, March 15, 2011 (retrieved 24 August 2012).

Permissions

All chapters in this book are published with permission under the Creative Commons Attribution Share Alike License or equivalent. Every chapter published in this book has been scrutinized by our experts. Their significance has been extensively debated. The topics covered herein carry significant information for a comprehensive understanding. They may even be implemented as practical applications or may be referred to as a beginning point for further studies.

We would like to thank the editorial team for lending their expertise to make the book truly unique. They have played a crucial role in the development of this book. Without their invaluable contributions this book wouldn't have been possible. They have made vital efforts to compile up to date information on the varied aspects of this subject to make this book a valuable addition to the collection of many professionals and students.

This book was conceptualized with the vision of imparting up-to-date and integrated information in this field. To ensure the same, a matchless editorial board was set up. Every individual on the board went through rigorous rounds of assessment to prove their worth. After which they invested a large part of their time researching and compiling the most relevant data for our readers.

The editorial board has been involved in producing this book since its inception. They have spent rigorous hours researching and exploring the diverse topics which have resulted in the successful publishing of this book. They have passed on their knowledge of decades through this book. To expedite this challenging task, the publisher supported the team at every step. A small team of assistant editors was also appointed to further simplify the editing procedure and attain best results for the readers.

Apart from the editorial board, the designing team has also invested a significant amount of their time in understanding the subject and creating the most relevant covers. They scrutinized every image to scout for the most suitable representation of the subject and create an appropriate cover for the book.

The publishing team has been an ardent support to the editorial, designing and production team. Their endless efforts to recruit the best for this project, has resulted in the accomplishment of this book. They are a veteran in the field of academics and their pool of knowledge is as vast as their experience in printing. Their expertise and guidance has proved useful at every step. Their uncompromising quality standards have made this book an exceptional effort. Their encouragement from time to time has been an inspiration for everyone.

The publisher and the editorial board hope that this book will prove to be a valuable piece of knowledge for students, practitioners and scholars across the globe.

Index